THE BOMBAST TRANSCRIPTS

THE BOMBAST TRANSCRIPTS

Rants and Screeds of

RageBoy®

Christopher Locke

PERSEUS
PUBLISHING

Library of Congress Control Number: 2001098257
ISBN 0–7382–0633–4

Perseus Publishing is a member of the Perseus Books Group.
Find us on the World Wide Web at http://www.perseuspublishing.com
Perseus Publishing books are available at special discounts for bulk purchases in the U.S. by corporations, institutions, and other organizations. For more information, please contact the Special Markets Department at the Perseus Books Group, 11 Cambridge Center, Cambridge, MA 02142, or call (800) 255-1514 or (617)252-5298, or e-mail j.mccrary@perseusbooks.com.

Text design by Jeffrey P. Williams
Set in 10.5-point Fairfield Light by Perseus Publishing Services

First printing, January 2002

1 2 3 4 5 6 7 8 9 10—04 03 02

CONTENTS

AUTHOR'S NOTE AND LIST OF UNINDICTED CO-CONSPIRATORS

Valued Readers:

In 1996, I started a webzine and Internet mailing list, which I named Entropy Gradient Reversals—a title that had occurred to me nearly 30 years earlier while deeply immersed in the study of psychotropic particle physics. The pieces collected here were posted to EGR over a five year span. However, through the vicissitudes of intertextual indeterminacy, this span has since been subjected to the unpredictable influence of what Kurt Vonnegut once called the chronosynclastic infidibulum. Any attempt to unravel their original sequence will therefore encounter certain quantum effects whose results tend to frustrate normal expectations of temporal linearity. This is intentional.

It is also my intention here to thank everyone who has assisted in this often questionable undertaking, whether through cheering or jeering—those who opposed it from the start having provided no less inspiration than those who encouraged me to keep it coming. Sadly, naming everyone I've met in this life would be impossible. However, a handful do stand out.

First and foremost, the Valued Readers themselves: the few, the brave, the EGR Irregulars. You know who you are.

Liz Locke, sorror mystica and all-around wellspring of arcane lore, who assured me I could do it before I even dreamed I wanted to.

Lauren Locke, who was the first reader of many of these pieces, and who helped me understand, by laughing, where the funny bits were.

Selene Locke, my wonderfully smart and rascally daughter, who never ever called her Da a butthead or anything like that. And who never displayed the least dread of the fearsome Anatidae Overlord.

David Weinberger, who greatly encouraged my madness by naming me "the official Scourge of JOHO" (www.hyperorg.com).

Eric Norlin, who joined me in laughing till we nearly choked over The Titanic Deck Chair Rearrangement Corporation (www.tdcrc.com).

David Miller, my agent provocateur, who never ever told me that I'd never sell this book, but sold it for me nonetheless.

Perseus Publishing, who took a walk on the wild side and lived to tell about it. So far, anyway.

Don Williams, who reads between the lines way better than most, and knows what it means to be human (www.cgjungpage.org).

And while it may go without saying, it goes so much better with: my sky, my fire, Laurie Doctor.

Thank You,
The Management

Introduction:
Dr. Paracelsus, I Presume

A certain humility has been lacking of late in American letters. I'm here to fix that.

Finally, the perfect moment has arrived to write this introduction. One has to wait for these things. The precise moment of creation is rare, to be treasured, to be savored, to be taken advantage of. Today I woke up at 10 A.M. feeling like homemade shit. I stayed up all night for no good reason. I have a cold I can't shake. I am feeling worthless and desperate about my life. If I had the energy, I'd hate myself.

Many seem to believe that such a state of mind is an impediment to writing, that it inevitably precipitates a fatal blockage of the creative impulse. Not so. Seeing oneself in the cold light of arbitrary personal depression is, in fact, the deeply yearned for opportunity. The inspiration of all true art.

Take Li Po, for instance, the ancient Chinese poet-sage. Perhaps the best known story about this shadowy literary genius, now shrouded in the swirling mists of time, is that he would get drunk as a parboiled ostrich and feed his poetry to the fish. Big old golden koi, most likely, in the formal gardens of some kingdom long since crumbled back to dust. "Look upon my works, ye mighty" he would write, I imagine, "and have a nice day." Actually, one of these poems was recently recovered from the belly of a fish that had inadvertently swum into a pool of molten amber directly after lunch. It reads:

> *This plum wine has fucked me up again but good.*
> *I can barely see my hand before my face.*
> *What a relief!*

What do those hosers in the Court expect of me?
That I will set them straight in the ways of Heaven?
Here, fishy-fishy . . .

Of course, this fragment is hotly debated, and many scholars believe the fish story to be entirely apocryphal. But so what? Those people are just playing with themselves, as always. What does it matter if this antique poet, about whom we can never truly know dick, couldn't decide if he was Li Po dreaming he was Chuang Tzu or Chuang Tzu dreaming he was Li Po? Have we not passed beyond the naïve tropes of high modernism with its art for art's sake. The hand that rocks the cradle rules the world, as any psychoanalyst will tell you for a modest fee. And who gives a rat's ass whether it was Tim Robbins or Tom Robbins or Tony Robbins who had the big insight? The real question before us is how any of this connects to the fact — and it is a fact, inescapable — that the UPS guy just rang your doorbell, a car crashed into a telephone pole three blocks over, the toilet is backing up again and your girlfriend thinks you're boring.

Life is so much richer than it seems on the surface.

Contrary to popular belief, inspiration does not usually come announced by sunbeams breaking through the darkening storm and the beating of angelic wings. No. It comes at moments like this, when everything is about as messed up as it can get, you've forgotten why you exist — was there a point? — and can't figure out if you have anything remotely worth saying to say. At such a juncture, inspiration is merely the willingness to keep putting words together. It's a kind of faith: that something will occur to you if you just keep making sentences. Don't give up, you tell yourself. This is important work. The human race will be enriched if I just don't falter now, if I can hold out five more minutes against the sickening paralysis of unavoidable despair.

Of course, it's all a crock. Jesus, lighten up! Think of the poor bastards who, for some reason that eludes you, feel compelled to read this stuff. Do they really want to be reminded of the impenetrable morass of confusion their lives have become? Of their broken dreams and unrealized potential? Fuck no! So have a little compassion for Christ's sake. What's it to you to bend the truth a bit? Revise history? Make it up as you go along? It's not like anyone's going to sue you. Though, yes I know, some days it'd sure be nice if someone did.

Still, we have to make the best of it.

The real enemy is self absorption. Few have come to appreciate as much as I the benefits of making fun of other people. It is impossible to adequately express how much this has helped me to stop focusing so much on myself. When I began writing Entropy Gradient Reversals — the self-explanatory title of the webzine from which these pieces were selected, some might say culled — I was working at IBM. Scant months earlier, I'd been proud to have been invited to join this awesome globe-spanning colossus of the computer industry. Soon enough, however, I found myself once again in the company of fools.

Perhaps this has happened to some of you. You read the annual reports, the press releases, the confectionary prose describing these corporations as havens of intelligence in a world hungry for their insight and acumen, their ability to cut through complexity to find simple, elegant *solutions*. And yes, you think, that is what the world needs. Solutions. Not idle talk. Not endless theorizing. But actions that speak louder than words. Bold and fearless answers to the pressing challenges of our times.

Then you discover you are surrounded by shit-for-brains losers with the courage of sheep and the IQ of pygmy shrews. Once, and you figure it's an anomaly, a bad call. Don't give up, press on. Don't falter now. But when it happens 30 times in ten years, it can really begin to get you down. My resume looks like the routing manifest for some displaced person after WWII. I am merely a high-tech migrant worker, following the harvests like Sisyphus rolling his rock. Rocking his roll. Locking and loading and finally going postal from the high bell-tower of a mind at once unhallowed and unhinged.

First it was artificial intelligence, expert systems, robotics, then document management and Standard Generalized Markup Language. SGML was the precursor to the World Wide Web, so then it was that:

the Internet, e-commerce, EIEIO. All the companies I worked for were uniquely positioned, without exception. Each offered solutions to unimagined problems. Which was usually the trouble. Most potential customers had no idea that recursive backward chaining was the answer to their most fervent prayers. Or that their businesses would soon be replaced by a cadre of kids so green they squeaked, who nonetheless were holding advanced degrees from places like Stanford and MIT and who, moreover, had suddenly become magnets for venture capital so prodigious it threatened to overturn the world economy. But then it all suddenly dried up and everyone lost their jobs in global capitalism's equivalent of "heh-heh, just kidding." At times, it's enough to make you wonder.

When I began writing this sort of stuff, I used to wonder if it was just me. Was I maybe a little cranky? Perhaps a tad unrealistic about my career prospects? Was I simply whining in the desert that the high places should be made low? Actually, the high places seemed to be high on dope far more powerful than the crack cocaine that was flooding our major urban centers. Money is speed, they were saying, speed money — from the show-floors of industry conferences and exhibitions that were indistinguishable from the Mad Hatter's Tea Party. Legends in their own minds, they slavered and slobbered in Pavlovian fugue. The closing bell would ring on Wall Street and they'd go into orgasmic paroxysms of hallucinatory avarice. Stoned on greed. Stoned on denial so deep there was no coming up for air. Hermetically sealed. Insane.

As I slowly came to grasp that this is indeed the way things are, I began to feel much better. You know, because for a minute there, I thought it was *my* fault. Whew!

But it's not all comedy in the real world. Of course not. Let's be realistic. Some things hurt. There is pain and suffering, separation, death. There is loneliness. Hey, what're ya gonna do, uh? What *can* you do? Be a man about it, that's what. Semper fi, motherfucker. Don't let em see the whites of your eyes. Don't wear your heart on your sleeve. It's a military op, take evasive action. Dive! Dive! Like in Tom

Clancy's *Hunt for Red October*. Remember that one? Or Dostoyevski's
Notes from Underground. Or Kafka maybe, but hey don't get all highbrow on us now, OK? Sure everybody gets the blues sometimes. Yeah,
so? We've got it good here in America. At least nobody's shooting at our
kids. Unless you live in certain parts of Colorado. Or Oklahoma. Or
LA, DC, New York, Chicago, Atlanta, Dublin, Beirut, Bosnia, Beijing,
Tehran, places like that. Places where everyone seems a little uncertain about the meaning of life. OK, so some of those aren't American
places. What's the diff? Computer and telecommunications technologies are collapsing distance, bringing us all together. And timewise too.
George Gilder meets the Brothers Grimm in a spirit of nihilistic irony
that's as familiar and user-friendly as your local Wal-Mart. It's a small
world after all. Thermonuclear core dumps from Three Mile Island to
Chernobyl. C3P0 cutting policy decisions while the ghosts of Wernher
von Braun and Werner Heisenberg look on. We got Schrödinger's cat
smiling inscrutably. We got 101 Dalmatians. We got it all. A screaming
comes across the sky: Do you Yahoo?

What does it matter if I speak? What would I say? One of the
pieces collected here was originally titled "The Bombast II Transcripts,
Run 1: I Was a Teenage Brain Surgeon." Part of this was a joke, though
probably not the part you think. I really was a teenage brain surgeon.
It's sort of a rarity these days; you just don't get that many of us anymore. No, the joke was Bombast II, which I introduced thusly:

> The following manuscript was produced *in its entirety* using arti-
> ficial intelligence techniques developed over the last 15 years in
> the world's most advanced AI research centers and from specific
> work on machine translation, computational linguistics, case-
> based reasoning and automated narrative generation. In devel-
> oping our system, BOMBAST II (after 16th Century arch-mage
> Philippus Aureolus Theophrastus Bombastus von Hohenheim),
> the commonsense/world-knowledge background was derived
> from Douglas Lenat's CYC system, first developed at the
> Microelectronics and Computer Technology Corporation in

Austin, Texas. The generative strategy involved encoding lexical-ized tree-adjoining grammars with a nonmonotonic inheritance hierarchy, and deployed higher-order logic programming for semantic interpretation of coordinate constructs.

It seems to us that BOMBAST II was only partially success-ful in creating a cogent narrative that might pass the Turing Test at a reasonable level of expectation. Of course, especially since the widespread popularization of the Internet, willing suspen-sion of disbelief has become a fast-moving target. Experimental subjects are encouraged to read this text *as if* it were the output of an actual human being, and to report their reactions to the publisher.

A number of readers expressed surprise that these technologies had become so advanced. They said it really did sound as if someone had written it. Which just goes to show that if you use arcane terminology and lay on the bullshit thick enough, you can get people to believe just about anything. For example, that you are uniquely positioned to write an industry newsletter exposing the scariest bits of your tortured psy-che to public view — and that it will someday become a book. Not unlike the one you are currently holding.

I remember the feeling or terror as my mouse-finger hovered over the SEND key on that one. How could I do it? My valued readers surely weren't expecting anything like this. One wrote to me later — because of course, I did send it — saying he'd have to unsubscribe from my zine if I planned to continue writing about my private life. I told him he'd be missed. Another summed it up beautifully: "I like to hear what you think, but I don't care about your personal thoughts." To his credit, this person agreed, after I put his unintentional bon mot on the site's homepage, that it sounded stupid even to him.

Making it sound stupid, however, is quite a trick. Usually, it sounds perfectly reasonable. And we hear it all the time: We'd like to know what you think, but we don't care about your personal thoughts. Well fuck that. The inspiration of all true art is a blank screen and a bad attitude. What does it matter if I speak? What would I say? As I've already quoted from the first Bombast transcript, here's how it ends . . .

"Later. Radical scene-shift. I am sitting on the floor of some-body's apartment playing the strobe over the Major Arcana one by one. Everyone seems to have gone somewhere. The Lovers. The Fool. The Hanged Man. The Magician. They flicker in the light, they move through time, floating on the trust you either find or die. Walking out on the thinnest mirror-ice of memory reversed, I flash for an instant on my future. It is always the hour of the wolf; that room, this room. Writing it down tonight, thirty years later, our eyes meet. Some spark leaps the synaptic gap, some circuit closes, and the echo it makes lasts for a little while before it fades."

So join me now, won't you, as we explore the draconian spawn of Albion's seed, from Puritans and Quakers to movers and shakers. From shamen and tax collectors, healers, takers, to warheads and heat-seekers. Finders, keepers. A sort of shockproof Schadenfreude with a side of Weltschmerz and a schmear. Where Christopher Hitchens and Henry Kissinger kiss and make up. Where Peter Drucker meets Kublai Kahn. Zubin Mehta meets Mickey Rourke. Where Jimmy Breslin meets Jimmy Olsen under the smarmy All-American gaze of Superman — out of the closet of his Kryptophobia at last, looking sharp in his bright green boxer shorts.

I dunno. It's a kind of faith, I guess. Don't give up. Don't falter now. Write on . . .

RageBoy®
Boulder, Colorado
June 2001

DISCLAIMER

Nothing to disclaim at this time.

Reading the Dictionary

Though I had passed the same buildings nearly every day, walked and driven the same streets, they now appeared alien, even threatening, as if some inimical wind had swept away whatever significance I had once attached to shops and intersections, old meeting places, the houses of friends long gone, or worse, unable to be reached. Whatever love I had woven into these scenes was suddenly lost, the town become a cheap tapestry of mistaken memories, unraveling at the edges. I remember standing on a corner that winter day, whatever naïve beliefs I'd cradled undermined at last, whatever vague hopes I'd casually entertained finally and completely shattered. The city looked somehow flat, deflated, like a cardboard stage set after the filming's over. Grief hit me like a blow to the stomach, and an aching sadness too exhausted for tears. Yet I was mesmerized by wonder at where I might have been these past five years. Had I really lived in this picture postcard dream-turned-nightmare? Without words to say why, I was invaded by the memory of a place I'd never been, and of a gate repeatedly slamming and swinging open in an empty yard, no longer separating the space it once enclosed from the now abandoned road.

That road was waiting for me when I left the place, first going into the high range 40 miles to the north. For nine months of healing silence, I lived in a rough A-frame cabin tilted out over a rocky slope. The Aztec-psilocybin rocks a mile across the valley formed a backdrop to the Buddhist shrine below my south wall window. While the Milky Way burned itself into the winter night, I would fill the shrine bowls and light incense and candles to forces I tried not to imagine. I sat like a mirror sometimes, no flicker, no breath of wind, holding the crystal reflection of flames in the water. Outside, beyond the falling snow, the forest was haunted with the sounds of other lives which became my familiars, my wise and terrible brothers.

It was in this place, 10,000 feet above the heartland of America, that I began to read the dictionary. I read it as if it were a mystery novel, turning from word to word for clues as to what it might mean when we speak to ourselves together, for a hint as to what had gone wrong somewhere along the way. Slowly, I began to see that the book was a work of archeology, an inventory of artifacts our race has picked up from its own ancestors, often without understanding their use. And I began to sense a deep movement across time and the world time weaves, a wavelength greater than the span of our life on earth. I began to know language as a music so profound it is impenetrable except to those who speak what they hear in it, and whose words are no longer their own.

Six months later, through a tangled concatenation of nearly random choices and chases, a demented search for heaven down innumerable blind alleys, I found myself standing on the platform of the Yamanote-sen, the train line that encircles the city of Tokyo. I remember especially the flashing window-glass reflections of my face, twelve layers deep, as the trains pulled in and out of Shinjuku station. There is no reason for this, I thought, and felt unreasonably alive in those ruins of my own rationality. No reason for me to be here reading signs that make no sense, I thought, reading them nonetheless: a mountain in flames, the book of the sun, a stranger at the gate. This was the beginning of an awareness that we are verbal fish awash in an ocean of language, unable to taste its salt. Except perhaps in rare moments, on the edges of an island understanding where sea meets land.

Well before I reached Japan, I had come to such an island, not so much through longing as through a series of losses that had systematically removed my family, my home, my friends and lovers, my tools, my livelihood, a large measure of my sanity, and very nearly, my life. Arriving in Tokyo, I realized that the last thing I had to lose was my language, and for the first time I saw what language was: a shared dream of the world from which its dreamers seldom ever wake, a virtually seamless emblem representing the accreted memories of a billion years of biological evolution, twenty-five millennia of human culture, and a few dozen centuries of historical wars and wanderings filtered through the personal fantasy of a single lifetime.

In Kawasaki, I taught English for a short time to the giggling receptionists of Fujitsu Electronics. I told them to pick a word, any word, and to repeat it over and over aloud until all sense had vanished, until they felt completely foolish and had to finally wonder at the meaning of the sounds they were making. If you listen closely, I told them, you will understand a great mystery. You will know what it's like for a fish to go to heaven. Management was not pleased with this approach, so we went back to practicing dialogs: "Hello? Mr. Smith? I'm calling about your appointment. Will three this afternoon be all right? Fine." And I circled the island from a great height, imagining I was a flying fish imagining it was a man teaching English. So I spent my youth in Asia.

Just as the dictionary had previously appeared as a fragile map of the territory I was about to venture into, on the eve of my departure to Japan I discovered a guide from another unsuspected quarter: artificial intelligence. The Japanese had just launched an ambitious research project in this relatively new and exciting area of computer science. I read a book about AI before leaving the U.S. and was immediately captured by some of the ideas it described, especially "knowledge engineering" and "natural language processing." Much later I learned that the philosopher Ludwig Wittgenstein had written "Die Welt is Alles was der Fall ist," which is to say: the world is everything that is the case. That covers a fair amount of ground, but given the rapid decomposition of everything I had assumed to be the case, perhaps it will be immediately obvious what so attracted me about artificial intelligence.

Here's the situation. Suppose you want a computer to solve a problem that human beings typically use their intelligence to understand. First you have to describe what's going on. Remember those story problems everyone always liked so much in algebra? "Johnny lives in Trenton, New Jersey and Pauline lives in Paris. If the Eiffel Tower's shadow measures 987 feet at 3 P.M. Eastern Standard Time, when will Johnny meet Pauline in Paris if he leaves New York at 6 A.M. and travels at a speed of 750 miles per hour?" Give up? Well, the computer gives up at "Johnny." It has literally no idea what a Johnny is, and no way at all of interpreting this tangled query. The computer's memory is a blank slate of millions of logic gates which can flip to 1 or flop to 0. That's about it. Try building a representation of everything that is the case from that.

Teach a computer to speak English. Now there was a challenge, especially for a sky-bound fish who no longer knew up from down, who had lost practically all sense of what people meant when they spoke to each other, could no longer tell how they knew when they knew — if they knew — what was going on in the words they used to send and receive signals representing internal states and the desire to modify same. We're talking an information-processing model of stone solipsism here, if you catch my drift. Immense storage, exquisitely sensitive receptors, sophisticated parallel architectures, representation schemata that loop back on themselves like infinitely nested Russian dolls: people. All dressed up and nowhere to go. "Good morning. . . . Fine, and you?"

The idea that captured me was not that this confusion of transmitted signals and their generators could be reduced to some sort of algorithmic explanation and the problem of language finally put to rest. Quite the contrary. I began to see the AI approach to modelling mind as allegorical proof of the power of ambiguity. The attempt to represent the world encounters deep paradox; the representation ultimately points back to its own symbols in a great circle. The language cannot escape itself. Likewise with human beings. Something happens in the heart and we don't know what. We see the moon and it tantalizes us, reminds us of something we once recognized somewhere else. But where? Is it a million-year old memory or the momentary resonance of deja vu? We assign symbols to our longing and build entire worlds from the names of our desire. There is a period of childhood wonder, for the individual as for the race, then a kind of blackout and we awaken in the ocean of language. "Good morning. Good evening. I love you too."

The solution is poetry not expert systems. AI and computational linguistics have tried to reduce language to formal logics, to a tractable system of rules and conditions, but it hasn't ever worked. We have been told for years to expect highly capable machine translators, natural language understanding systems, intelligent computers that can correctly interpret the full meaning of human speech. But they haven't come. The systems that have been created have turned out like brain-damaged genetic engineering experiments, lisping a few words that seem to make sense, then launching into demented gibberish. A few more rules here, a couple more conditions there, perhaps a brand new model, and maybe it'll work. What drives this search for intelligent computers? Is it simply the enormous profits they could generate by cloning the experientially acquired knowledge of expert human problem solvers? Or are the researchers looking for something else in there, some *one* who could answer all our questions, some reflection of our own original face? Does the fear ever arise that the ghost we find in the machine might be insane? Or that we may create a reflection of our own insanity, a la the Star Wars project? "Good morning. I love you too. Launch all delivery vehicles. Have a nice day."

The solution is poetry.

Winter Solstice

"And the earth was without form, and void;
and darkness was upon the face of the deep."

GENESIS

Before there were years, I wonder when people started to notice it was getting darker. Were they human even? You don't usually think of years as having been invented, but they were. By people. Much later than we're talking about here. Then, the days were only dwindling, getting shorter. No time to hunt. No time to gather. No time for much, except to notice it was getting dark, and colder.

There was a pattern here. Each day was less day than the day before it. The people knew colors, tastes and smells. They felt the wind. They saw constellations in the shapes of animals. They had no idea like our idea of time (and whatever you've heard, it's still an idea). But they noticed a pattern. How long did it take before someone did the math? If the sequence held, soon there would be no light at all. And the further north you traveled, the more this was true. Until, if you hunted far, very far, there was only darkness.

Perhaps some returned to tell about it, the land of endless night, with only sometimes an icy moon to see by. And maybe once, a burning ship, some local chieftain's funeral barge heading out from the coast forever. Like a dream. Like a life where the edges of death are uncertain. Where the land ends. Where the sea begins. When the moon disappeared and the storms rolled in, how black was that blackness? What was it like to huddle alone in a skin tent on the edge of the edge of the world and wonder?

We lived through this. Many times. Many years. And for long years we wondered if this year would be the last. A "year" in fact became the period of our recurrent meditation. And it was marked and pinioned at the four furthest quarters of the light: morning, noon, evening, straight-up midnight. The last not the least. The darkest the deepest. The hour of greatest danger we hang all our hopes on in silent dumb-struck vigil, praying as we've never prayed, before or since, for dawn.

Too much. Too many masks. Too many eyes. Too many voices. Too many lies. Too much neurosis, politics, religion. Too many saviors. Too many cooks. Too many formulas. Too many truths. Too many cigarettes. Too much coffee. Too many lovers. Too many cures. Too many births. Too many deaths. Too many dreams. Too many broken hearts. Too many hopes. Too many fears. Too many channels. Too many offers we just can't resist. Too many signals. Too much noise. Too many words. Too much endless everlasting silence.

There is no surer hell than glimpsing paradise.

I Was a Teenage Brain Surgeon

You may not believe this, but it's true: I *was* a teenage brain surgeon. It was my job for a while, though it's not what I was hired for. What I was hired for was to clean up monkey shit.

I had just dropped out of the University of Rochester and I needed work. As I'd had some lab experience, I figured I might try the teaching hospital at the college. In high school I designed an experiment that proposed to attenuate a certain strain of bacteria using gibberelin, a recently discovered plant growth hormone. I didn't know much about the biochemistry, but I figured that, bacteria being simple plants, hey, this stuff might do weird things to them. It sure grew big watermelons! Only problem was, I picked an organism called Pasturella Avicida. And the only problem with that was its common name: fowl cholera. If it got loose, it could easily waste the entire city. Thanks to the superior wisdom of the lab director, the city survived, but I never did get to find out what germs and watermelons might have in common. For a long time afterwards, I was sitting on five grams of pharmaceutically pure gibberelic acid. I guess I could have grown some killer tomatoes, but I finally lost the stuff somehow.

My first job interview went very badly. I could tell the guy thought I was a total fuckup loser. Finally, he asked me whether I'd taken any biology. I said it had always been my favorite subject and yes, I sorta took Bio 101. "What was your grade in that?" he asked. I looked at my shoes and mumbled, "I got a D." Unaccountably, the guy brightened for the first time. "Well, there *is* an opening in the Brain Research Center . . ." And that's how I got the gig.

As I said, the work was cleaning out monkey cages and doing other menial jobs around the lab. Sometimes they let me polish lenses. Boy, that was fun. But the guy I worked for, one John Bartlett, since deceased, started doing this weird thing. Once a week, he'd take me into the surgery and make me sit there while he implanted electrodes in some poor squirrel monkey's brain. The monkey was totally zonked on Nembutal and didn't seem to give much of a shit — with one dramatic exception. Most of the wires, Bartlett stuck into visual centers like the optic nerve. Later, when the monkey had recovered, he'd record from the optic radiations, which are at the back of the head. But he'd also implant an electrode in the reticular formation. This is old reptile-brain stuff and has mysterious things to do with arousal: fight, flight and fucking. When he sent a couple of microvolts down that baby, the monkey — this is under deep anesthesia you understand — would scream at the top of its lungs and shit all over the table. It wasn't pain. It was arousal. Think about that the next time you see a really hot number in some singles bar.

But I digress.

While working — these operations took hours — Bartlett would sometimes quote Shakespeare, generally long soliloquies on the death of kings. One time he got so carried away with this he overshot the structure he was driving the electrode into and the monkey died. Instantly. John was grieved. It wasn't that he was embarrassed — though that too; he knew he'd been showing off. He was genuinely remorseful. I didn't hear any Shakespeare after that.

One day he said to me, "I can understand you kids fooling around with LSD, but this thing I've got is completely beyond that." I didn't know what he meant, so I said, "What do you mean?" It turned out he'd picked up some weird virus from one of the monkeys in the lab. The squirrel monkeys were in the minority; most of our animals were great big badass Rhesus Macaques. One was named Romeo, and he'd been there forever. Romeo got loose one day and it took five guys to wrestle him down. The teeth on a Macaque make a German Shepherd look like a gerbil. He probably got it from a Rhesus.

The one you worried about was Virus B. Nobody knew what the fuck it was, except that it killed you pretty quick and there wasn't anything anybody could do for you if you got it. Not real contagious or anything, like Ebola, it just vitiated your personal career in big way. But this wasn't Virus B. Nobody could figure out what the hell Bartlett had, and it didn't kill him — not right away. I went back to visit a few years later and was shocked to hear that he was dead. He was a pretty young guy, much younger than I am now.

So evidently, what this virus did to John Bartlett for a long time before it killed him was make him trip. Continuously. He said he'd never come down since he got it. His wife drove him to work because he couldn't operate a vehicle. There were tunnels under the University Quad, but he couldn't walk through them. If he did, they would begin to vortex and he couldn't get out. I guess someone had once had to rescue him from one of these episodes. He was tripping all the time, and he was dying. He was also doing serious brain research and, as I would discover much too late, trying to teach me everything he knew.

One night he called me at home and asked what I was doing. This was highly unusual, and it kind of freaked me out. I told him I was drinking beer. I was probably smoking a big Jamaican spliff, but we didn't tell anyone about shit like that in those days. Paranoia was part of The Code. "Whatever you're doing, stop doing it and go to bed," he said. "I want you in here at 7. You're doing the surgery tomorrow. Solo."

I totally lost it. "WHAT!!! I can't do that. I don't know how!" As I recall, I was literally sputtering. "Why do you think I've had you sit in on the surgeries every week for the past two months?" he asked, rhetorically I figured. "Weren't you paying attention?" I didn't know what to say. But he did. "You're on for tomorrow," he said. And hung up.

I did go in at 7, gowned, masked, scrubbed, gloved, and did the operation, which I finished just after 1 the next morning. Almost 18 hours sterile. If I needed to take a piss, I had to re-scrub and go through the whole gowning dance again. At the crucial moments, I'd turn out the lights so I could see the blips on the oscilloscope. While an atlas of a sectioned squirrel monkey brain was some help in general orientation, the distinctive waveform signature of the optic nerve was the only reliable sign you were really hitting it. The monkey's head was fixed in a stereotaxic frame, and I had a microfine drive to sink the electrode a fraction of a millimeter at a time. In the room alone, the animal dreaming of some lost forest in South America, I would watch the green phosphor trails track across the scope's face. Where the hell is it? Am I already too deep? No, there, what's that? Yeah, maybe. Yes, I think so. Coming up now, easy, easy . . .

John told me one day, much later, that I'd done both the worst and the best surgical preparations he'd ever worked from. His post-op work (the monkey was *supposed* to survive) involved paralyzing the animal, propping its eyes open, and recording from the optic radiations. Bartlett had headphones that he would plug in — sometimes for as long as 10 hours at a stretch — as he presented bars of light of different widths, lengths and colors, sometimes vertical, sometimes horizontal. He was tripping on monkey virus in a totally pitch black lab, and listening to the neuronal music of a single cell, signaling, signaling . . .

It was around this time that I started doing psychedelics in a rather serious way. Some friends got hold of a bunch of Sandoz tabs, the world supply of which is gone forever kids — not much chance of trying this one at home, even if you wanted to. Not at the dosages we did it anyway. Sandoz was the only pharmaceutical outfit ever to produce pure lysergic acid diethylamide–25, and they stopped production long ago. Except maybe for the Army or the CIA. Ergotamine is a precursor, as the chemists say; it comes from a fungal rust that grows on certain cereal grains. Weird that these things occur naturally, in the wild so to speak (as if which part isn't?), yet slot so perfectly into the complex serotonin metabolism of the primate cortex. Must be some sort of accident. Some random stochastic happenstance, some entropic slippage whereby you eat some ugly looking mushroom that tastes like cat piss and find yourself looking into the eyes of god.

Yeah, that must be it.

As you may have read, the more you take this stuff, the higher the probability that you will begin doing Really Strange Shit. And, as the year was 1966, a wave of such shit was just about to break across the social fabric of America the way a tsunami takes out a Japanese fishing village in the dead of night. The morning after my first trip, I remember feeling some nostalgia for the sleepy details of what had been up to then a fairly boring normal life. It was Winter. The sunlight on the snow was intense coming down. The sky had become much larger. And I finally understood colors.

By the way, the reason I'd dropped out of school, or the best excuse anyone will ever have at any rate, is that some redneck cocksucker had recently murdered my best friend. There were two of them that waylaid us outside the bar as we were leaving — it had been too full to get in. Though I didn't remember it until days later, I had met them, once, a couple months previous, and had made the mistake, after the fifth beer, of telling them marijuana didn't give you a hangover. My friend had never laid eyes on either of these high school football heros, and they'd killed him before I could make the proper introductions.

In the Grand Jury hearing, some hausfrau asked me why I dressed and wore my hair "that way." Was I trying to start something? I basically told her to shove it. The kid who killed my friend testified at the trial that we were trying to sell them marijuana, which was odd, because when they jumped us from behind, we didn't have much of a chance to sell them anything. The killer got five years. And the judge then immediately suspended the sentence. After all, we were clearly dope dealers.

In fact, neither my friend nor I had ever sold dope to anyone, though we'd certainly smoked plenty of pot. Maybe it had been a mistake to tell that particular part of The Whole Truth to the jury. Now, though, I figured the lily-white City Fathers of Rochester, New York, were due a little payback. I privately vowed to turn on as many of their kids as I could get to. And in fulfilling this resolve, I was hugely successful. To start my new career in the role in which I'd been typecast by The Law, I scraped together whatever money I could by hustling nickel bags, and pretty soon worked my way up to Serious Weight. If you couldn't afford it, but looked like a jock, hell, I'd give you an ounce of decent weed just for the good feeling it gave me to imagine your folks finding you blowing up in the rec room.

In the storied Summer of '67, I lived in this house with a bunch of totally over-the-top acidheads. I put a sign on the front door that I'd ripped out from a local newspaper ad. It said, in five-inch high letters:

USED RUGS

One time the cops came looking for me — I was avoiding the subpoena for the trial described above. I slipped out the back window when I heard them introduce themselves to one of my compatriots. They later told my parents that "places like where your son is living can lead to drugs." I shit you not: five-inch type and they were looking right at it.

Oddly, I can't seem to remember how this happened, but I once got my hands on an entire pint of liquid LSD. This was the stuff that freaks in California were using to make blotter acid back then. But I had to be different. I decided to bottle the stuff. Of course, it *did* hit you a little harder that way . . .

By this time I had quit the Brain Research Center. Something about a girl, as I recall, but I got over it 20 years later. Anyway, near the Brain Lab was the Chem Building. Aren't Universities wonderful? They have everything a growing mind needs. What this particular mind needed was a 1000 milliliter burette and a couple hundred 5cc vials with bakelite caps. I sneaked down this basement hallway in Chemistry, and went over the chain link fence barring access by normally law-abiding students to the chemistry stores. Aha! Here's a nice big burette now, and lookee here! Little glass bottles! Back over the fence, I beat it back to an accomplice's apartment with my loot and jug of acid.

You're not expected to know what a "burette" is, but you need to for the story. It's a long glass tube about a half inch in diameter that has graduations up the side indicating how much liquid is in the thing: 50 milliliters, 100, 150, etc. It's also got a ground glass stopcock arrangement at the bottom so you can portion out small quantities of whatever you've got inside — in this case, as Led Zeppelin would soon be jamming out, "A Whole Lotta Love."

It was one of those things that seemed like a good idea at the time. But damn, it was painstaking work filling those hundreds of tiny bottles. Turn the stopcock just a little, drizzle one full, cap it, next. There did get to be a rhythm to it after a while. But nothing is perfect; there's that entropy again. Each time, a little bit would dribble down the side of the vial, and pretty soon my fingers were drenched. I couldn't wipe it off — this stuff was precious — so I just let it build up into a sticky goo, eventually all over my hands.

Skin is porous, did you know that? It actually breathes, which is why you will die if you paint yourself all over. I wasn't dying exactly, but my hands were starting to breathe. I don't mean like your skin is always doing that. I mean like, BREATHING. It was fascinating just watching them, but I knew I couldn't afford to get into this right then — I had a hundred vials left to fill and I needed all my concentration. Without it, I knew there was a high probability I'd be counting the molecules in the tabletop inside of a couple minutes. But oh man, this was getting difficult. Little peripheral flashes at first, you know? Those darters you get? And then there was that optic nerve thing. I could always tell it was going to be good acid when I could close my eyes, sort of bear down on the muscles behind my forehead and an electric purple Major Fifth chord would arc across the inside of my skull. Right now, I wasn't attempting this, but it was happening anyway. Whoa, good count!

I got nearly all the bottles filled before I started floating out of my body. Almost. I always hated being half high. That's the place where you're taxiing, and the runway is going on forever and you're neither here nor there, so to speak. The tension is incredible. Like before a storm. Big thunderheads rolling in, the temperature is dropping and the wind comes up, turning the leaves over the way it does, rustling through your hair and clothes. Wildness coming on but not quite here yet. I couldn't stand it any longer. I licked my hands all over, drank what was left in the burette, then knocked back a couple vials just to make sure it kicked in good and solid.

With my wares in a shoulder bag, I headed out into the night just as an enormous lightning bolt struck no more than a hundred feet away; thunder spoke in tongues. Rain came slashing out of the sky and I was running though it, laughing, crying, crazy, sane. Illuminated as the night. Higher than God Herself.

Back at the University, I stashed my bag of tricks down that same dark underground hallway where I'd pinched the chemistry set. Nobody'll ever find it here, I thought. And I was nearly right.

The band was an animal clawing at the walls when I hit the club and it took me by the balls like a cocksure lover. Good. Rock with it. Hey man, wanna get as high as me? The guy takes one look at my eyes and says wow, how much? Cheap man, five bucks one vial. It's liquid. Liquid?! Weird, man. I never heard of acid coming like that. . .

But these qualms are quickly overcome and soon I have twenty orders. OK. Now all I gotta do is find my stash, and. . . . Wait a second! I am back outside, not sure this is the same planet I entered through. I look back at the door. Yeah, same door. . . . Slowly I realize I am simply a LOT higher than I thought possible, but also that basic geographic coordinates still hold. Moon overhead, a good sign — not that the rain has stopped, but that gravitation is still in effect, so now I know which way UP is.

Finding my way back down that chemistry hallway was a little more challenging. It was a great stash because it was totally blacked-out dark, though that turned out to have its downside too. Like not being able to see, period. I edged my way deeper down the tunnel. Estimating distances in pitch blackness is not easy even under normal circumstances, which these definitely were not. I tried time. Let's see . . . isn't this about half as long as it took me to walk this when I was down here this morning? This *morning*!!! Wow. What did *that* mean?! No, the Temporal-Slicing approach clearly wasn't going to get me anywhere.

Somehow, I made it to the stash. After a few minutes, I found it wasn't really as dark as I'd thought at first. Must have been a dark adaptation kind of thing. But it was funny that when the light got better it was so many different colors and seemed to be coming from inside my head. Cool! I've got Super-Power Acid Night Vision, I was thinking — among various and sundry other things. To some extent, this was a false ebullience, as in the background, between the pretty trails and streamers, there were, well . . . possibly certain other . . . things in there with me. Some still find Jimmy Hendrix's quintessential question a little odd. Not me. I was definitely Experienced at this. I knew better than to concentrate too closely on the scales and teeth.

I must have made this trip about twenty times during the evening's revelry. No sooner would I get back with another dozen vials than they'd be gone and people would be saying like hey man you got any more of this righteous product? And I'd say you know I do, and go back to my cave. I was feeling a little like Golem, my precious, with my good things hid deeply in the dark. But the impulse to share was a strong thing in those days — or at least to see just how many people you could get precisely how wrecked. The answer to both those questions was shooting for some kind of local record that night, and whatever straights might have been in the place had long ago vacated. There's something about seeing some guy screaming full-face into an overdriven guitar amp, so hard that his neck veins are standing out, that makes you want to take your date just about anywhere else. So the Greeks were gone. The jocks were gone. Which is not to say the chicks were gone. The bravest and most beautiful always stayed with us, which invariably drove the Normals to the brink. God, what women! So anyway, it was just us freaks and we were ripped and tripping as the night came down and the band, still cooking, slipped into an altogether different gear.

But for myself, I thought, you know, this is so . . . East Coast. What we really need is a strobe to get things *moving*. So I went back out again to get one, knowing just where to look: the Brain Research Center. We used them on anesthetized monkeys to synch their psycho-optics to the oscilloscope. However, this was going to take some doing as I no longer worked at the place and therefore didn't have a key — pretty much a necessity unless I planned on breaking through two feet of concrete; the place was a bunker. So I called up the campus Pinkerton office. They didn't know I didn't work there anymore.

"Hey, I wonder if you can help me. I just drove all the way over here from my home in . . . mumble . . . and I seem to have forgotten my keys. I need to get into my lab to pick up some equipment for an off-site experiment we're running in the morning . . .

"And what is your name, sir?"

Oh fuck! I panic. Then just in time, I remember I have super-power acid night vision, so it stands to reason that I may have other unsuspected abilities, like cognitive invisibility to Pinkertons. To tell the truth, I did suspect this already, and pretty strongly, or I never would have called them. But then, I'd forgotten the part about *why* I'd called them. You know how it goes when you're that blasted. Better get it together in a hurry . . .

"Uh . . ." and I gave the guy my real name: Zaphod Beeblebrox.

"OK, Dr. Burblebrash, we'll send a car right over."

It wasn't a car I needed, of course. What I needed was An Official who could help me rip off a stroboscope from a locked University laboratory. When the prowl car showed up — seemingly before I put the receiver down, but that could've just been me — I remember thinking, I wonder if this doesn't look a little suspicious. I was wearing jeans with the knees ripped out, though the holes were nearly covered by a beautiful dark blue thigh-length frock with red piping across the bodice. I had an enormous full beard, hair down to my ass, and I was flipping through a deck of Tarot cards. "Thanks so much," I said, slipping into the shotgun seat. "Can't tell you how much I appreciate you saving me the extra trip!"

"No problem, Doctor. Where to?" Hooo! This was going to be a piece of cake.

I guess he figured the faculty was so goddam weird anyway that I didn't set off any of his onboard alarms. I'm playing it casual. Hmmm-de-dum-de-dum . . . I hold up Death to the car's dome light to get a better look. "Interesting. . . ." I say to myself. Just your typical whacked out academic weirdo, he's thinking, being careful not to look at the card too long. But I know he's thinking, "Jeezus, Mary and Joseph what the hell IS that thing?!?!?"

We get to the lab and I go into All-Business mode. I head straight for Bartlett's back office and carefully tear down the strobe setup. But wait, this is vandalism! All of a sudden I feel guilty as hell. Just as suddenly, it passes. Acid is like that. I get the Pinkerton to help me carry the stuff to his car, and then — the good part — into the club wherein by now every single soul has passed beyond the orbit of the moon. The place is literally rocking, the windows threatening to give under the high-decibel barrage pouring off the stage. And here's this fully uniformed Rent-a-Cop shouting over the din, "You want I should set it down here, Doc?"

There's a sudden lull. In fact, the place pretty quickly falls into dead silence and everybody's looking at me like, "Maaaaaaan, I do not believe this, man . . ." Of course, I'm enjoying the hell out of this wave of telepathic kudos. And to celebrate appropriately, I drink off a few more vials, then thank the Pinkerton and see him out. At this point, everybody else decides — we are of one mind in this — that more is a thoroughly excellent idea. So I am forced to make one last trip down my stash tunnel. When I bring back what's left, it's gone almost instantly. I was supposed to be collecting money, but that's way beyond my current capabilities.

There is a kind of blur, a synesthesia of events and motion, sound and silence. The eye of the hurricane approaching. Then: white light.

Later. Radical scene-shift. I am sitting on the floor of somebody's apartment playing the strobe over the Major Arcana one by one. Everyone seems to have gone somewhere. The Lovers. The Fool. The Hanged Man. The Magician. They flicker in the light, they move through time, floating on the trust you either find or die. Walking out on the thinnest mirror-ice of memory reversed, I flash, for an instant, on my future. It is always the hour of the wolf; that room, this room. Writing it down tonight, thirty years later, our eyes meet. Some spark leaps the synaptic gap, some circuit closes, and the echo it makes lasts for a little while before it fades.

Funny, isn't it?

*"After the First Death
There Is No Other"*

Dylan Thomas

RageBoy® Tells All

Entropy Gradient Reversals is just a couple days away from its first anniversary. Funny what stock we put in the accidental periodicity of our particular rock in its tireless circling of that big yellow star whose life-giving warmth and light, whose very gift of vision and the world's immediacy, is always eight minutes old. Other planets take much longer to make the annual pilgrimage; some far less. Mercury, for instance, has pretty much always operated on Web Years, but as the temperature there requires a level of sun block not yet invented, no one has ever expressed much interest. Whatever; wish us a happy birthday. We are one.

Irrespective of the ultimately inconsequential nature of the occasion — more probably because of it — we feel it necessary to do something new, different, mark some kind of departure here. Or embarkation. For starters, we are going to drop speaking in the first person plural. The Royal We has become such an ingrained habit that this may prove difficult, but we are going to try. I am going to try. . .

Christ only knows why. But then, the same applies to having started this thing at the end of April 1996, which already seems about a thousand years ago. Here's how it happened.

I had been working at IBM not more than a few weeks before I was approached by this guy who was some kind of ranking individual in the company's corporate public relations machine. "I've heard a lot about you, Chris!" Already I was worried. He takes my arm and claps me on the back in that infuriating demonstration of patronizing paternalism that passes for camaraderie among "the guys." Why don't they just cop a feel of your crotch to see how big it is? "Whoa, nice set!" But that would be too overt. Instead they wink and ask if you've been getting any. More than you'll ever see, scumbag. So, you should be getting the impression from this that we were off to a great start.

He wants to do lunch sometime. Where have I heard this before? But in contrast to the usual case, we actually do lunch — in the company cafeteria. Which, in this particular nook of the IBM empire, tells me everything I need to know about the company. Every time I walk into the place I get flashbacks of my elementary school lunchroom. Eisenhower is still president.

That's something else you probably don't know about me — the other things being everything there is to tell, outside of what little you may have gleaned from reading EGR. In November, I will turn 50. As in: years old. Are you picking yourself up off the floor? Did you figure someone who wrote stuff this whacked could only be a precocious teen with a dysfunctionally large vocabulary? Well, the truth is that I'm pushing the final days of my fifth decade in this cosmic penal colony and — would you believe? perhaps you would — this trashy zine is the best I've got to show for it. But back to our IBM flack.

He says he understands I have a wonderful collection of contacts in the business press, as if I picked them up like interesting seashells on some remote postcard beach. Yeah, I said, I've run into a bunch of writers, what about it? And this was his opportunity to rhapsodize on the subject of the Fourth Estate and the marvelous things I could do for The Company with those connections. I had assumed this was among the (to be honest, rather mysterious) reasons IBM had hired me in the first place, so none of this came as any surprise. The stunner was what came next: that I was never, ever, under any circumstances to speak with any of these journalists again without, a) direct permission from himself, or b) someone official listening in on another line. And with that he folded his napkin, gave me a winning smile and a little punch in the arm and disappeared into the bowels of whatever organization this company can lay claim to in the misty senility of its twilight years.

Wow, I thought. That's really fucked.

More to the point, *I* was really fucked. Because for whatever twisted reason, and I really don't know what the reason is, I write. I have always written one thing or another. Once it was poetry, usually when I was so smashed I could hardly hold the pen and couldn't make out the next morning what I'd been trying to say. Sort of like the signatures on my bar tabs in those days. The bank would call to say they thought someone was forging checks in my name. Reeling, crazy, out of control. But I'm getting ahead of my story.

So to feed this penchant for connecting words into sentences and seeing what kind of paragraphs these sentences might lead to, I had gravitated to other writers in what they call the working press — evidently to distinguish themselves from the non-working louts who litter their ranks. Language, as it transpires, is our only clue to many otherwise occulted truths.

But I was not a journalist myself. No, I was something far, far worse: a PR sycophant. I don't mind telling you about the acid, the drinking, the women — there is definitely something to be said along these lines for never getting old, as seems to have happened to me while I was paying inadequate attention. But to admit that I was once in Public Relations . . . well, try to imagine how painful this is for me.

It wasn't like I had aimed for such a career. I didn't wake up one morning and say to myself, hey I've got it! I want to be a loud-mouthed asshole who goes around collaring innocent people to tell them about The Product! I want a plaid sports jacket and some really nice white bucks and, above all else, I want to play a lot of golf! It wasn't like that at all.

Instead, I wanted to be a knowledge engineer and monster Lisp hacker. At this distant remove from the heady days of AI's ascendancy, the allure may be a trifle difficult to grasp. But during the early eighties I stumbled — literally in some cases — into the innermost sancta of this priesthood and became instantly addicted to a particularly bizarre and virulent new form of raw intellectual power worship. This was not my initial target either, truth be told. What I really wanted to be was a rock star, more specifically Mick Jagger. Sadly, the job was already taken, not to mention that — while I managed some reasonably decent blues guitar for a white boy and once even got stoned out of my mind with Buddy Guy's sideman, Luther "Snake" Johnson — my sense of rhythm was definitely marching to a different drummer, and I was therefore forced to seek other career options. Artificial Intelligence seemed as good as anything, especially as earlier experiments in certain drug-assisted magickal rites had not entirely panned out as expected. Which is to say, they worked a bit too well.

Confused? If you know anything about Lisp, what we're doing here is opening parentheses, so to speak, many of which will no doubt wait forever to be closed. This came to be seen by many — at least those not on the receiving end of Major Government Grants — as *the* Non-Trivial Problem for AI. As the challenges to reasoning get more interesting, closure becomes what is technically known as a Total Bitch. Fair warning: this state of affairs is likely to continue into any foreseeable future, the opinions of *Wired* magazine notwithstanding, especially with reference to this little one-sided discourse we are having. So here's where things stand so far. EGR has anniversary coming up. How did EGR get started? IBM. How did I end up at IBM? Something vaguely to do with public relations. Yeah, and what about that? Well, it started out as an AI kinda thing, but that was really just displacement activity driven by despondency over the patent lack of viable arena-rock options. If this doesn't exactly clarify everything, believe me, you're not alone. Just be glad that EGR is a sometime thing for you; imagine living this 24 hours a day!

Anyway, I came back to the U.S. from Tokyo in 1985 after a couple years there. When the plane touched down in Portland I thought it significant that Aretha Franklin was singing Pink Cadillac into my headphones, something to the effect that the girls should pop the top (on said Cadillac, presumably) on accounta Papa was back in town. Not that I was any longer much of a threat along such lines, having been much chastened by the experience of the couple years preceding my self-inflicted exile to Japan.

She was blond, from Texas, liked the red lizard Tony Lama boots I bought her, the diamonds, the cocaine — not necessarily in that order.

She would say she was not that kind of girl. Trust me: she was that kind of girl. To be fair, I was that kind of boy, which is why the attraction was so mutual, so instantaneous. And so deadly. From the words alone, you'd think "meeting your match" was a *good* thing, right? God, she was beautiful. It still hurts to talk about it. As far as I know, she still lives here in Boulder, to which I just returned (for the third time) six months ago. Sometimes I think about picking up the phone. Sometimes I think about picking up a drink. But it's been 13 years in the latter case and 15 for Texas. In neither case is there any doubt what'd happen after the first few hits.

This sort of thing is sometimes referred to as a Valuable Learning Experience — ranking right up there with not sticking your finger into electrical outlets. Some people just need to learn the hard way, I guess. But damn, the voltage was incredible!

Skipping lightly over the fact that this may be more than you really wanted to know, we now jump to Pittsburgh — The Land That Time Forgot — which is where I ended up mere days after Aretha's false prophecy in Portland. While Japan was in many respects enlightening — everyone should have a chance to be suicidally deranged in a totally foreign culture where nothing makes any sense — I had been itching to get back to the U.S. and into a red-hot AI startup. I understand that the logical progression of concepts may be a little thin here, but that's the way it was. And I got my chance in the form of an offer to work for Carnegie Group, a spinoff from the geeky University of similar name.

It is by now painfully obvious to many that none of this should have ever happened. I sassed my teachers in grade school. I dropped out of college. I dealt drugs to minors. I spent time in jail — though not for that. I kissed the girls and made them cry (and not for that either). I have never been a Team Player. I do not Question Authority, I piss on it at every opportunity.

But it did happen. I ended up working for Larry Geisel, Carnegie Group's then-CEO, with whom I had interviewed six months earlier wearing blue jeans and a dirty sweatshirt well after midnight at the Imperial Hotel in beautiful downtown Tokyo. It's a long story which maybe I'll get into later as I unpack and expand the contents of these telegraphic parentheses. Larry is CIO today at Netscape. I owe this guy. He didn't know I had less than a year of white-knuckle sobriety under my belt at that juncture and was in fact crazier than your average shit-house rat. What he saw was that I could write. So he said, "We think you'd make a good director of corporate communications."

"Cool!" I said. I had no idea what he was talking about. If he had explained it in simple terms — "You'll be our PR monkey" — I would have bolted right there and maybe I'd still be at Fujitsu fixing broken English in badly translated documentation about reverse-engineered IBM mainframes. Or pounding 16-penny nails, my previous job before Japan. But he was smarter than that. He just said my first challenge was to write the press release on the Ford deal. "OK, just two questions," I said. "First, *what* Ford deal? And second, what's a press release?"

As I soon discovered, the Ford deal involved a whacking big investment by that auto maker in artificial intelligence. Live and learn, eh guys? And the stuff I wrote played on Page-one Financial in *The New York Times* several days later. Oh, I thought, this is going to be easy! As fate would have it, it was five years before I hit *The Times* again — a full page story on the Mars Rover robot, on which I worked with John Markoff for thirteen months. But very early on in those five years, a horrible realization struck me like a sharp blow to the head. I had somehow become . . . that's right: a PR guy!!!

This was brought home to me in the first conversations I tried to initiate with the press about the wonderfulness of Carnegie Group's approach to artificial intelligence (the exact nature of which utterly escapes me today). I would call some guy I'd never heard of at, say, *Time* magazine, and start pitching him on whatever it was that was so exciting it just wouldn't keep. The problem was, I could hear the pitch too. It didn't sound very good. It sounded like telephone spam. And, I could tell by his slightly less-than-patient silence, the guy on the other end of the line thought so too. I remember this specific call because it marked a distinct watershed in my just-begun career as corporate flack. I can't do this, I thought after I hung up. It is sleazy. It is despicable. I will never make a call like that again. Ever.

Now if you are paid to "get ink" for a company, and that pay is your sole source of life-support, such a vow hardly constitutes a happy circumstance. This sort of predicament is often called being Up Shit Creek Without a Paddle. The excuse I used for continuing at all was the same all-purpose rationalization you've likely used yourself in similar circumstances: I needed the money.

Nonetheless, the vow had been serious, and I therefore had to answer the Scylla-and-Charybdis conundrum of how to keep both my job and what little was left of my self respect. Having had some Zen-ish sort of meditation training — this was during the worst days of my alcoholism; don't worry, it's a Tantric thing — I used this to good effect in solving my problem. And it went like this. I would get furiously working on my media database and wait until my mind was a complete blank. As I maintained this as a flat Emacs file on a Vax VMS system, I never had to wait very long. Then I would quickly grab the first number I saw on my screen, dial the phone and find myself voice-to-voice with some stranger — with absolutely nothing to say. That sure took care of the spam-script problem in a hurry.

Hello?

Yeah, uh, hello. My name is Chris, what's yours?

Charlie Smith. Look, what's this about? I'm on deadline.

I dunno. What's it like working there at Time? I just got back from Japan and everything seems kinda weird in the U.S. these days.

Oh yeah, what were you doing over there?

I was in the Japanese government's Fifth Generation Project for a while, and then I worked at a new lab Ricoh set up to study AI or something.

Really? That's interesting. Are those guys getting anywhere?

Nah, not really. It's a lot of bullshit for the most part. Making useless Prolog machines, faking results, the usual . . .

So what are you doing now? You're back in the States I assume . . .

I work at an artificial intelligence software company in Pittsburgh. Carnegie Group. Maybe you've heard of it . . .

No, but I'd like to chat with you sometime. Gimme your number and I'll ring you back when I've got this story about IBM and Microsoft put to bed. Man, this OS/2 thing is gonna be really big!

Sure, OK. It's (412) 555-1212 . . .

And so on. Now this may not exactly seem a breakthrough in the history of human communications, but it sure beat what I was doing before, which was basically reciting a canned spiel. And the effect was almost instantaneous. I started having real conversations. In some cases, really *interesting* conversations. At first, this was with small fry: *Oswald Spengler's DARPA Policy Tracker* or *Case-Based Reasoning Report* or — my personal favorite — *Intelligent Command-and-Control News*. Loser pubs like that. But later I got talking with real journalists at places like *The New York Times, Business Week, Forbes* and *Fortune*. The first thing that struck me was: hey, some of these people aren't half as dumb as they sound in print!

And I was writing too. Mostly stuff I was ghosting for Geisel, though it was a good collaborative setup. He'd tell me what he wanted to say about something like, say, Computer Integrated Manufacturing, then I'd go off and make up all this wild shit about how AI was going to save Business's collective ass. One day, as I was patching together one of these thumb-suckers, I wrote a paragraph that stopped me cold. Jesus, did I write that? I can't remember what it said, but it had fire, passion, and — this was the kicker — I actually *believed* it. Wow, I thought, and that was the end of the ghost writing.

Around the same time I also abruptly ended my dewy-eyed-groupie romance with AI and began overtly attacking the foundations of its know-nothing materialist catechism. The constellation of ideas and attitudes this precipitated — think of it as The Birth of RageBoy® — proved so spiritually cleansing I wondered why it hadn't occurred to me sooner. One piece I wrote in this vein was published in *IEEE Expert*, one of the journals chronicling the ever-upward advance of The Field, and could reasonably be inferred to constitute the proximate cause of an invitation I received shortly thereafter: to seek employment elsewhere. I had been working as "Director of Industrial Relations" at Carnegie Mellon University's Robotics Institute, and the guy I had so rabidly attacked in this article turned out to be CMU's star graduate in Computer Science. How was I supposed to know? Not that it would have stopped me if I had.

Then I wrote a bunch of other stuff, some of which is reprinted on my "other" page (http://www.panix.com/~clocke). I hope to God none of this smells of flackery. That was the whole idea: to keep earning a living doing public relations without ever doing any PR. It's complicated, but unless you're stupider than I suspect, you catch the general drift. (Just because I'm speaking in the first person doesn't mean EGR plans to drop its patented Reader Abuse Programme®.)

So all this takes us back to the guy who just folded his napkin and departed our table in the IBM lunchroom, leaving me staring slack-jawed at his retreating back. The Desire for Revenge was a large emotion at that moment, as I recall. Because not only had I been forbidden to talk to the only interesting people I knew — there sure weren't many among the business pukes I worked with — but, by obvious extension, I'd been specifically enjoined by this visionary corporation *not to write*. I freaked.

You hear this stuff about authors going cold turkey if they can't write. Yeah sure, I always thought, what a crock! But it turns out to be true. If you so much as get started with words — c'mon, the first one's free! — there's no end of the pain you're asking for. It must be an endorphin kind of thing, like runner's high. Of course, it's not like dropping 1000 mikes of Sandoz pharmaceutical — but then nothing is. Sometimes it comes close though. Too goddam close!

What was I going to do? I could either cop, and write chocolate coated PR lies for IBM — rather than do which I would have preferred to choke myself with a well-plied toilet plunger — or I could just plain shut up. For a while, I tried the latter tack. I watched the Internet industry from the sidelines. I sat on my hands. I stifled my shouts with a dirty sock that I always kept handy for the express purpose. I tried. God knows I tried! But finally — and inevitably — I couldn't take any more.

I first achieved Total Cognitive Meltdown on the last day of April '96, though because of my political beliefs — several degrees to the left of Kropotkin — I prefer to remember this as May Day. I decided to start a newsletter and invited a slew of online friends to sign up for it. The intention was pretty straight at first. I would deliver my precious insights on The Online Industry to like minded people concerned with the development of the medium. But first I started Capitalizing Things and making snide asides — and then there was the bit about aromatherapy salespersons and ritual axe murderers.

The response was amazing. Over a hundred subscriptions the first week! I was spooked at first, thinking IBM would find me out and the paychecks would precipitously cease. Then I reasoned with myself. What's your biggest complaint about this outfit? That nobody's online, except on those Neanderthal systems they've got running behind their 10-foot-thick firewalls. Well, what does this tell you? Hmmmm, you've got a point! They'll never find me on the web *because nobody ever goes there!*

For what it's worth, that's how EGR got started. After ranting for a year about Internet Cluelessness in all its multifaceted glory, I have no illusions about the impact of my work. Clearly the commercial world is finally realizing the error of its ways. That's why you see RageBoy® quoted so often in *The Wall Street Journal*.

Rather than keep on doing this though — anything can get to be a rut — I plan to write more on a subject I'm sure will be of enormous interest to you all: myself. Another reason for this change is that EGR is still woefully short of its initial goal of two million readers. This has so bummed me out that I've decided to retaliate once more, and this time to inflict Real Pain. If you've ever watched MST3K, and moreover understood the fundamental premise of the thing, think of yourself as Joel and me as Dr. Forrester. If you don't know what I'm talking about, just go away. In fact, that's the main idea: to end this whole Koyaanisqatsi thing by driving subscriptions back to zero. Then and only then will Life return to Balance. Then and only then will there be Rest.

The other reason of course — just in case the above strategy is somehow unsuccessful — is to amass a sufficient bulk of lurid autobiographical fodder that I can package into a book and hoodwink some publisher into making me filthy rich *that* way. Clearly, the Webzine Path is a total cul-de-sac.

So that's the new plan. Repent now! Only the Unsubscribers will be Spared.

Next time out in EGR — RageBoy® on Jungian Tarot and Goat Husbandry: Casual Connection or Global Conspiracy? Until then, do like me and my personal buddy Al Gore . . .

Be A Good Citizen!

Pattern Recognition

I grew up on the streets with a headful of Homer, Herodotus, Ovid, Virgil, Coltrane, jazzed in the knowledge there was greater knowledge and a way to know it. Beowulf, Thomas Wolfe, *Steppenwolf*, *Magister Ludi*, *Das Glasperlenspiel*. Between Beethoven, Mingus, Bach, Monk, Palestrina, discovering the archeology of secret long dead libraries and dusty bookstores. Alexandria, New Directions, City Lights. Dylan, the first one, wording his birthday shroud from the morning surf and dark drunken midnights of Wales and New York, 20 years older than I was then; 16 years younger than I find myself writing this now, for some reason trying to remember.

John Donne, Bessie Smith, Zen, amphetamines. Japanese calendars, Child ballads, southern spirituals. Getting high on cheap wine, bad weed, and watching the cars at night from the overpass, taillights streaming into the night and wondering where I would travel, who become. Gerry Mulligan's baritone sax bopping and blurting, talking back to the night, to Kerouac, Clellon Homes, Ferlinghetti, Ginsberg, and ending up on those negro streets myself, looking for something altogether else. Apollo, Dionysus, Delphi, Styx. Crossings and counterpoints. Toynbee, Spengler, Robert Graves, Jane Ellen Harrison's dark Prolegomena. Books turned and weighed, their secret geometries imagined.

And dropping finally in the slums of Rochester, best Sandoz product ever made. Not knowing how to take it, how to be, joking and poking at the great snake sleeping, kundalini uroboros, under my little life. I picked up the first book that came to hand, *The Interpretation of Dreams*, read from it aloud, my voice strange in the great space opening out inside my head, but Freud, long since dead, still made too perfect sense. And I knew what I needed then: more acid.

Love and sadness, nights on the road and in empty rooms, so empty they echoed with absence. A night on the rocks down by the river, in it actually, all words gone and reason blown, only the water rushing past in the darkness. Forgotten how I'd gotten there or where I might ever go again from that place, turning inward, falling, back through time, unwinding, back to my own conception, disappearing. Then further back through geologic time and evolution, watching as terrifying beasts first became extinct and then emerged, and then had never been. Back through primitive swamps and forests, then oceans and only oceans, then swirling gas, no earth yet, no sun. No one to see. No one at all. And shocked: no God. But further unstopping something watched as time uncoiled back to its beginning and beyond, poised on the trembling brink, that endless moment before Before. Holding, holding, but rumbling now with silent immanence. Then everything exploding screaming streaming out of endless darkness light forever. Slamming across all that had ever been, creating, impossible, I opened my eyes and looked directly into sunrise. Found myself sitting on that rock, seeing my hands again, feeling my body, face wet with amnion fluid or tears or the baptismal waters of the river that had carved its way into my life all night. At the end of the endless telegraph road, the universe finally getting its own message. And it was the morning of the first day.

Later, sitting on my porch cupping hot tea to my cheek, the world so suddenly huge, watching the grass grow. Watching myself change, become lost and not caring. Taking off my shoes, most of my clothes, taking my wallet out of my jeans, setting aside anything that would identify me, bring me back. And dropping. Traveling. Tripping unconditionally. Never planning to return, and if returning ever, then not to this place or body or accidental frame of mind. Dying so many times. I grew up on those streets.

Wandering barefoot on the Lower East Side of New York, over a thousand dollars cash in my pocket, looking to score, bring back for the holy freaks the one good thing. Odysseus adrift. Also in my pocket, the Tarot, the Waite deck I'd just bought that day. I went into The Eatery on Second Avenue and my waitress saw the cards. "I was raised by Gypsies," she said. "I will tell you about the trumps if you like." I had just dropped another tab and had little time left I knew, but she sat with me and pointed to each of the major arcana, the Lovers, the Fool, the Tower, Death. Then stopped. "You have two Magicians," she said.

"It came like that."

"Heavy," she said, and looked at me fully now: "use it well." Pentacles, Cups, Wands, Swords. As above so below. The Magician stands between heaven and earth, connecting them. The Magician does not fuck around.

In those days I would find cards on the street. Regular playing cards, though I knew pretty well how they had evolved, clubs from Wands, hearts from Cups. Queen o' Diamonds is a hard card to play. And even in some cases, the particular Tarot image lost in the modern versions. A cup proffered by a hand extending from a cloud to an unwilling youth, ignoring it. A black-draped body lying in the mud, pierced by many swords.

I would be standing on some street corner and I would hear in my mind the sound the moon might make if it were a gong. And invariably, turning, I would see a card, face down on the street. I would pick it up wondering: what now? What next? At the end of some days I would have six or eight in my back pocket and would take them out, arrange them, try to fit them with the dozens of others I'd picked up during the weeks and months when this was happening. Something was happening, that much I knew. When was the last time you found a card on the street like that? For me, it's been many years now, and I've had to find other ways to tell my fortune.

Magic was natural then. Some door. Some key. Some way to see beyond and behind the events and circumstances into which we'd been thrown. Into which all of us have ever been thrown. So naturally, I Ching, the antique Chinese book of changes. Trigram hexagram, sun moon, man woman, the well. An obvious guide for 20th century orphan teenagers with too much love, too little experience.

And Egypt — of Isis and Osiris, Justine, Balthazar, Clea, Mountolive — and Tibet and India, Alan Watts, D.T. Suzuki, Heinrich Zimmer, Joseph Campbell, Erich Neumann, Carl Jung. Tracing the stages of some journey we were taking anyway, whether or not we'd bought the ticket. Your face, your eyes, your ancient ceremony. I touch the stone to my forehead again, address the directions, the seasons, bow to you deeply and as best I can.

Abdul Mati Klarwein, does anyone remember that? Bitches Brew? Impossible anima, lover beyond breath of life. Fingers curling into the corn, the world at flood, proliferation and profusion, emblems that had been hidden, waiting centuries, icons, madonnas, archetypes, demons, gods, sex, longing, seed, birth, death. It wasn't the '50s anymore, kids, nor were we in Kansas, troubadours arriving out of nowhere like Medieval mummers, but with electric axes, amplifiers, walls of sound more powerful than the horns that brought down Jericho. Don't you want somebody to love? Don't you *need* somebody to love?

Stones, Beatles, Byrds, the Doors, the Dead, and Dylan, the other one, abandoning the blues and tin pan alley, chartbusters, the screaming fans, the stadiums. Let me take you down cause I'm going to . . .

Strawberry Fields, the prison, the escape. War in Viet Nam, in the streets of America, and everybody stoned, everyone feeling the napalm on their own backs, the gasoline igniting Buddhist monks in Asia and on television. We were tripping for the '68 convention, history, the moon walk. Out into the universe, we don't care who gets there first. Loving, dying, wondering as ever. But with a difference this time: that we knew it. That we were for once awake.

Then days in the country. Years. Pulling weeds and planting, having children. My daughter Shanti maybe three years old then, laughing under a tree so brilliant it was on fire. Fall in the Catskill mountains. Spring in Maine, and a remembered photograph, a picture of myself with long hair and a bandanna wrapped around my head, my dreams my freak flag, wreathed in white apple blossoms, looking right at you. No mistake. Ancient winters in cabins and brokendown houses, but so warm, so close. Cutting wood, splitting it. Milking the goats, their udders swollen full. American lotuses on the pond ringed by cedars, bathed in the billion-year silence of the undiscovered earth. Breaking the ice to drink. Deer and porcupines at the door. And *Atalanta Fugiens*, Michael Maier. Woodcuts and copper engravings, alchemy, magickal music. Of the spheres, of the sky at night while I'm taking a piss at the edge of the woods, the Milky Way wheeling overhead. Then hegira once more and more goodbyes. To friends, to lovers and whatever I'd found of a place. Those taillights again, but this time beckoning Orpheus into the underworld, into the Bardo between this life and some darkly inviting other.

Break, the film breaks. I am sitting overlooking a valley in Vermont. Nothing is happening. In the morning, cold, there is incense and a larger space that feels like home but has no location. Wrathful deities, mind unfurling like a prayer flag atop Everest. White light. Dawn.

Leaving again, for Colorado, Boulder, some strange place where I would get to see Alan Ginsberg dancing in his underwear (I swear I really did). And the Jack Kerouac School of Disembodied Poetics, inside which, if it has an inside, I never set foot, feeling too disembodied myself behind Country & Western beer joints and cheap booze. Plus I became a committed proletarian, a working class hero priding myself on my tools and trucks and worldly tricks and saying things like jes' burn that sucker in there, fuckin A!

Drunk and forgotten and broken to have found it: a door I could never pass through and live to tell about. No more stories, no more dreams. No history, no lineage. Just Say No. Just stay stuck at heaven's door, at the gate, and what to make of the rusted hinges, weeds in the yard? No one had ever lived here in this lie. In the night I would hunt and hunt well, bringing you down in my teeth, the blood thick and good in my mouth. Your neck arched back, your breasts pressed into me, and coming together into our each and only darkness we would sleep.

Until I met my match. Sweet irony. Sweet Jesus. And I still don't know who you were, or who you may be today if it matters. But damn girl. So much pleasure, so much pain. And too much time already spent replaying each word, each gesture, until memory blacks out and turns to fabrication, fantasy, our words and visions lost in the storm of other conversations, other eyes. It would be easier to think I never knew you if not for being able to see your smile, hear your laughter, echoing somewhere between us still.

I awoke on the road to the south, to Santa Fe and Phoenix, where even mushrooms in the high desert would not release you. Then suddenly I was in Tokyo, emblems of fire and mountain and water and earth the radicals of everyday language. And I had to begin again at the beginning, building a world, a place that might match the patterns of all before. An algebra of the heart and a taxonomy of words to tell it in.

Meanwhile back at the ranch, I found myself stroking the star maker machines, the dumb mainframes from which would emerge, we all hoped, some intelligence not our own. A kind of SETI project of the soul, though none would admit it. None but I, and I only whispered it, because even then I knew it was insane. But artificial intelligence led straight back into the deepest mysteries of language, without which no Turing Test was ever possible, and so to conjugations of the verb to be.

It was parallel processing, you could say, a joke, though we both had different objectives all along. Mine to bring back from the cold dead cycles, the blind iterations of if-then loops through random access and all the rest, some spark of life, some however uncertainly beating heart.

So then back to "the States," as if I had come from there once upon a time, to Pittsburgh and Chicago, Connecticut, New York. Familiar words that had lost all meaning. Whose only meaning is whatever happened there, more than I could write if I lived forever. And I will not.

But something else. We are strangers always, all of us to all. And yet in the words and traces, there is memory that is not our own. Stranded here, not knowing how we arrived or what will happen next, there is still a chance to meet again, against all odds, to recognize each other even now, to wink perhaps, as if to say: I told you so.

Shake!

> *"Love is not love*
> *Which alters when it alteration finds,*
> *Or bends with the remover to remove.*
> *O, no! it is an ever-fixed mark,*
> *That looks on tempests and is never shaken."*
>
> **WILLIAM SHAKESPEARE**

> *"Shake the shake with all your might*
> *and if you don't do it right . . . Shake!"*
>
> **SAM COOKE**

To presume to speak at all is already dangerous. Best first to make obeisance, burn whatever incense you may have to hand, draw up the circle, huddle in it, wait. Submit.

Talking to a friend once — this must have been around 1977, '78 — I said something I'd been trying to say for so long I couldn't remember. Trying and not being able to get it out. Not sure if I can now. The words went something like: if I lived for a thousand years I couldn't describe what I've experienced. It would take a year to express the thoughts and feelings of a single minute.

If this had been merely passing observation, the sort of smarmy self-important realization one might write into one's unwarranted memoirs, it would be trivial. Or worse. Yeah? So what. Lighten up. Have a snack or something! But it was said in desperation and the desperation is the interesting thing.

I drank in those days. I drank a lot. Not to forget but to remember. We used to laugh when they said psychedelics led to heroin, but there's a lot of truth in that, though for all the wrong reasons. There is no surer hell than glimpsing paradise. Rivers of silver and turquoise flowing free, snaking the world together in its own dark curious liquid wisdom. Look on the tree of life, of knowledge, unseparate at last, ancient and eternal. Look on your own vision then, within that mind, within some impossibly larger heart loosening finally from the iron grip you once thought was yourself. Helpless, leaving, unraveling out into the night. Dying, being born.

She was so kind to me in those fragile moments. Fierce but never false. Learning to walk again. Learning for the first time colors, elements, seasons, moonrise, where the sun came up. I would go down to the water and pray into it. I would encounter other animals and we would recognize each other.

And now this, I would think. Not the endless tapestry of complexity unbound, but just stupid ordinary confusion. Embarrassing. Not knowing how to hold one's hands. Like posing for an awkward photograph when you're already in a bad mood. Leave me alone. Shall I hold my face like this? Or this? And nothing felt right, and nothing felt true. No surer hell.

So I drank.

They don't call em spirits for nothin, pardner. Certain kinds of music are like sex. You go back for more because you know there's something about that, but you just can't put your finger on it. So to speak. It's not a remembering kind of thing. If you do it right, drinking is like that. I did it right. Or as right as it's possible to do. What this entails is going where it takes you, which can be further than you bargained for. And I don't just mean nights in the drunk tank, or that real bad feeling that something uncommonly weird went down and maybe there are people looking for you.

No, I mean the certain knowledge that comes at some point that you're unmoored anyway. There's no turning back and death is the sound of those falls in the distance. But that's far too melodramatic. Death is the next moment and the succession of moments whose beginning you can never quite recall. Might as well be down for the whole nine yards. Might as well ante up.

The last time I "took a drink," as the old-timers say, was in the kitchen of my Tokyo apartment in 1984. I knew we were bound to part company, and soon. I was either going over those falls or I was gonna stop. Stop? Stop what? I couldn't imagine life without the connection. Without plugging in. So I got high one last time and I could feel it coming on so strong. I saw what it was that time. I felt it.

Big snake comin' baby. Yeah. Big worm comin' through the sand tonight!

Maybe I'm still riding it. I hope so. Sometimes I wonder, just like you do. How do I know? C'mon!

If you think you can't take it for another second, at least you're asking the right questions. At least you haven't knuckled under, given up, told yourself it was all a dream and after all there's that mortgage payment, presentation, trade show. Whatever it is we waste our lives on. Making dumbbell cracks in gonzo zines, for instance.

Every once in awhile, we have to come through, if you get what I'm saying here. It's an inside joke, hold the irony — then lay it back on even thicker. It's a belly laugh though, not one of those thin self-conscious snickers. It's a big ol' Mars Bar, honey, and it's all for you.

Strangely, the desperation's gone. Knock on wood and get my mojo workin. Where's my rabbit's foot? But really. Gone. Something happened somewhere in there and I know I can't say what, even if I had those thousand years. But it's OK. You know those songs that go like "everything's gonna be alright"? A lot of songs say that. Well, they're right. It is gonna be alright. You and I may not survive it, but that's alright too. At least it's alright with me. Forgive me for not mourning your inevitable passing. Think of it as an acceptable tradeoff. Best I can do anyway.

But is it? There's still some sense that I should try to say what it is — whatever it is that came, that went, that changed. People ask me to. Hell, even you guys. Actually, only you guys, which is why I keep doing this. And which is nice, believe me. I mean, that you believe me enough to ask in the first place. But I'll let you in on a little something here that I really shouldn't talk about at all. I distrust art.

Yes, I know that's pretty shocking, but I've never been comfortable with the whole idea. Maybe it's because I'm really not a writer. A real writer would make it all seem effortless. You'd get all the insights with none of the peeled-up edges. It'd be second nature to write the real, the truer than true stuff. The stuff that's not just clever e-zine tricks for the terminally disenchanted. All the human tragedy would still be there, of course, but with the rough bits filed off. Honed down. Polished up. Otherwise, it wouldn't be . . . well, art.

Loops within loops within loops. Such is our entrapment. I thought I said I said I thought I said . . . Somehow I just stopped caring. Maybe because I finally heard what she was trying to tell me. Maybe because I finally saw the light. Maybe because there really is no turning back.

So here we are. The world is fucked up, true. The environment's in such a muddle. Dear! How will we ever cope?

Dunno. But here's a thing that's interesting. Here's a bit of comedy that's downright anthropological. Look how the natives dress, how they speak. How they defer, without acknowledging they are deferring, to the ghosts of their long-dead ancestors. How they walk reverentially in the presence of money. How they elevate certain magical symbols in times of great collective fear. Yeah, that Y2K thing sure is gonna be a whopper! Better move away to Arizona. Better move to Timbuktu! They hide their pain. They hide their broken hearts.

When context fails completely — flatlines — it's as if you just landed from another planet. And anyway, you might as well have. Do you remember how all this got going? I sure don't. I do recall one day I was going to the grocery store. This was in Sunnyvale, California, circa 1956. I was maybe nine years old. I stopped stock still in the middle of the road and suddenly knew I was alive. That's how it happened for me. Don't know about you.

But I do know about you. A little. You think you're lurking at a safe distance, reading me. But I'm reading you too. I could be wrong, it goes without saying, but I say it anyhow to defuse the potential creepiness of feeling that I'm stalking you in my rearview mirror. Here's what I think I'm reading.

Some of you are on your fifteenth Major Strategy for Dealing With Life. You discount the others as laughable. You were younger then, naive. Now you've got it nailed.

But hold the phone. Maybe not. Didn't you just recently catch yourself thinking something you can't possibly admit to yourself that you were actually thinking? Didn't you see this and immediately convince yourself it hadn't happened? Fast, huh? The mind is so fast. Yet there are those peeled-up edges again. The Chinese puzzle looks like a lacquer treasure from some ancient dynasty, but then you look closer and the pieces don't quite fit together and they're some kind of plastic. Not to mention that it says "K-Mart" on the bottom. Strange that you'd never noticed that before. So maybe by now you're thinking it's getting time for #16, but you can't imagine where that one's gonna come from. Why else would you be reading EGR?

You're in love and this time it's going to last. Cue Stevie Wonder. You finally left the bitch, the insensitive bastard, and you won't make that mistake again real soon! You're floating in limbo, your emotions unpredictable, unwieldy. You snap at people for no reason, then invent a reason. A really good one.

You're beginning to suspect this is all a bit too random. Or long ago suspected it and now you're not taking no wooden nickels from nobody. You're ready for anything, you've seen it all. You love your kids, you hate your life. No wait. You love your life, you hate your kids. You've even considered Scientology. Or joining the Psychic Friends network.

In short, in fact, *in flagrante delicto*: you're at the end of your fucking rope. Admit it.

Contrary to popular belief, which is even more obsolete than primetime news, this is not such a bad place to be. It just takes a little getting used to is all. Have you ever been experienced? Well, I have. And I can tell you for a fact that dealing with inordinately large doses of LSD, even when ingested by accident at loud indoor sporting events, is nothing compared to dealing with plain old ordinary garden variety reality. Naturally, some farting is involved, among other humbling functions. But perhaps more important is the *recognition* of farting, neurosis and suchlike as unavoidable consequences of having incorporated. And I do not here refer to anything with IPO potential.

Perhaps this all seems too pedestrian, though. Maybe you really did learn everything you need to know in kindergarten. If you truly believe this, just go away now. Unsubscribe. Kill yourself. You are a hopeless idiot and you've learned nothing. You are wasting valuable floor space.

But you don't believe it. No one does. No one. Everyone looks up at the stars and wonders. Everyone remembers falling in love. It's corny and you don't like to admit it, but there it is. It's true for your most hardened killers. It's true for your most chichi ennui-ridden webhead hipster neophiliacs.

. . . yeah? And then what? Then you give yourself absolution. You forgive yourself for being human, for being confused, for not knowing the right answer. You weep for your life. For having been so shut off and hard hearted. You get down on your hands and knees and kiss the fucking earth for having you one more day is what you do.

And then you're free. That's all she wrote. Amazing isn't it, that anything so apparently complex and long-term-debilitating could turn out to be so simple in the end? Trust me on this one: it is. So slap your head, kids, and have a V-8, cause that's all there is to it.

I'm sitting here thinking, "Well, I could end it there . . ." but knowing full well that's not what you came out for this time. It's too neat, too reductionist. Even if it does add that certain hint of surreal Vermouth whispered across the vodka of verisimilitude, straight up and straight out of the freezer. Hey, I quit. I didn't forget.

Once I was trying to get my head around rock and roll. I mean, I was trying to understand it. People have strong reactions to this music,

I reasoned to myself, tapping my foot to the beat like a good little white boy. Uh huh. Uh huh. But I just didn't get it. And I only mention the white boy thing because when I was a young dude, I used to hang out in places where that was very obvious. Painfully obvious. Because I was the only white boy there.

I used to score from this guy who worked in the local grocery on Plymouth Avenue in Rochester, New York. It's all upscale gentrification now, and even that's gotten tacky and frayed. Back then, this was the hood, though no one called it that. It was the black ghetto. Once it had been the best part of town, and many of the slum houses had stained-glass windows in the entryways. I guess I liked it for the same reason I like the net. All the bad people hung out there. People I could tell knew more about how to be alive than the people I grew up around. I remember Friday nights down in literal pits dug into the ground and covered with tarpaper, filled with barbecuing ribs and drunk old blues guys with cheap guitars knocking out shit *your* ass never copped from no Tower Records, Jack.

And this guy I used to score from started inviting me to these dances. I went to like one dance in all of high school and it was a disaster. I went home early, much to my date's chagrin, and put on some Buxtehude to settle my nerves. But this was different. You'd do up a little Robitussin AC, smoke a little weed, and eventually you got into it. It was dark in that hall and all the chicks were dressed up like something out of a movie. The guys too. They would have, some of them, like powder blue tuxes and outrageous satin cummerbunds, patent-leather shoes you could comb your hair in. But you didn't laugh. You were just a guest, a tourist. You were respectful. Or you died.

And then here came the band. Who *were* these guys! They could really play. They could sing better than anything I was hearing on the radio. Soul, rhythm and blues. Wilson Picket. Otis Redding. Where had I been all my life? And I was only 18.

This is where I figured out about rock and roll, or whatever you call it that does that. And a whole lot else, I guess, though it's only just now sinking in, now that that world is dead as a burned out supernova ten million light years somewhere back behind yesterday. And the thing would sorta build up as the night wore on, the band getting hotter, the lovers getting hotter, the hall getting a *whole* lot hotter, until you were dancing your ass off, sweating like a motherfucker, stoned, exhausted and you didn't care anymore, and then the band would know they had you and they'd kick it over the edge, driving the beat like a blinded animal, the lead guitar suddenly sliding up from tasty to insistent to full-throttle roadhouse and just when you thought that was the top, the horns would come in, a whole line of them wailing blasting blowing the fucking roof off and they'd cook like that for so long you could not believe it, as it defied the very laws of God and man, shredded the fabric of space and time, and you'd find yourself shouting "Yes! Yes! Yes!" like a goddam madman just like everybody else, and that wall of sound, of crazy joyous noise, was all the reason you needed, all the reason you'd ever likely get, and everybody knew it. Which was the whole point. The heart and soul of rock and roll. And all the rest of it. If you didn't get it then, you never would.

I got it. And so do you, or you got no business being here.

"get it while you can . . . "

Howard Tate

Signs and Portents

Awash in panic. Alone in my cabin in the high Rockies, I had clearly eaten too many of the innocuous looking little mushrooms, and now I was veering out of control, alarms triggering down every internal subsystem, neural klaxons going off like explosions, each calling for more adrenaline. Suddenly removed from the sky, white clouds, impossible summer sunshine, mountain air: all were mocking, distant, alien. Lost between heaven and earth, I was falling headlong into the wreckage I'd created of my life. Unable to hide, to beg forgiveness, to continue living.

I stumbled out from the cabin to my truck, testing just how self-conscious it was possible to be. Deeply embarrassed by the trees, so obviously belonging there unlike my stupid interloping self. What was I thinking to have come here, done this? And how would I survive the next eight hours? A meaningless temporal division in a life so abruptly terminated. More to distract from my patent doom than anything else, I slotted a tape into the deck and hit the play button, closed my eyes.

It took forever for anything to happen after that. Hell is for eternity, just as they say. Curious that Pat Metheny was in hell along with me, plus someone on vibes, a drummer heavy into cymbals, a piano. Maybe it was "As Falls Wichita, So Falls Wichita Falls"; that was the right year, 1981. The music began as random sound, unbearable, without purpose or direction. I thought to turn it off, but my hand was so far away it wasn't responding. More panic! I was paralyzed, gripped by iron bonds of aimless yet inevitable consequence. Nothing was worth doing. Yes, I could move my hand if I really wanted to, but why bother? What would it prove, cut off from the human race forever, sitting alone in some automotive contraption on the side of some random mountain in East Jesus Colorado, that I could turn a cassette tape player off? Nothing. I slipped deeper into whatever lethargy had stoned my heart and sapped my will and tried not to fear the fear any more than it seemed to be demanding as its due. I blanked and disappeared. Then back then gone again.

The noise of the music was all there was, and maddening interminable time. Because there was nothing else to do I found myself watching the notes unfurl. I remember noticing the stereo was much better than usual. As I blindly drifted closer, each bit of sound took on a shape, an iridescent color, almost a personality. They were moving against each other as if confused, searching for some better arrangement. Then, wait — even though all was lost, though nothing mattered — this was very nearly interesting. They were forming into patterns, then falling back apart. Hard to describe the constellation this created. It held yet shifted, twisted, flowed, like the edge of a Mandelbrot set, fractal recursion collapsing in on itself only to repeat, the same yet different on every iteration. Like rattlesnakes suddenly in fallen leaves. Because of this movement my vision was drawn to something larger that the local piece was just a part of, and in that moment the music shifted focus, dropped into gear and somehow *opened* to reveal a huge ring of synchronized diamond fire hanging in black space, beginning to turn, to glow, to become one whole and living, breathing mandala. Sharp edged, terrible, immediate, real. Beauty beyond all pain and sorrow. Not of myself or other either: original face.

Nothing left, I rode the music right on through forever and was almost thrown again when it began to slow and faded, finally ending. "Fifty-five . . ." someone called out matter-of-factly on the tape. And in the far background, ". . . let's do it again," then laughter. They know, I thought, amazed I hadn't seen it sooner. Skillful brothers and sisters always bring you through.

I opened the truck door and got out. The clouds had massed the sky and the wind come up. My eyes were liquid with ancient knowledge, and the world they took in was no longer outside. I opened my hands to the earth. I breathed and stretched, a certain animal once more. So good to be back.

55

Later, coming down, drinking hot peppermint tea, exhausted, drained, absolved of my humanity, I see the great million-year rocks upthrust across the forest valley. Aztec rocks, it's instantly clear. Jagged, electric, brooding, dangerous. Blood sacrifice as natural to them as the slanting light of sunset they are redly bathed in. It is fifteen years later and I live less than 50 miles from this place. If I went back today, I know they would be there still. Watching.

The plane had left LAX in the middle of the night. What is it about leaving the earth that precipitates such melancholy memories of one's path up to that point? Cusps and passages. Departures. I could see moonlight on the clouds and maybe water, miles below. High over the Pacific, headed for Tokyo.

A few days after the trip described above — not the one to Japan — I drove down from Red Feather Lakes to Fort Collins, 40 miles to the edge of the Great Plains where a part of America's manifest destiny had finally thrown in the sponge. I was after two things: a dictionary and a thesaurus. While I didn't have much money, I wasn't looking for anything all that fancy, just simple paperbacks. This is curious in light of the 20-volume Oxford English Dictionary and the several dozen other unabridged lexicons I've collected over the intervening years — fundamental documentation for the mother of all operating systems. But that day all I wanted was the bare bones, your rock-bottom basic starter kit.

It seemed to me that no one really understood what anyone else was saying. It still does. We are locked up in our heads with our ideas: memories, longings, aspirations, disappointments, dreams. We try to explain. We fail. This disconnect is so dependable it has become our closest bond.

We make noises we act as if we do not own, or even comprehend. For perhaps a million years, human beings have lived and died and, in the course of all that time, have constructed and preserved this legacy of presumably useful signs, first uttered, then inscribed. I tap the keys, you read the words the letters make. This is not given. We created it.

So these things were going through my head in the days after my illuminating descent into a hell I could no longer deny, and my undeniable, even if temporary, rebirth. And I figured the dictionary was as good a place to start as any in examining these sounds we use in trying to convey the things about ourselves we least of all understand. But I would start simple, with "bread" and "tree" and "love." No, not that last one. Way too compound.

It's like archeology. You take a word — say "word" — and wonder how it got into your mouth, how it tripped off your lightly typing fingers. So you look it up. And you are back on the steppes of Asia 10,000 years ago. "Word" it seems comes from "wer," a sound invented by a people so obscure we call them only "Indo-Europeans" with little idea of what that means or who they really were. Also from "wer" comes man, a complex concept (from whence also "werewolf"), as well as oath, in the sense of bond. There you are holding your testicles (where applicable) and swearing fealty to some berserker liege who will otherwise lop your freaking head off. You laugh. But this is precisely the derivation of "testament" — giving your word on your "manhood." As in "word up!" Also as in Old Testament and New. Hang onto your cohones, compadres, we are riding into history. The Internet is not a new thing, though the pipes are certainly faster now. No matter where you get on, though, the Telegraph Road stretches back in time, time out of mind, and in a shimmering mirage of might-have-been, drops below the limen of our collective consciousness. 28.8, X2, T1; doesn't matter.

I grew up in an erudite family. There were books everywhere and I poked through them all, well before I understood why they put all those black marks on the nice white pages. I learned to read early and well, as I am watching my daughter do today. But even before that, there were pictures. As of the cave paintings at Lascaux and Altamira, those bulls and horses still running in the flickering Neolithic torchlight. And one that remained with me even more powerfully. It's a painting of a monk, or maybe an alchemist if there's a difference, sitting deep in thought at his desk, which is strewn with manuscripts and bones, a skull, a set of cartographic dividers, maps and charts of stars and ocean voyages, stones and various unrecognizable minerals, hand drawn tables of elements and corresponding icons — earth, fire, water, wind — an open book, a goose-quill pen. And all about the cluttered room are other arcane artifacts, each of which serves as an entry point into a secret and otherwise unknowable universe. Symbols we call them, for lack of a better explanation.

Symbols represent something that isn't immediately obvious, or perhaps that we'd rather wasn't. Words represent mental constructions, concepts, which try in turn to justify experience to itself. Experience is the trace of something that has passed — always a little while ago — through the sensorium of touch, taste, smell, of hearing or of sight. Think of a tree falling in the forest of your solipsistic psyche. But is there something else? If you try to find out by tracing these nested representations far enough in either direction — through introspection or the analysis of socially potentiated memic propagation — you will either go stark staring mad or become enlightened. Quite possibly both, depending on your expectations of the latter state.

Abruptly, I was awake again and the plane was banking over Tokyo Bay. The next three years would be a blur of artificial intelligence, Lisp, knowledge engineering; zeros and ones concatenating into increasingly complex data structures until, presumably, they would speak back to us from that space beyond which we cannot see. At the time, reinventing God seemed a noble enough vocation.

And then . . . then I forget. Some other things happened, some of them important, and the next thing I knew I was sitting here writing this issue of EGR. It had to be today, but this is all there's time for. There are so many tasks and projects nagging at me that I knew I wouldn't have another chance for weeks. Whatever this installment may be about — and I leave it, of course, as an exercise for the reader to decide — I must get on to these other pressing matters. For one thing, I have a brand new Intel 266 MHz Pentium II Processor w/ MMX Technology (fool!) sitting in my hallway unassembled. It will let me rip through information at demon speeds. It will store 6.4 gigabytes of raw unpurposed data (or as one salesman enthused, "six jiggabytes"). It will let me assemble and deconstruct codes and semaphores, tokens, pointers, arrays, whole documents, websites, networked archives, cultural repositories. But first I have to clean my fuckin desk.

There are papers, the printer that spits them out, a fax machine, a phone. There are notes, reminders, magazines, scattered software packages, their registration papers never registered, books on regular expressions, Unix, Perl and Java, Javascript — and one on Indo-European etymology. There are Zip drives and Jaz drives, cables everywhere. Ashtrays and cigarette ashes, because I often miss. Coffee cups and CD-ROMs — and even, still, a pile of floppy disks, though they don't flop anymore. Perhaps they've died. There's a picture of my wife holding the cat — with a two of spades hanging inexplicably in thin air — and pictures my daughter drew for me, as well as a note she left on my terminal last week that says, "Da, I think your system locked up." She is seven.

Worst of all is what's *inside* the box I'm writing this on today. I'll have to move it all over to the new machine. Tools for making words and tools to take those words apart to see what's inside, if anything. Tools to wrap them up and unpack them. Tools to upload, download and distribute them. Tools to read them, store them, categorize and recall them. Tools for trying to engage with a language and those who continue to create it on the fly without stopping to wonder what it is they're doing half the time, but who might wonder, if it ever crossed their minds, why anyone would sit and type on a beautiful sunny Colorado afternoon in a cave of a room so far from the sunlight and the cries of the people — good, bad and indifferent — who make up the world, or fondly assume their ideas do.

One off these days I'm going to have to get all this organized. But hey, in the meantime, it's sure good to be back.

"Let's Drink to the Salt of the Earth"

The Rolling Stones

Dust My Broom

> *"I've seen things you people would not believe.*
> *Attack ships on fire off the shoulder of Orion.*
> *I watched sea-beams glitter in the dark near the Tannhaüser gate.*
> *All those moments will be lost in time, like tears in rain.*
> *Time to die . . . "*
>
> **ROY BATTY IN *BLADERUNNER***

There's a storm coming in over the Rockies, a sheet of gray forerunner clouds already stretching to the eastern plains where the sun is still shining. The wind just came up and the temperature dumped 20 degrees. Brooding thunder from the West. Feels good. Suits my mood today.

Do you ever feel that something's shaking but you don't know what? Could be you're gonna die or fall in love. Could be nothing. Then again, it could be something's trying to signal to you. Get your attention. Something you forgot.

Trying to remember then. Standing here feeling the wind come on, the elements talking to themselves. Always feeling like an eavesdropper. Always feeling this must be meant for someone else. Maybe not.

A couple months ago I went to see that IMAX movie about some expedition to the top of Everest. I don't recall too much. Somebody died. The rest of them made it. Why, I wondered. What kind of person would you have to be to do something like that? Crazy I guess, but in a way the world gives points for. We made it. Look at us. And the crowd goes wild.

But there's something wilder. Something bearing down on you, but uplifting at the same time. Something uncanny yet so familiar. Across the street someone's mowing a lawn. The sky is getting darker. It is

going to storm now, but good. The Fed-X guy just dropped off two
packages from Amazon. Wanna know what was in them? OK:

- *The Experience Economy: Work Is Theater & Every Business
  a Stage*
- *Mass Customization: The New Frontier in Business Competition*
- *Net Worth: Shaping Markets When Customers Make the Rules*

See? It really is me. It really is EGR, bringing you that same old
endless pointless pitch. This isn't art, folks. You can click the buttons,
buy the books. They won't help you any really, but hey, Hemingway
never gave you that kind of option, did he? And besides, he blew his
head off with a shotgun one afternoon in 1961. That Captain of Your
Fate routine is often less than it's cracked up to be.

Meanwhile back on Mt. Everest — the thunder is getting louder,
more insistent here — there are prayer flags flying everywhere. My
heart leaped to see them beating against thin sky, impossible sunshine.
As close to heaven as it gets.

Somewhere down below is Katmandu, almost everything I know
about which I learned from Bob Seger, who also asked the somewhat
less than immortal question: "Who Wants to Go to Fire Lake?" —
shades of the I Ching leaking through early-80s American radio — and
the answer was pretty much nobody, but the night was young back
then and so were we.

Prayer flags against the wind. Think about it. This is a Buddhist thing.
They put em up all over the place and they say things like "May All
Beings Be Happy" and "Om Mani Padme Hum," which roughly trans-
lated means: <cosmic sound> the jewel in the lotus <cosmic sound>.

Depending on your point of view, the cosmic sounds either mean
everything or nothing. Independent of your point of view, they mean
both. The rest refers to the fact that the lotus, a symbol now fucked up
forever by an American software company since acquired by IBM — are
we talking Global Economy here or what? — is this awesomely beautiful
flower that blooms in the mud, but is not, you know, like, sullied by it.

But even that's a throwback, because by the time the Buddhist teachings had reached Tibet, the whole notion of pure v. sullied had taken a couple of serious turns. The mud is as good as the flower. Both are empty. Both luminous. That's the jewel if you look deep enough inside.

For one thing, the Tibetans were far too earthy and practical to buy into the intellectual logic chopping of those Indian scholars to the south. Or accept it completely at any rate. They already had these bad-ass demons and shit, and neither side really felt like parting company. Let's just say they came to an accommodation. To me, what happened up there in like the 10th Century or so — close enough for government work — resulted in the only religion I've ever run across that has any balls.

Thank God.

Speaking of Whom, the funny part is the Tibetans don't have one. Weird, eh? What are all those prayer flags supplicating then? Because make no mistake, that's what they're there for. Calling out to the start of things before before, back to some uncreated primordial space that predates any bang, big or small, by a trillion times a trillion years but that's also happening even now while the coffee's making and the rain has already rained while I wasn't looking and I'm wondering what I must have been thinking when I ordered *Net Worth*. The Jewel in the Lotus maybe. It is all one. All empty luminous stupid beautiful. All sacred beyond compare. All one big thundering cosmic belly laugh.

Such fine distinctions aside, though, where does that leave us? Right back at Reality Central, sad to say, with work to do and schedules to meet and nobody speaking to me from the clouds. No message waiting in the wings. And it's the same for you I bet. All product placement notwithstanding, you do *not* have mail.

Is this perhaps the right place to say that the greatest invention of the 20th Century is not the microchip, not extra-orbital flight, not bio-engineering? Sure, why not? The the greatest invention of the 20th Century is rock and roll. Specifically rock and roll performed at extremely high decibel levels in humongous sports stadia that thereby finally inherit some legitimate human use. Or late at night in a car alone going as fast as possible on hot summer residential streets with the windows rolled down all the way and the speakers shredding under the gain. Oh . . . start me up!

And nothing personal, you know, but fuck you Microsoft and fuck you Nike and Wendy's and VW and all the rest who've ripped the music that didn't mean anything but that we were alive and knew it, and strapped it into the blind dark service of your fucking cars and fucking shoes and fucking hamburgers.

Balls means balls.

Is it a gender thing? Yeah, probably. I mean, how would I know? Like those old blues dudes always liked to say though: the men don't know, but the little girls, *they* understand. And Jim Morrison, if you got him high enough, would say the same thing between sessions of calling up numinous Aztec reptiles to come eat your daughters.

While I'm waxing ecumenical and all, let me back up and admit it's probably not true the Tibetans have any corner on the market for spiritual cohones, if market there be. Those Muzein guys belting out the Koran from their morning minarets, Jews davening with tefillin or whatever that's all about, Pentecostal Christians speaking in tongues and screwing around with rattlesnakes in tent-show revivals down in Arkansas . . . there's something dark and spooky in the human soul, and it's hard to blow off with some casual handwave of above-it-all rationalism. Scratch the surface and it's right there every time. One way or another, we're all baying at the moon. But maybe that's not as dumb as it sounds. Maybe there's some atavistic longing that runs so deep we just can't touch it any other way.

Can't you hear me howlin? Callin on my darlin . . .

So imagine some clever segue here into whatever it was I started out to say. There must have been some point to all this. Or maybe I just got lost. Yeah, that's it in fact.

I was driving past my old house today. I woke at noon. I was feeling that odd tug I tried to tell about before. I lived there nearly twenty years ago, four blocks from where I'm writing this now. And there was a guy out front getting the mail. I stopped.

"Do you live here?" I asked. He looked a bit confused for a second, like why are you asking me that? Who wants to know? But ". . . yeah" he said.

"I used to live here a long time ago. I put on the addition there, and built the kitchen. Does it still have those green counters?" It was an amazing green. I can still see it. The color of karma. "I used to have my cabinet shop out back."

"You want to take a look around?" he said, real friendly now. "You could come in and see how it's changed . . . "

I wasn't going to. Maybe some other day. But I parked the car. I knew the place had long ago been turned into a kendo or whatever they call it for teaching Japanese archery — the kind everyone knows about from bad business metaphors. Plus, "You Are Not The Target" Laura Huxley said, and maybe she was right or maybe she felt like one from all that mescaline her old man kept doing and maybe she just couldn't see in through the doors of *his* perception. It can happen.

His name was Chris also. Really, would I make that up? But odd, too, isn't it? We walked back through the grounds, larger than I remembered, but it could be that old Jap trick where everything just looks bigger than it really is. There were trees, pretty good sized ones, that hadn't been there when I used to stumble outside at night to take a piss. Ah, that always felt so good. And the stars went so well with whatever I was drinking. I was always drinking. Or coming down. There was a moment there, suspended. And suspended still.

He unlocked the kendo and we went in. That looked smaller now, though a lot neater than when it'd been loaded to the rafters with particle board and tools and sawdust everywhere: my craft. Now it was lined with targets down one side, and a shrine at the far end.

I recognized the picture of the guy at the top of it all. My teacher, Trungpa Rinpoche. You could look him up. You could buy his book, *Cutting Through Spiritual Materialism*, along with *Mass Customization* or *The Experience Economy*. It is all one, motherfucker.

I walked up closer and looked at him. He was smiling that smile. This was the funniest and scariest man I ever met. I loved him. I still do. He drank himself to death. I've been sober for fifteen years now. So we were a little different.

One time he said, "The teacher carries you across the great water." It was one of those I Ching numbers again. Sure, everybody knew that. "But the Vajrayana teacher carries you across and then burns your boat." He chuckled to himself. For a long time, as if it were a private joke. I bowed to the shrine. I started laughing. The other Chris looked sideways at me like I was nuts.

"I was supposed to make these cabinets for him," I tried to explain. "We worked out this complicated design together." On the doors, in black lacquer, I would inset the seal of the Trungpa Tulku, of which he was the 11th incarnation. "But I never did it. The materials were all in here once, in this building." Before he died he told me, "You're still going to have to make those things you know . . ." Now he'd taken over my shop. It was why I started laughing. Sort of.

We walked outside and I saw half a dozen prayer flags tacked into the branches of a tree. This was just before the storm came up.

I know all this must sound alien as hell, hard to relate to. I can dig it. You don't have to. I just keep asking myself why it all still seems connected. And, if it is, what's the connection? Whatever has happened in your life, I bet you have days like that too.

He was talking again, Sensei this, Sensei that. We came to the gate and it struck me suddenly because of the Kanji on the post, and in English too: Shibata. "*Shibata* Sensei?" I asked, amazed now. I figured it was just some faked up hoser. Boulder is full of them. Shibata Sensei, on the other hand, is a National Treasure of Japan. Officially. Not a metaphor.

"I saw him once," I said. It was maybe 1979, on midsummer's day, high in the mountains a couple hours north. There were flags and tents and horses everywhere, hundreds of people. He drew back his enormous bow and everything stopped then. Completely. The day stood still. The sky so blue, the clouds so white. After an eternity, the arrow flew out, thunked into the target. Maybe it was a bull's-eye. I can't remember.

"He had cancer," Chris was saying. "Years ago. He beat it, but he was never the same."

"Jesus," I said, "How old is he now? He must be ancient."

"Seventy-five, but he looks ninety-five."

And he was living in my old house. In the house where I played Blondie so loud it rattled the windows, and a band called Thin Red Line slamming out "Can't Get Over You" (let me know if you've got a cut of that one). The place where I threw Gravity's Rainbow across the room into the bookcase, drunk again, and figuring it was all Tom Pynchon's fault. Where I first kissed that blond Texas Dakini who opened my heart, dashed my hopes and flipped my ass across the ocean like a flat rock. I ended up in Japan of all places, almost able to touch that mythical crane I saw one afternoon at Rikugien, the Edo-era walled garden a block from my Tokyo apartment building. And now I am standing here again, boat burned for sure, and wondering what to make of it. A life if possible. Maybe not too late.

There's so much you don't know about me. Cannot ever, no matter how hard I try to make it otherwise. I have been places, done things impossible to recount. I remember nights of love, each different from all the rest. I have sat beside the dead in the room with the open windows. I have seen those ships on fire off Orion's shoulder.

Yeah well. I wrote something into *The Cluetrain Manifesto* that must have raised some eyebrows among our more knowing cousins. And it went like this:

. . . People of Earth
The sky is open to the stars. Clouds roll over us night and day.
Oceans rise and fall. Whatever you may have heard, this is our
world, our place to be. Whatever you've been told, our flags fly
free. Our heart goes on forever. People of Earth, remember.

So I should end this now, but that's way too dramatic and drama is the wrong note to end on. I think I need to put in something ordinary here, pedestrian. A joke maybe. A duck walks into a bar . . .

Because, whatever it is, it's just the normal regular passage of time. Nothing mystical. Nothing shocking. We are born. We grow old. We die. In between, we sometimes get a glimpse of something. If I knew what it was, I'd tell you in a second. I don't know. Take this piece of writing as my prayer flag flapping out in the wind of a day that came on sideways. Who knows where it's headed? Tomorrow I have a con-call at noon, a website to build, and forty-one phone calls to return. Possibly lunch.

What I do know is that if you're lonely and you're hurting, then you're human. What am I telling you this for? Hell if I know. To cheer you up maybe. Let me know if it worked.

Bad Science, No Pictures

I must be more fucked up than I thought. I had a dream last night that I was a kid again and my world was falling apart. I was pleading, begging for it not to happen. There weren't any people I can remember. Instead, there was this intense purple electricity. Whatever was going on, it sure seemed important. I woke up angry. I'm tired of being angry. I'm tired of being scared. It makes me angry.

Maybe it's all just in my head. Always a winning bet. Maybe I'm locked in some lifelong fugue that doesn't relate to anything outside itself. Never sees daylight. Turn it back in, wrap around the wound. I get this psychotic image of an animal suddenly caught in the headlights, eating its own entrails. Hour of the wolf is a fine game to play, an outstanding role — long as the wolf's not really dangerous, not somehow broken or deranged. But then that's usually the central question, isn't it?

I pretty much know how the world works. I just don't like the *way* it works. The world is its own darkness. But it disguises itself as clearest day. The way it is. The way it's always been. It's only you and I that just don't get it. Because we're damaged. The logic is seamless, almost beautiful. Almost. All it really needs is something like baptism, some kind of assurance that yeah, you're fucked, but it's not really anything you did. As long as you don't look back, into the darkness you crawled out of, the bad place that birthed you and left you hanging. Umbilicus, omphalos, whatever. Quick, pretend you're not stranded! Even though those strands are all you've got.

What I believe — sometimes, on a good day, which this is not particularly — is that I am healing myself of this madness. It is not real, but it's not a dream. Not something I can just roll over and wake up from.

What I believe about my writing — sometimes, when it's not just flatulent exhibitionism — is that it's a way to turn those headlights on myself. Not to shock anyone, but to cease ignoring, fearing, hating what I am. After half a lifetime doing that, one day fourteen years ago I stopped. And right before I stopped, I got truly angry. It wasn't anger born of fear, for once, but of understanding. Understanding how I'd been complicit with whatever it is we go along with, buy into, lay on ourselves and others constantly: the shameful guilty knowledge that we are licking our own secret wound in private, in the dark, and no one must ever see. No one must ever know.

Well, maybe not you. Maybe you're what they call well adjusted.

But others — I suspect many others — see this freakshow of crippled psyches every day, like some medieval *Danse Macabre* out of Bosch or Brueghel. Some work in mental hospitals where their patients perhaps see it clearest of all. The phenomenon is hardly limited to institutions though. Its sickened spirit haunts the laboratory and the stadium, the whorehouses and great tabernacles of commerce. It is welcomed outright in those cathedrals still offering salvation, not just Bingo.

Jesus died for your sins, the story goes. You wanted. You craved. You had this gaping need. And because you couldn't hold back, control yourself, he was nailed to a cross for you. Personally. It was very personal. You were involved. There was blood everywhere, not like they show it in the churches. It was ghastly. Visceral. Not something you'd ever want to look at really. Get out the incense and the flowers and the whitewash then. Shine your shoes and comb your hair and straighten your goddam tie!

Did it get off-track someplace? Or was Christianity always just fundamentally weird? Is there a mystery here we really don't, really can't comprehend? Unless we surrender, as they say? And who are these "they" who presume to comprehend enough to say it? Let them cast the first stone. Let them, after Einstein, dice with God.

What I was going to say about writing was . . . What? Something about art perhaps. I used to think art was just another trick. A crock.

Another form of posturing — just more clever, more obscure. Another pretense to cover up the fact you didn't have a clue what was going on. Now I'm not so sure.

Entropy is simple stuff at base. The stone once cast, rolls down the hill. It stops at the bottom. There is no perpetual motion, no friction-free anything; there's the rub. In a closed system, heat transfer is a losing game. All energic transactions are headed for absolute zero. Steep is the path; downhill the gradient.

But what's this about a closed system? The physicists always throw that in, like some kind of legal rider, some incantatory caveat. Here be dragons — beyond this point we cannot take responsibility. The thing is, they don't really know, and this is the place they have to admit it. They're talking about the universe, you know. Isn't that great? Science is so cool. You get to say shit about the very fucking universe no less! Not like religion, which is so mysterious and all, so unnecessarily complicated by the things you get to know and the things you don't. Since the Enlightenment, we get to know it all. Except, of course, those bits we can't. Like, for instance, whether the universe is open or closed.

If it was all just energy and mass, it wouldn't really matter much. If it was all just suns and clouds of interstellar gas and light shifting red with nobody there to measure it anyway, I mean, who'd give a crap? It could be beautiful, in a theoretical sort of way I guess. It could be meaningless. Neither of those could possibly count for much unless there was somebody there. But suddenly there was.

Because something forgot to run downhill. Maybe it was some rogue carbon. We can find out what, but not why. Or maybe why, but not *how come*. There was DNA in the oceans one day that wasn't there the day before, and it was linking, headed somewhere. The fact of the matter, no matter how you cut it: it was headed for us.

Nature abhors a vacuum they say. Now, where the hell did *that* come from? What an anthropomorphic notion. Moreover, what a peculiarly Western, Northern European, *adversarial* form of anthropomorphism. Nature, whatever that is, looks around one day and says:

man, I just can't stand this vacuum! Motherfucker! And I am surrounded — no, worse — I am defined by it.

Seriously, go outside, look up! Between all those stars out there, you know what that is? That's vacuum. And there's quite a lot of it. More than anything else. Of course, the scientists will tell you that's not something you can really say — "there's a lot of vacuum" — because it isn't anything at all. It's just "space." But the universe, which must be coextensive with nature — you'd think, huh? — and which is mostly space, supposedly hates this space. Abhors it. If you take just this one thing, you can see how a lot of problems get started . . .

"What? Do you think I'm working this hard just to heat the whole outside? Shut that friggin door!" This is how Dad first explains entropy and the closed universe. It *must* be closed. Space must be contained by *something*. Otherwise, there would be — my god! — no borders, no boundaries, no Heavenly Kingdom! Bummer.

But it isn't all just energy and mass. Look again at your animal in the headlights. There is something else. Intelligence in the eyes and that purple electricity. There is something awake in there, some urgent purpose. Look closer. This is hard, yes. You're not supposed to even notice it's there. It's not polite to stare. But if you do, you might realize that the animal is not eating its own entrails as you first thought. It is chewing its leg off. The leg that binds it to the trap.

What trap, you say. What animal for that matter. What in christ's name are you talking about? You must be crazy. There is no trap, no animal, no look in its eyes you thought for a second that you might have recognized. It's all just a bad dream. An open and shut case. A shut universe. Go back to sleep. Tomorrow we're taking you to Disney World!

Then what is this pain in here, Mommy?

Don't kids just say the darndest things? They've got that special light in their eyes too. Until it goes out. Until they stop asking those innocent America's-Funniest-Home-Video-type questions, like: Who am I? Where did I come from? How am I connected to those stars up there? Will someone please tell me what this is all about?

We've got to protect our kids from the facts of life. The dirty little secret of how they were conceived. Well, the chemistry is OK maybe, the molecular biology. But you take it to its natural conclusion and — whoa! — it's all attached to that *thing* down there. Nevermind Billy, nevermind Sally, run along and play! And such *nice* kids, too. But oh, the blood and sweat of it, the awful want. The longing that's never satisfied. The horror, the horror . . . (June turns abruptly from the disturbing reverie to complete her household chores, knowing Ward will soon return from work to play baseball with the Beaver.)

It's not just the Catholics, either, and their virgin mother who never got laid. The embarrassment runs much deeper. It's there in the whole Big Bang thing too. Funny how they call it that. There couldn't be any, like, Freudian overtones you don't suppose? Just for the hell of it, try asking sometime what happened just before that. Just before everything came slamming out of that singularity 14 billion light years roughly to the north. And the answer is — ta-da! — it's all Mind-of-God stuff, kids. Don't ask; don't tell.

That's one edge of the box. The others are a bit more iffy. In fact, it might be open or it might be closed. We're not sure. We are uncertain. But if it's closed, then the energy is running down, running out. Must be closed then, right? Because it's late now and we're getting tired. Because love never works and everyone dies. Because . . . well, because nature abhors a vacuum, that's why! And the trap closes. The light goes out.

While this has the advantage of not being messy, like the reprehensible agenda of DNA, and not as outright spooky as religion, it's still just too depressing. What are some other options, then? Well, we can remain outside it, we think. Though quantum physics suggests otherwise, we can opt to be observers. After all, what's a little denial between friends? We can separate body from mind, then prove that mind does not exist. We can use logic. We can be objective and precise. We can make fine distinctions. We can be professional about it.

Or we can just shoot smack. One path seems about as legitimate as the other. There is no pain, you are receding . . .

One way or another, like the guys and gals in the antiperspirant commercials, we can finally be *sure*. We can reach closure. We can attain certainty about what's outside and what's inside: in both cases, a bounded space that abhors itself. As above, so below. It's not much, but it's a *kind* of redemption. Something to make the voices stop. And all it demands is a little surrender.

Maybe there's another way, though. I've been thinking about art as a possible candidate. Exploring without knowing. Looking at what's actually there, not what you expect will be. Allowing for the possibility of magic.

Why bother though? Who needs another way? Wow, you forgot already didn't you? Amazing. The fear? The pain? The howling emptiness and desolation? Remember? Oh right, you took two Tylenol and had a nice hot bath and it went away. Lucky you.

Whatever five out of six doctors may say, Tylenol somehow didn't quite do it for me. I never used heroin either, because my junkie friends told me I was a natural, and I believed them. I figured I'd be strung out in a week. I ended up doing mostly alcohol — and acid. I used to joke that the hangovers kept me grounded. Probably true. But the hangovers were hell. And the high got pretty weird too.

Basically, it just stopped working. That's the worst part about addiction. The shit quits doing what you used to take it for. And then what?

Then you either quit or you OD or you go off a bridge. Bridges are quicker. Anyway, when this happens all you know is: something's gotta give. Which leaves you in a really strange place, because the so-called Real World is a lot different from the world of booze and dope — or whatever your drug of choice happens to be — and if you opt to keep on living, you're gonna have to do it *somewhere*.

But what really pissed me off was the assumption that, if you were going to stop taking, you were also going to have to accept the reality of all those sexless heartless high-entropy androids you found yourself surrounded by and the twisted belief systems based on *their* weirdass addictions: Money, Work, Fame, Beauty, Sports, Science, Religion, Higher Education, Television, Relationships, Satanic Bondage,

General Niceness. The prospect kept me out there a lot longer than I needed to be. Yeah sure, cop, buy in. Make a genuine effort to be a more all-around reasonable human being. Beg their forgiveness for attempting to escape all those wasted years. I never thought they were wasted. Escaping those zombie vampires had always seemed like a good idea to me. In fact, it seemed like a hard-wired survival imperative. After 14 years sober as a goddam hanging judge, it still does.

So the question becomes: is it possible to live in a world that is not pre-defined in the kind of philosophic depth you might expect to find articulated, say, on the back panel of a box of Wheaties? A world that is hugely uncertain and whose principles of operation, if any, are largely unknowable? Well, like the man said, when you got nothin, you got nothin to lose. Why not?

You might end up a little on the feral side. You might have to gnaw a limb off to get free. But hey, you can get around just fine on three legs, trust me. And the best part is: it's your world. No excuses, no bullshit. Somebody fucks with you, they only do it once. Somebody's in pain, you understand they're suffering, not having a bad hair day. Somebody's born, somebody dies, you know who you are, you know what to do. Plus there's luminous night again, the mountains, water, wind, those stars. That amazing light in people's eyes. Coming back in yours.

And you say what you see along the way. That's the art of it. That's the reversal.

She Moves in Mysterious Ways

They were not memories yet, though he wished they were. It was January and the road wound upward through the rocky passes bound in snow, almost impassable in places. Desolate. What was she doing now? He turned quickly from the thought, pressing his forehead against the cold glass of the passenger window. The driver was silent, knowing he didn't want to talk.

People spoke of living in the moment, as if that was something — if only you were a better person — you might want to do. He was in it now all right, one seamless and interminable stretch of agony, its eyes wide open watching him, detached, observing its interesting experiment in pain. Hell is curiosity without compassion. What does it feel like when you cannot breathe it wanted to know. What does it feel like when you think it could go on like this for another hour, for a month, a year, forever?

The car finally arrived at 12,000 feet, someplace I'd been but hadn't been. Faces I recognized the way you recognize the mailbox, or a stop sign. There was a cabin and a bed. I had three Valium left. Good thing. I slept.

What happened in the days that followed was like everything that's ever happened, only you didn't usually notice how it went. Waves. It all comes in waves. Ride when you can, hang on when you need to, but they never stop. Voices across the fields, people walking, going somewhere, what does it matter? Breathing matters though. Back in, back in. Holding together, but against what? Why is it so frightening to be this lost?

Also days when the ice began to melt and there were whole hours when it seemed this was the life. Didn't need anything except the sky, didn't have to stay. Then night would come down and the wind would talk to itself through the rocks, the stars. I am too close I thought. There is nothing between us.

In the mornings sometimes, stumbling down to the kitchen half a mile away for coffee and a little warmth, a cigarette, there would be signs and signatures along the trail, windfall pine cones, delicate wild-flowers pushing through the snow, patterns of stones that hadn't been there yesterday. It might be possible to read these things, I thought. It could be a language of some kind.

In the same building with the kitchen there was a sort of meeting hall with a platform at one end and lots of pads and pillows arranged in rows. On the platform there were sticks of incense burning, bowls of water, rich brocades, and an antique painting of two people fucking. He was blue and she was arched in his arms, enfolding him in her embrace, head tilted back beneath his kiss. They were so deep in love. So gone.

And what you did in there was learn to breathe again. Sit down. Fold your legs, pull yourself up straight as you could manage. Then somebody would ring this gong they had, and it would ring for a little while, finally reverberating off to total silence. You could hear the birds out-side, not too often a car from a couple places over. You slowed up, you slowed down. You breathed in, you breathed out. You paid attention to your mind, but not too much.

Sometimes I fell asleep. A lot of times I fell asleep. That was OK. I learned to sleep sitting up, to dream that way. But then I'd wake up suddenly and wonder what the hell I was doing there, what was hap-pening to my life. I would panic and believe I needed to be some-where else, to be doing something I'd forgotten how to do. Then I would remember what I had forgotten — how to let go of whatever it was I was so desperately hanging on to, holding out for. Maybe how to at least die gracefully, as winter was doing right about then outside the frosted glass and knocked-together walls. Somewhere in all that, gradually, there was forgiveness. Not so you'd notice, really, or right away. Not with a name and a return address. Just the beginning of a hunch that this is what it must feel like to be human.

I almost got used to it. I lived in a wooden house alone, up against jagged mountains to the south, looking down across a valley to the east. You learn these things. East is where the sun comes up. It's hard to remember what I did there though. Bits and pieces, yeah, but nothing too continuous. I worked in the kitchen. I sat sometimes. Nobody ever called it meditation, except when they were getting ready to be assholes.

One day a bunch of lamas showed up out of nowhere, from Tibet I guess. I'd been sleeping in another cabin with this girl I'd met and I woke up late. When I staggered outside, it was already afternoon and the light was blinding. I was still dreaming, half hungover, walking around in a haze — the sort of not-all-that-unpleasant confusion you sometimes give up wondering about and just decide to see what happens next. What happened next was I wandered straight into this tangle of monks and I am thinking how in hell's name did *these* guys get here? I must have missed something. Especially as they are chanting, right out in broad daylight, in this incredibly low and guttural drone. They are also ringing these little bronze bells and making various weird hand gestures. I have no idea what I am looking at or hearing, but I can tell they are calling on something, and I can tell it is something powerful. The air between us has suddenly either disappeared or gotten thicker, hard to say. The sky is blue and the wind is moving big white clouds around up there. Forest, mountain, pasture, lake — and then I get what's going on. They are invoking the world.

One night before I left that place — I lived there for nine months — I was sitting in my cabin. I didn't want to be there. I wanted to go out drinking and get really ripped. But I was in retreat, something I decided I had to try, you know, it was just so fucking tantric. So I sat there in front of this shrine made out of a cardboard box. It was covered with some pretty fabric, had some incense burning on it and a couple candles, plus these little glass bowls filled with water. Just regular water, you can get some from the tap. There was also a picture of my teacher and of Vajradhara and Vajrayogini, those two. But I wasn't looking at any of that. That's not what you did. What you did was breathe out, breathe out. Something always breathed back in for you, so you didn't need to worry about that part. I probably looked over at the clock to see how much longer I was going to have to be there doing this, and it probably told me I'd only been sitting for about three minutes, so forget it.

It was pointless to begin with and you stopped asking why you did it after a while. It even had its moments sometimes. Like that night. Time had apparently stopped as far as my clock was concerned so this was going to take forever anyway. I let go some more, wondering then how far you could do that. Was it possible to leave for good, just vacate, never mind the stuff you left behind? Most of that stuff was gone already and no one would really miss me if I split, I thought. No one would even need to know. But that was just more thinking, thinking.

I unwound out into the night somehow. I don't recall the shift. All I remember is being still at last. So still. I could feel the world around me like a blanket, like a cloak. And it felt like home. Fire in water, crystal light reflected from the glass, the colors sharp and pure. Everything come back to its senses, to itself. In focus. Perfect. Better than any drug.

A couple nights later I did get drunk, though, as a fucking lord. Falling down stupid puking wasted. Then I went to Phoenix and to Tokyo, where I got sober, then to Pittsburgh and Chicago and New York. Later, I ended up back here. Maybe you've noticed it too: you always end up back here.

Oh baby.

Just wanted to say how much I miss you. These days so different yet so much the same. We were happy then and suicidal. Meeting briefly, edging away. I try now to remember sometimes. We were you and I, I think. Folded in aboriginal darkness, oriental light. Drifting, dreaming, deathless for a second there. Just wanted to say how much I miss. How much I miss your point.

Eli eli lamma sabacthani anima mundi yoni padme hum.

For one last look I'd loot the Aztec temples, burn the scriptures, sacrifice poetry and myth, complex ecologies, the wind, the river, life itself: to your eyes.

Here and gone today oh dancer, red shifted always, tilting out of control, out of sight in your spiral arms tonight, the air unopened, incomplete, yet hanging on your every word, tip of your tongue the entrance to the field, dragon in straight lines, mother, death, ancient jailbait flash your mocking invitation, jaguar by the forest verge, sunlight on water, shadow, the rattling gourd, the feathers arranged just so, left-handed spin, approaching, coming, coming soon . . .

Stirring my coffee this morning, looking up, the mountains still here, the sky. Where were you ever?

Sybarite renunciation. A cultivated taste that's not for everyone. For every one she turns, she passes. Periodic. A table spread with pure delight, an empty room, a metaphor unto herself. And laughter echoing down whatever's left.

Word

It was twenty years ago today, or close enough. I had gone over to the school to pick up my son Jesse, who must have been around seven at the time. My cabinet shop was around the corner, but all I had to do to get there was cut through a waste lot and jump the stream that ran along the riverrun past Eve and Adam's. It was getting on in the afternoon and I seem to recall that I'd taken along a rock glass half full of scotch and ice. It was a very liberal school.

I saw her standing there. Talking to another woman I must have known well enough to say hello to, but have now long since forgotten. I said hello. Hello. But I was looking at her friend. One look was all it took. You hear about these things. Poetic license you figure. I can't remember what anybody said. It's like an old scrap of silent film found in an attic. I remember the light though. Of the day, of a particular moment in my life that would change my life forever. It was coming from her eyes.

After she left, I asked "Who was that?" Trying to be casual about it. I was never good at casual. Also, I had a reputation and it wasn't good. I got the look. But I also got her name. Laurie.

I wanted her more than any woman I'd ever seen, and I wanted most of them. My reputation was not for wanting in vain. One of the great gifts of alcohol. Dionysus touch me. Light my fire. Bonfire, bone fire. Ashes on my forehead for sins not yet committed, but committed to. Steppenwolf basking in the Colorado sunshine. On vacation you might say. Waiting for the world to begin. And where are you from, my lovely? How do you arch when the last fuse arcs and the night short circuits do you cry out for your life or look away? Here, let me show you. But in one flash she was in past defenses I didn't even know I had. It wasn't anything she did. It was something she was, and I knew it instantly. I also knew she was out of my league. I could never have her. There was a barrier here, a boundary I couldn't cross. Unless I was invited. And little chance of that. I didn't like fences, especially fences that kept me out. What's a stronger, deeper word than frustrated? But I think I was also a little relieved.

A few weeks later I saw her again and asked if she needed a lift home. Oh that's OK she said. Really no trouble I said hop in. No trouble at all. But I knew she was bigger trouble than I'd seen coming in a long time. Maybe ever. She lived with her daughter Rachael, Jesse's age, in a little house on Mapleton Street. Rachael's dad lived in Arkansas or maybe Texas. Far enough I thought. But I didn't run into her again and I had no excuse to call. I forgot about it.

Until, a few months later, she called me. She was selling something. Photos maybe, I forget. I couldn't believe it, a telemarketing job. She told me her name and said you don't know me. I said don't count on it. What are you making at this gig? A percentage of sales? That can't be much, you've got a daughter to think about, come work for me. I hired her on the spot. I was thinking fast. Nowadays I'd go to jail for it.

I'd just bought an Apple IIe — actually, traded it for the cabinets I built for the first ComputerLand store in Boulder. I had no idea how it worked or what it even was. Come work for me, I said, and I'll train you to manage the data processing for my business. At night, I'd read the manuals. In the day, I'd sit next to her and explain. You see . . . And here . . . Now for this . . . And she'd say wait you're going too fast. But she was way ahead of me.

If you'd wrapped an orgone accumulator around that room, you could have powered New York City. I had the libido monitors dismantled after the first week as they would have topped out and fried. And I was being good. I stopped working in the shop though. I only wanted to work with Laurie. Work having always been a relative concept. It sounded good though. How many ever truly plumbed the amorous potential of Visicalc? We were pioneers. It was like living in a steam bath. Now to sum this row of cells . . . brushing her hand. Oh excuse me.

It went on for weeks like that. One day I brought out the scotch. Have a drink I said that's enough for one day. She said no that's OK. Don't mind if I do I said. Maybe that was the afternoon we couldn't stand it any longer. I didn't know there was any "we" about it until I kissed her. The grid went down right up into Wyoming. I looked at her. Who was hunting who here? It wasn't exactly a wink she gave me, but that sparkle, Jesus. And after that things got explicit pretty fast.

One day I was there alone. Late afternoon in the spring of 1981. The sun was setting over the front range and the air felt . . . what? Expansive. I'd had the first drink or two and I thought at first it was that. But this was better than the usual first rush. Much better. More connected to the world, the sky, the . . . and I suddenly realized I was in love. It hit me like that. A complete surprise. The real thing, you never see it coming. And I let it hit me. Wash over me. Take me.

It took me. The summer was a blur. I remember shopping with her in the little market on West Pearl Street. Touching the plums, turning to ask would you like to have lunch at my place? Yes. I would like to see you cook. I would like to watch you in different kinds of light. To hear your voice and your laughter. I would like this to go on forever. And it did. It seemed forever. One day we came back from the store, maybe it was the same day. I like you I said. Very much. I am on this road alone. Walk with me. Yes she said.

She was like that. Always right there. Later, I thought maybe she hadn't really heard me or hadn't understood. But she was right there. More than I was, as I was about to learn. Early on she said whenever we've made love you've been drunk. It was a statement, not an accusation. I drank. Yes, I said, and? And, she said, you're not drunk now. I was confused. What was she getting at? It was maybe 3 o'clock in the afternoon. She took my hand and led me to her bed. She took my clothes off, then her own. She was beautiful and she loved me. When we came she was looking into my eyes.

You kept your eyes open I said. I was surprised. It's better that way she said.

Arc of a Diver was playing. Spanish Dancer. Smokey Robinson singing "I've heard the warning voice / from friends and my relations /

they've told me all about / your heartbreak rep-u-ta-tion . . ." She would sing along and wag her finger at me in mock admonition. I was going down. In flames that afternoon. The light was everywhere. Secret flower of golden eternity. Georgia O'Keefe wasn't even close. "Arc of a diver, effortlessly, my mind is sky and when I wake up . . . "

And when I woke up it was ending. I began to hold on. I could never have her I'd thought that first day, and I was right. She was free in a way I couldn't imagine. The light turned around on the solstice. Thunder abides in the earth. I remember casting the I Ching a lot. Waiting in blood it would say. Nothing furthers. I got the DTs for the first time in her bed. I didn't know what it was. What it was was I was dying. I began to know I would lose her. I drank more. The plum tree outside her house had lost all its leaves. The snow was coming. I went to the clinic with her, hung over that morning. I sat in the waiting room. Waiting. Waiting for the world to end. The doctor asked if I was OK? No I said. He looked worried. I could tell what I must have looked like. My face at first just ghostly. I brought her flowers afterwards. It hurt she said.

A world of hurt. Like the boys down at the bar would have said. Those rednecks I used to hang out with just to prove I could. I'd wait till one of them was about to kick the shit out of me then I'd yell, bartender, drinks all around. You're one of the good hippies they'd say later. Let me buy you a drink.

Lot of good that did me now. Steppenwolf flayed and nailed to the barn still alive. Look, you can see the heart beating. I'd try to go five minutes. Just keep breathing. Nothing ever hurt that much. And it didn't stop. Ever.

All this I've written about before here in EGR. That backs you up, huh? Only of course, you didn't know it. I left Boulder in 1982. Phoenix, Tokyo, Pittsburgh, Chicago, back to Boulder for a while in 1992. When I was leaving, I called her. I loved you I said. I'm leaving here. You won't hear from me again. She said goodbye. Maybe she said take care of yourself. I can't remember. Four years later I came back to Boulder again. 1996. I bailed on IBM a week before they offed the whole division. I was always good at that. Keeping one step ahead of it. I knew she was there. Ten blocks away. Sometimes I'd think of her, amazed that I could. Amazed I could breathe again. I'd been sober for a dozen years or so. That helped. I wasn't dying anymore. Not like that anyway. I never thought I'd make it to the year 2000. I was going to die young. I knew it.

It's funny about things you just know like that. Especially when they turn out to be wrong. What then? What else was I wrong about you begin to wonder. It's also funny what happens when you get sober after drinking and taking drugs as long and hard as you can remember. Everything you stuffed into your heart, everything you burned to burn brighter, you get back. But slower. Slow the way crucifixion is slow. Not that I ever tried it. People ask gosh how did you manage it? Must take a lot of will power. Wow. If you're smart you just say yeah, that's right. I'm a hell of a man.

If you're not as smart maybe you try to explain. First, to yourself. It's because I wanted to write, I guess. There was something I was trying to say. But it was so big I couldn't find the words. So intricate, so com-plex. So I drank. And then one day I knew I was dying. Knew it, the way you just know those sorts of things. And it's not like I was afraid. What a pussy reason to keep living. I'll drink to that. It was because . . . I was standing on the platform in Shinjuku station thinking about you. How lost you were to me. How lost I was to myself, my reflection floating in twenty layers of glass down the rows of trains pulling in and out. Laurie. You will never know this moment. I was alone with that. I didn't believe I would ever write it down. I couldn't put two sentences together. Maybe because I thought I had to tell it all. Make sense of it somehow. Despair has an interesting texture when it gets right into you. When you stop trying to hold it back. When you know you no longer can.

I don't know why I stopped drinking or how. I tried for years. I could go about seven weeks. I went that long three or four times. The last time I drank I remember feeling it kick in. Paying attention to the power of it. One old guy I met in the program years later he says in a meeting one night I came to AA because of the bit about Higher Power. I came for the power. Brother.

I quit so many times I lost count. But I couldn't drink anymore. I couldn't get high or shut it off. I couldn't pretend I hadn't found what I was looking for. And lost it. One night in Tokyo I came to the end of the line. I couldn't stand myself any longer. But I couldn't get away either. You know. Shit. What do you do then? Go off a bridge? Put a gun in your mouth? I thought about it. Got close a couple times. I finally had to look at myself. What a fucking mess. I kept trying to change but I knew I wouldn't. I knew I wasn't going to change who I was. I looked at that then and I forgave myself. I said fuck it that's it. I'm not going to beat you anymore.

I didn't notice until a few months later that I wasn't drinking. It's not like I forgot. It was all I thought about. But I never drank again or smoked another joint or dropped another hit of acid. I never forgot any of it though. Never saw the error of my ways. Never recanted. I just stopped caring what happened next. Take me.

That was 1984. How did I get there from here? Or here from there? I mean, in writing this. I guess it's getting pretty long. Let's see, I came back to Boulder in '96 . . . That was the year after I began writing EGR, in the back pages of which, if you read between the lines, this same story is told over and over. Trying to get it right I suppose. And then . . . one night last April I was sitting at this terminal, as usual, and out the blue I thought I wonder if she's online. I started searching around a little. Nothing. OK, I like a challenge and I'm good at this. I searched deeper. And deeper. Somewhere in there a voice in my head said Chris you realize what you're doing here, right? And I answered that I was just surfing around. Not making any commitment to do anything with the information. Just bits in a welter of bits. Uh-huh.

Two hours later still nothing. I found her phone number, but I'd had that for years and hadn't used it. I knew I wouldn't. What I wanted was a website, an email address. But nothing doing. I was about to give up when I remembered Google. Now I use Google all the time because she came up bam! the first hit: www.lauriedoctor.com

For the rest of that night I wrote to her. Hey where did we go? Days when the rains came . . . And the next day and the day after that. Slowly at first, she began to write back. I didn't think she would. I told her I loved her and there wasn't a damn thing she could do about it. I laughed. She laughed back. I held my breath. I went to see her work at a show at the public library. I was amazed by what I saw. I took detailed notes and wrote to her about it: "My, how you have grown."

Let's run away to Majorca and live naked on the beach I wrote. I don't even know where Majorca is. She went to New Mexico and nearly died on the way. I didn't know. Around the same time, I went to Hawaii to give a talk. On the beach in Maui, straight-up midnight it all came back. The planets were doing some big convergence number I found out later. I didn't know that either, but it made sense. Something was shaking. You get it all back. Everything you've stuffed and burned. Everything you couldn't feel. It comes back slow, but then it comes all at once. I'd never prayed for pain before. I never had my prayers answered like that. When it was over, it was over. I knew I loved her. Knew I always had.

Between April and June, we wrote 80,000 words to each other before we met again. We'd been living a mile apart for nearly five years, hadn't spoken in nearly ten and, once so close you couldn't see daylight, had not touched each other for nineteen. We went out to dinner on the summer solstice. It seemed an auspicious time.

Which brings us by a commodius vicus of recirculation back to . . . where else, the present. Today, tonight, whatever time it is, she's somewhere on the south island of New Zealand. Has been there for over a week, in which time I haven't heard anything from her. No phones. She's trekking, tramping, camping out, driving around in a rental car. I don't know. Or she's taken up with some filthy sheep herder. Or dumped me for some guy with a catamaran and a slick rap. Doubtful though. Slick raps never worked with this woman. And besides, she loves me.

It's not often in your life you get to write something like that and know it's true. I love her too. I miss her. But against all odds, I didn't miss her. It turns out the big thing is not really so big or so hard to say.

Well no . . . it is big. It's huge. It's just ordinary huge. I finally uploaded the pictures I took in Europe. The one called out below is my favorite. When I look at it, my heart leaps. I know what that sounds like, but really. It does. It may look like just another photograph to you, but I know what it took to snap this one. A lifetime.

I dedicated my book to her. *Gonzo Marketing: Winning Through Worst Practices*. How romantic, huh? But it's a hell of a book (I'm a hell of a man). There's a chapter called The Value Proposition. You may have already read this bit. I ran it first on EGR. The section starts with two quotes from Homer . . .

"Sing, O goddess, the anger of Achilles . . . "

"Tell me, O muse, of that ingenious hero who traveled far and wide after he had sacked the famous town of Troy."

. . . then ends with this.

Who is creating such stories today? Whose voices will draw new listeners the way Druids drew down the moon, the way Greeks drew a wooden horse to the gates of Troy? Tell me, O muse, of *those* ingenious heroes. Sing to me, goddess, of anger and estrangement. I'm a motherfucker, baby, your mind my sky, your eyes my fire. This world, this life so intricate, delicate, complex. Precious beyond measure. I'm slamming my head against the walls of empire, the habits of power, enraged. Blasting and burning for your love. Imagining the network finally connected. Imagining joy. A wall of horns and drums and dangerous magical noise. I'm bending over my Fender, working the circuits, incendiary, incandescent. Rocking in the free world, serving notice on Babylon. Ain't in for a dollar, ain't in for a dime. Ain't going down for no two-bit dream. Armed only with imagination, I'm back in your spiral arms tonight. Everything has at least two meanings.

But one thing girl that I want to say, love is love and not fade away.

Here's the picture I took of Laurie in Zurich in November 2000. And my dedication.

www.rageboy.com/laurie3.html

not fade away

I laughed. She laughed back.
I held my breath.

Desiderata

Go wrathfully among the poised and chaste, and recall what mindless stimulation may be had in noise. As far as possible, without surrender, alienate as many of the timorous little bastards as you can. Prevaricate at volume with byzantine obfuscation, and listen not to others' smarmy bilge: the dull and ignorant; say yo, what's up with them? Avoid passive-aggressive personalities as you would the plague; it's bad enough they are so deadly boring; they're also a royal pain in the butt.

If you compare yourself with others, you may become vexed and bitter. Some news flash there! For always will these bungling fools be lesser persons than yourself, and nine out of ten times better paid to boot.

Enjoy your achievements, for what that's bloody worth, and plan to be reassigned now any day. Keep interested in your career, and don't neglect to eat more Humble Pie; it is a real nutritious snack say recent articles in *Fortune* and in *Time*.

Exercise acute paranoia in your business affairs; the world is full of high-strung corporate psychopaths. But let this not blind you to what fate truly holds in store: demented zombie fascist ghouls whose vaunted high ideals conceal bloodthirsty plans for jingoistic genocide.

Be yourself, but do not risk detection. Never tell the motherfuckers what you really think. Neither be clinical about love, especially not with that enchanting Sweet16 on AOL, or your ass is grass.

Eschew the questionable counsel of decrepit hosers, nor willingly follow their drooling downward stagger into the depths of sadly premature senility.

Nurture unhinged hallucinations that everything's A-OK to shield yourself from suddenly wising up. Neither be distressed you are imagining things: the recurring fear that fatigue and loneliness are merely prologue. Beyond a wholesome discipline, slip fully into voluntary mental bondage.

You are an orphan of the universe, no less than the trees and ozone layer and the buffalo. You are cattle. You are chattel. You are in the way.

Whether it is clear to you or not, the economy is growing as it doubtless should. Therefore, say your prayers, whatever you hope to gain by that, and whatever your deluded aspirations may have deemed, finding you are a certain loser in the bedlam of life's little lottery, now kiss your sorry ass goodbye.

And yet for all its rampant spam, its government-sanctioned drug cartels and tranquilizer-stifled screams, it's just too beautiful a deal. Double down, cheer up, dream on; as if you might ever get to cop a slice.

Starve to be happy.

I Have a Dream:
An Interview with Corporate Legal

What a nightmare! We woke up in a cold sweat recently after having the following conversation. What a relief to realize it was only a bad dream.

Could an exchange like this really take place? Of course not. It is inconceivable that any individual or organization could be this out of touch with reality. But because Entropy Gradient Reversals is committed to exploring the far-fetched and improbable, our delirium is here presented in its entirety.

By the way, there is no actual 666 Corporation. Just in case you wondered.

Was It the Phone or the Alarm Clock?

incessant ringing

EGR: Hello, Entropy Gradient Reversals.

LEGAL: . . . uh, I'm calling for a Mr. Christopher Locke. Is this Mr. Locke speaking?

EGR: Yes, we are Mr. Locke. Sometimes.

LEGAL: Mr. Locke, I am Midas Welby, Under Assistant Counsel to the Executive Vice President for Legal Affairs at the 666 Corporation. I believe you work for our organization, is that correct?

EGR: We do, yes.

LEGAL: "We"? Are there more than one of you there? Are you referring to a department I am unaware of?

EGR: We represent a plurality of perspectives.

LEGAL: Well, let me get straight to the point, Mr. Locke. I am in receipt of what appears to be an electronic distribution of some sort, originating from yourself. Among other things, it names you as chairman of something called Entropy Gradient Reversals. Do you know what I'm referring to here?

EGR: Yes, we are Entropy, Inc. The "Inc" is for incarnate, by the way.

LEGAL: Mr. Locke, I don't understand. You say you work for 666, yet you also have a position with another firm?

EGR: Well, it's not much of a position, really — or firm either, if you must know . . .

LEGAL: It says here "Chairman," Mr. Locke, and "Chief Executive." I would say those are quite high posts. Are you aware of 666's position in such matters?

EGR: No, I guess not. Can't I be chairman if I want?

LEGAL: Mr. Locke, I hardly know where to begin. The fact is, you cannot maintain formal ties to any other organization while you are in our employ. Was this not made clear to you in BARFS-note 3892C/P?

[NOTE: BARFS (Binary Algorithms for Redundantly Formatted Strings) was originally developed in 1949 on ENIAC. Since ported to 666's OU/812 operating system, it now constitutes that corporation's primary information infrastructure.]

EGR: We don't read BARFS-notes.

LEGAL: What do you mean, you don't read them? All employees of 666 are required to read all company directives, including cafeteria menus and snow emergency notices, and to respond to them, where appropriate, within one business day.

EGR: Well, I did respond at some length to one about nine months ago. It was about the tuna casserole being served on Wednesday — sorry, I can't remember the date now — in our Backspace Key Division in Dubuque, Iowa. I was quite proud of it, but I never did get a reply.

So I stopped using the system. It seemed kind of a one-way broadcast channel for corporate spam-mail.

LEGAL: How can you possibly work for us and not use BARFS? And what's this about spam? What does lunch meat have to do with it?

EGR: Well, you wouldn't want someone *else* eating your lunch, right?

LEGAL: Mr. Locke, I have the distinct feeling we've gotten off to a bad start here. Let me make this clear. 666 takes very seriously any infringement of our intellectual property rights.

EGR: I'm confused, I guess. What property?

LEGAL: This so-called "EGR newsletter," Mr. Locke. Anything whatsoever produced by any individual in our employ — be it program code, documentation, patentable ideas — automatically becomes the property of 666 Corporation in perpetuity, notwithstanding death or termination.

EGR: You mean like, if I draw one of those really funky wide open beaver shots on a lavatory stall, it should say underneath "Copyright 666 Corporation, All Rights Reserved"? I already do that. Religiously.

LEGAL: Mr. Locke, this is no joking matter, I assure you. Not having cleared this with Management, you are in serious breach of contract.

EGR: I'm not joking. What contract?

LEGAL: Surely you can recall your employment contract, Mr. Locke? The "Assignment of Intellectual Property Rights" you signed during your hire process?

EGR: I recall the document. You got a copy there with my signature on it?

LEGAL: Well, no, not at the moment. But I can have Personnel fax it to me.

EGR: I don't think so.

LEGAL: How's that?

EGR: Well, it's still in my desk somewhere. My old desk. At work. And I hardly ever go there.

LEGAL: Let me get this straight. You did not *sign* our Assignment of Intellectual Property Rights? And why is that?

EGR: I forgot.

LEGAL: You forgot. I see. And what's this about not going to work? Mr. Locke, what precisely do you *do* for 666? And how do you manage to do whatever that may be without going to work?

EGR: I work on the net.

LEGAL: The net.

EGR: Yeah, you know: newsgroups, ftp, html, the web . . .

LEGAL: I'm sure those are very interesting for you, Mr. Locke, whatever they are. But are you suggesting that you're conducting official 666 business outside the protection of our network firewalls?

EGR: I'm not suggesting anything. And I'm not certain what you mean by "official business." But I'm curious . . . do you know what a firewall *is,* Mr. Welby?

LEGAL: Well, not in a precise technical sense, of course. I know they're critical to our corporate security. But I'm not going to debate these propeller-head issues with you. Judging from the whole tone of your response so far, I have to say you seem to have little appreciation or respect for the position with which you've been entrusted.

EGR: Just for kicks, do you know what that is?

LEGAL: Well, it says here in BARFS that you are Director of Online Community Development. I wasn't aware we had a neighborhood program in place.

EGR: It's not a neighborhood program. It's an Internet thing. And great whacking hordes of security freaks and paranoid barristers kind of conflict with the whole idea.

LEGAL: We'll be the judge of that, Mr. Locke.

EGR: No you won't. The market will.

LEGAL: Precisely which market are you referring to?

EGR: Good point. It's not one market, really. It's zillions of little ones.

LEGAL: And where do these "zillions of little ones," as you put it, exist, Mr. Locke?

EGR: Well, not inside your firewall. That much is clear.

LEGAL: Are you saying you presume to understand 666's market strategy better than Top Management?

EGR: Strategy? No, I wouldn't give you any back-sass about *that*. But let me ask you a question, OK? Where did your current CEO come from? Where did he get his understanding of the industry?

LEGAL: I'm surprised you don't know — this is all a matter of public record. And after all, he is your CEO too, is he not? But since you don't seem to have spent much time on your own company's recent history, before 666 he earned his well-founded reputation by turning around a major diversified holding company.

EGR: And what were they holding, if I may ask?

LEGAL: This was in the Food Processing industry.

EGR: If you could get a little more specific, what kind of food are we talking here?

LEGAL: Well, it was largely dog food, in point of fact, but I fail to see how that has any relevance. Business is business. The annual revenues of Bow-wow Bowser Chow exceeded those of most Fortune 1000 companies, and their P/E ratio back then was the talk of Wall Street.

EGR: Dog food. Uh huh.

LEGAL: You have a problem with that, Mr. Locke?

EGR: Well, it doesn't tell you a whole lot about the Internet marketplace, does it?

LEGAL: I have read all about the Internet, and I know we have some exciting offerings in that arena. But really, it's by far the tiniest of all our profit centers.

EGR: As any reasonable person would expect under such conditions. Let me ask you another couple questions. Have you ever logged in to the net? Downloaded a file? Sent email to anyone?

LEGAL: That's what we have secretaries for, Mr. Locke. Surely anyone with a Director's title should understand that much. But I suspect you really are not Management Material at all . . .

EGR: Have you ever, in fact, been outside of BARFS and Bloatus Moats?

LEGAL: I do not need to submit to this pointless grilling, Mr. Locke! But I will answer you anyway. Why would I want to use this Internet you seem so fascinated with? Our competitors could be listening in. Or hackers. Or perverts. To bring this ridiculous conversation back around to the issue at hand, this is exactly the kind of exposure you are creating for 666.

EGR: Cool!

LEGAL: Now see here, Locke, I'm beginning to get the impression that this may not be so much a legal matter as a medical one. I think you're in serious need of professional help.

EGR: You can say that again. Do you have anyone up there who can hack CGI? Or even Photoshop? The site really looks like shit. But I guess you haven't been there . . .

LEGAL: There's no need to use foul language. Been *where*?

EGR: To the EGR homepage at www.rageboy.com.

LEGAL: There you go again. I have no idea what you're talking about.

EGR: I know.

LEGAL: Mr. Locke, I think we are at an impasse here. Whatever other action may be required — and I can see this becoming rather complex — I must demand that you immediately cease and desist from distributing this . . . this trash! I will not even go into the ramifications of the gutter language you use, the copyright infringement, the false claim of being listed on the Nasdaq stock exchange for god's sake!

EGR: Yeah, I thought that one might cause problems . . .

LEGAL: So, do you agree?

EGR: Agree to get listed? Sure, why not.

LEGAL: *No!* To stop publishing this Entropy thing we've been discussing.

EGR: No way.

LEGAL: In that case, Mr. Locke, I'm afraid it's my sad duty to inform you . . .

EGR: That's funny, you don't *sound* sad . . .

WHEW! It *was* the Alarm Clock!

incessant ringing

Oh man, what a bummer! And that *noise!* Gotta get rid of this damn clock. What time is it anyway? Christ, nearly 2, and we've got a meeting in the office this week!

Ah, never mind — that's tomorrow. We really ought to look at that scheduling program once in a while.

Hmmm, let's see. Where do we want to go today? You know, maybe we could do something with this stupid dream for EGR . . .

a distinctly different kind of ringing

Oh no, the phone! Can we at least reach the switch on the espresso machine from here? Ah, good. Please god, don't let it take too long . . .

picks up receiver

"Hello, Entropy Gradient Reversals."

". . . uh, I'm calling for a Mr. Christopher Locke. Is this Mr. Locke speaking?"

"Yes, we are Mr. Locke. Sometimes . . ."

THE END

(or is it?)

Ships in the Night: The 666 Exit Interview

Entropy Gradient Reversals — the collective entity formerly known as clocke — is getting out! Out of the internet.web-as-surefire-money-maker biz, out of the whole sad software industry, and perhaps most significantly, out of the 666 Corporation. We feel liberated, as if a great weight had been lifted from us.

We'll soon be heading for the hills — the Rocky Mountains to be more specific — where we will magically transmogrify ourselves into the Vice President for Business Development of a little outfit so obscure that nobody's ever heard of it outside of a small coterie of individuals so technical they are only let out at night. Displaytech, among a number of other things we could barely grasp, makes really-really tiny hi-rez displays. Think CRT-on-a-chip. Think virtual screen real estate enabling full-motion cinemascope video perched on your nose in the form of modified bifocals that let you surf late-breaking business news with one eye while downloading the erotica binaries of your choice with the other. Think a nation of cross-eyed-but-happy digerati!

. . . though our new colleagues probably wouldn't have put it quite that way.

As we'll be saying all kinds of laudatory things about this company via other channels (we really *were* extremely impressed both by the core technology they have patented six ways to Sunday, as well as by the obscene amount of cash they offered for our services), we will probably never mention this outfit again in the pages of EGR. Conflict of interest sort of thing, you understand. After all, we wouldn't want to give the impression that we could be *bought!*

However, it bears mentioning that a Very High Official at Displaytech has been a charter subscriber to EGR from its inception, and that our latest issue played no small part in this mid-stream change of corporate horses. Readers may rest assured that this fine organization, while incurring no liability for our views — they remain ours and ours alone, as always — will also make no attempt to sway our balanced and independent editorial judgment. For that, we will continue to rely strictly upon informed industry sources, unstinting primary-source research, and whatever the fuck we feel like saying at any given moment with no regard whatsoever for those to whom our offhand opinions may do irreparable harm. We take our principled irresponsibility in such matters as our sacred bond with the ever-growing collection of eyeballs that you, our Valued Subscribers, represent.

But we digress from the theme, which — we can only hope — will cost your company the balance of the hour you've already decided to waste with us. In spite of the unbridled school's-out *joy* we feel at saying sayonara to 666, we also figured we owed it to our erstwhile employer to share something of what we have discovered during our brief tenure at this Fortune–10 monolith. We believe we learned quite a bit. Imagining, perhaps foolishly, that this experience might prove of some value to the firm, we rang up the company's Chairman, Lew Firstner.

It seems entirely fitting that, on the eve of this long-awaited Labor Day weekend — our culture's only formal monument to institutionalized slackery — we should present this heartfelt farewell to one of America's Truly Great Companies.

EGR: Hey there Lew! How's it hangin?

LEW FIRSTNER: . . . uh, do I know you?

EGR: Probably not. But I've been working for you for a year-and-change, and since I'm about to split any day now, I thought I'd introduce myself and share some of my experiences in your terrific company.

LEW FIRSTNER: Oh I see. Well, that's certainly good of you . . . (muffled, offline: *Lucy, how in Christ's name did this call get through on my private line?!*)

EGR: Yeah, it's been a real trip!

LEW FIRSTNER: Precisely where do you sit in the organization Mr. . . . uh, I didn't get your name . . .

EGR: You can call me clocke, but my friends call me RageBoy.

LEW FIRSTNER: Rage boy? (*Lucy, tell security to run a trace on this. I'll try to keep him talking . . .*) And which part of the organization did you say you were in?

EGR: The Internet division. I've been working with the infoSkag group.

LEW FIRSTNER: That's odd, I wasn't aware we had an Internet Division. Of course, I'm glad to know we do. If you say so.

EGR: Oh yes. It's part of the whole Network Eccentric Computing thing you got going last Fall when you were featured in that *Business Week* cover story. I must say, sir, that was a brilliant coup! Especially since the panel you had asked for some sort of recommendations about the Internet hadn't yet returned with anything useful. In fact, I wonder, did they ever get back to you?

LEW FIRSTNER: Now, which panel was this?

EGR: You know, those Good Old Boys you sent off on that Internet bug hunt in the summer of 95? You remember. It was right after you all decided that you couldn't afford to read one more *Journal* article about the World Wide Web without having at least some notion of what they were talking about . . .

LEW FIRSTNER: Oh yes, it's coming back to me now. Network Eccentric Computing is an important part of our message now, as you say. We feel it is the major contribution this company will make to the 21st Century.

EGR: That's real good to hear, sir. We feel that way too.

LEW FIRSTNER: So then why are you leaving us? You did say you were leaving 666, did you not?

EGR: Basically, I felt so inspired by your leadership that I decided it was time for me to make my own contribution — except I'm shooting for the 23rd Century. All the Major Contributions seem to be taken up till then.

LEW FIRSTNER: I see. So you're starting a new company of some sort. Is that it.

EGR: Yup. It's called Entropy Gradient Reversals. I wonder if you'd consider being on our Board?

LEW FIRSTNER: That sounds a little out of my line, actually. I don't really know much about high energy physics.

EGR: You're being too modest. After all, you don't know anything about computing either, but that didn't stop you from taking on 666.

LEW FIRSTNER: True. But I'm afraid a Board position is out of the question. (*Lucy, are they getting anything yet?*) Besides, you haven't told me much about this Energy Ingredient Replacements startup. What is it you plan to offer.

EGR: Oh, I don't know. This and that.

LEW FIRSTNER: I have to say that doesn't sound like much of a business strategy . . .

EGR: Well, we thought we'd emulate the Fortune 500 in that regard. You know, kinda keep em guessing.

LEW FIRSTNER: Have you done market research?

EGR: Oh yes, of course. We've been conducting online focus groups of a sort. You might be interested in some of the people we've spoken to and their attitudes about online commerce.

LEW FIRSTNER: Actually, yes, I'd be quite interested in hearing what you've found there . . .

EGR: Well, for instance, there's this one web site called Gap-Toothed — it's for people who have large spaces between their front teeth. They thought we were pretty cool. And Geek Girl liked us, but then she said she was too busy. It happens. I think you might like Geek Girl though. You want her email address in Australia? Maybe she'd do an interview with you or something. That could get you some credibility at least. Couldn't hurt.

LEW FIRSTNER: "Geek Girl" you say? (*Lucy, for God's sake!*)

EGR: Yeah, she's pretty far out. And then there's Media Whore. She's got a site that'd really fry your brainstem!

LEW FIRSTNER: I didn't think there were many girls online. Tell me, do they uh . . . Do they like pictures too?

EGR: What kind of pictures are we talking here, sir?

LEW FIRSTNER: Well, maybe we'd better not go into that right now. I have to say I still don't have any idea what this Enervated Gentry Rebuttals is all about. What are your product plans?

EGR: Oh that. Well, we plan to interview Industry Leaders like yourself and publish them for the many people now coming online seeking to better understand the businesses that serve them.

LEW FIRSTNER: Well, yes, I can see a need for that. By the way, was the purpose of your call to request an interview?

EGR: Oh no, sir. We would never ask for something like that. We would never make such a request.

LEW FIRSTNER: Good. Because we do only a very limited number of interviews and our PR people have to go through quite a lot of preparation first.

EGR: You mean like telling you what to say?

LEW FIRSTNER: That's part of it, of course. This is a large company, as I'm sure you are aware, and no one person can be expected to know it all. It's a team effort.

EGR: Since you mention that, just out of curiosity, is there any area you *do* know about? I mean, in a kind of non-team, personal sense?

LEW FIRSTNER: Well, I'm quite fascinated with this whole Web notion. Of course, they won't let me have a computer of my own, but I do see the occasional screen here and there in my travels about the company. Some of them are quite stunning, I must say. I once saw a thing where you could put in a credit card number. Maybe you've seen this too. Do you know what I'm talking about?

EGR: uh . . . yeah, I think I do recall seeing that site. (*I wonder how Lucy's doing. He's clearly beginning to crack . . .*) They've got these little boxes you can type into, and like that?

LEW FIRSTNER: Yes, that's it precisely! Of course, I don't know who did that work. I keep asking my people to find out for me but they can't seem to get outside our firewalls.

EGR: But what wonderful firewalls they are, sir. You have a lot to be proud of there. No hackers inside 666, that's for sure!

LEW FIRSTNER: You seem fairly knowledgeable in these matters. Maybe I can ask you a question. Do you think this whole online thing is really like CB radio? A lot of my lieutenants seem to think so. And God knows, we're losing money on it like crazy. But I'm starting to think maybe these Netscape people are onto something. I hear we even did a deal to let them use their browser in 0U/812. Frankly, I don't know why we'd lend them that kind of credibility — and we had to pay *them* to use *our* brand, which I really don't understand at all. But some of my people tell me our browser isn't quite up to snuff.

EGR: Was the word "dogshit" used, sir?

LEW FIRSTNER: How's that?

EGR: Oh sorry, that's a term we technical types sometimes use to indicate deep respect for cutting edge core technologies. You know how some African Americans will say "bad" when they really mean good? It's that kind of thing . . .

LEW FIRSTNER: What is an African American?

EGR: Never mind. Just trust me on this one. Dogshit's what you got.

LEW FIRSTNER: I see. I'll have to remember that one. So, would you say Bloatus Moats is "dogshit" too?

EGR: Oh yes, absolutely. In fact, perhaps this is an opportunity to share a little marketing idea I had recently.

LEW FIRSTNER: And what is that?

EGR: Well, you know how we said "Get Warped" with OU/812? Maybe we could say "Get Curbed" with respect to Bloatus Moats. It's just a thought . . .

LEW FIRSTNER: I'll run it past our Marketing People. You may have something there. Of course, I don't make those kinds of decisions personally.

EGR: If you don't mind my asking, what exactly *is it* that you do? I know it must be important because everyone speaks of you in such hushed — I'd almost say reverent — tones. But I never did get a very good idea of what it was . . .

LUCY (*offline*): *Mr. Firstner, they say they're getting something from the 203 exchange . . .*

LEW FIRSTNER (*hissing*): (*For Pete's sake, Lucy, write it on a goddam notepad! Don't let this cretin know we're tracing him! I've got him thinking I actually give a shit about some demented plan he's describing to me here . . .*)

EGR: Excuse me? I didn't catch that.

LEW FIRSTNER: Oh, I was just telling my secretary to, uh, give a shipping bill to someone cemented to the LAN.

EGR: Gosh, I just love it when you talk that way. It reminds me of those encouraging personal notes you always sent around to all 200,000 employees on BARFS.

LEW FIRSTNER: Yes, well, I think it's important to keep in touch with the troops.

EGR: Always appreciated. I'll miss those.

LEW FIRSTNER: So, uh, you still haven't really told me the substance of your business case for Tropical Graveyard Removals. Is it a sort of Rain Forest thing? My people tell me that's quite a hot area these days.

EGR: The tropics, sir?

LEW FIRSTNER: No, no. The whole recycling craze. You know, *eco-*whatever. Some very large opportunities there. Or so I hear.

EGR: Well, not exactly. EGR is more about memic amplification and enhancement, you could say.

LEW FIRSTNER: Oh that. I see.

EGR: Yes, we had some early successes, and had hoped this might follow in that vein, but frankly, it's turned out to be pretty boring.

LEW FIRSTNER: This? What do you mean, "this"?

EGR: Why, the recording we've been making of our little chat, of course.

LEW FIRSTNER: <click>

EGR: OK team, looks like that's all we're gonna get from the dude. Transcribe the tape and mark it up. It's pretty thin but our market boys are telling us only 3% of EGR subscribers read past the first graph anyway, so it'll probably fly as an issue and nobody'll take much notice.

EDITORIAL: You want we should work in the usual innuendos, boss? Like say some backscatter on the Olympic crash-and-burn fiasco? There's also some juicy stuff we could milk outta that 666 Argentine caper . . .

LEGAL: Nah, it's been done to death. The targets are way too easy. Just give us verbatim copy. We'll take care of the rest. Maybe some subtly actionable hint about lewd gifs. A racial slur, perhaps? That'd be more in keeping with our style . . .

EGR: Whatever. God I just hate this shit. But what the hell. *Somebody's* gotta do it I suppose . . .

50-Minute Hour

"If the nineteenth century was the age of the editorial chair, ours is the century of the psychiatrist's couch."

MARSHALL MCLUHAN

"In a completely sane world, madness is the only freedom."

J. G. BALLARD

"Do you understand why you're here?"

"Why, where are we?"

"I'll remind you again. The Lou Gerstner Memorial Hospital for the Criminally Insane. Does that ring a bell?"

"The name is vaguely familiar. Lou who?"

"Gerstner. He was chairman of some computer company. Generous philanthropist. Took a strong interest in our work because we ended up treating so many of his senior executives."

"This was before Michael Eisner became president, right?"

"Very good. But do you know _why_ you're here? That was the question."

"I get some kinda reptile flashes, but that's all."

"Let's go over this again. You kidnapped your last employer and fed him to Komodo Dragons you had specifically imported for the purpose. Premeditation played a rather large role in your trial. The police found six of them in that crack house you left the poor fellow tied up in. One was 10 feet long and weighed nearly 300 pounds."

"Oh that."

"Yes that. You still seem to display no remorse. But let's get back to what we were talking about last time. Do you remember?"

"Uh . . ."

The doctor pushes back from the desk, tenting his fingers to pursed lips. He looks at me intently for nearly a full minute.

"Let me refresh your memory then," he finally says. "You were describing how you felt invisible, as if no one knew what was going on inside your head. So tell me, just how long have you had this feeling that no one is watching you?"

I put hand to head trying to recall. Wasn't there something about this in my EGR To-Do folder from last week? "Oh yeah!" I brighten. "It's all coming back to me now. I guess it started in the sixties when we all thought the FBI had us under surveillance — you know, for drugs and shit — but then I began thinking it was just because we were lonely."

"*Lonely?*" he pounces. "How do you mean that?"

"Well, you know, sort of wishing someone would pay attention. Take notes. Keep a file or something. You know, like: 'The subject left his apartment at 2:35 P.M. dragging what appeared to be a bale of marijuana'. . . That sort of thing."

"But then . . . ?"

"Then I got it that no one was *really* watching. I mean, I was dealing weight right out on the street in clear daylight and the cops never hassled me except when I forgot to feed the parking meter."

"And now?"

"Now? Same thing. It's an attention economy all right, just like they say, but everybody's broke."

"What about me?" he asks. "I'm observing you, am I not? I'm extremely interested in your situation."

"No you're not," I reply. "It's a displacement thing. I *want* to believe I'm being watched, that someone would care enough about what I'm thinking to do that. So I'm making you up."

"*Really?*" He is visibly amused by this. "How so?"

"I'm writing you into this issue of my web zine."

"Your *web zine*," he repeats, emphasizing the words as if they are from another language. "And what does that mean — to you?"

"It's called Entropy Gradient Reversals," I tell him, immediately suspecting it may not help all that much.

"Ah hah," he says, and makes a quick entry in his notebook. "Then you'll know what I just wrote."

"Delusional. Increase lithium. Increase anti-psychotics."

"Well, you're a smart guy," he says, chumming up. "You could easily have inferred that much." But it's shaken him a little, I can tell.

"So tell me, what does 'Entropy Gradient Reversals' mean? That's an odd collection of words, don't you think?"

"Sorry," I tell him, "not again. We been over that too many times already. They'll never put up with another iteration."

"They?" he asks. "Who are 'they'?"

"The readers. The Valued Subscribers."

"I see," he says, trying to keep the excitement out of his voice. I can tell this is getting really interesting for him. Poor bastard. "Tell me more about these . . . uh, 'subscribers' you value so highly. Where are they now?"

"Oh, all over, really."

"All over. Hmmm. . . . Are any of them here with us now?"

"No, they haven't arrived yet. They come after we're done."

"By 'here,' do you mean here to this office? Will I see them?"

"No, you can't see them, but they're there. I mean here. Only later. It's kind of like a time travel thing."

"Time travel." He's giving me this really weird look.

"It's hard to explain, I guess. I never thought about it that much, but yeah, right now it's pretty much just you and me and then later there will be a couple thousand others. But by then, you won't be able to tell they're here. I don't usually know myself unless I look at the logs."

"Your 'readers,' as you call them? And they carry logs?"

"Well, partly right," I tell him. I'm thinking: how far should web literacy be taken? Does the guy really need to know any of this? Probably not necessary.

"OK, so say I take you at your word that you're making this all up, why would you write yourself into a mental institution? I mean, you could be anywhere, right? Why not on a beautiful beach some-where?"

"You may be getting the hang of this after all," I say. "Fact is, I *am* on a beautiful beach, being served Piña Coladas by an attentive bevy of Eurasian housegirls."

"Right, OK, and where is this?"

"EGR World HQ in the Yucatan Peninsula. Lovely place. Have you ever been?"

"Forget that. Let's get back to why we're here in a mental hospital instead of having this conversation there on the beach in Mexico, or wherever you think you are right now."

"Well, I imagine that's how my readers think of me. Locked up someplace safe for crimes too heinous to contemplate. Especially after that *last* issue."

"Oh? And what was that about?" he wants to know.

"It's kinda vague now. I'd hafta go back and re-read it. A buncha stuff about sex and alcohol and nuclear physics I think."

"Well, that's a very neat solution, wouldn't you say? No need to take responsibility for your actions if you've just made everything up. Isn't that it?"

How far can I take this character, I'm wondering. One false step and his willing suspension of disbelief could be shattered beyond repair. The results are not pretty to contemplate. Maybe I'd better take another tack.

"So what made you decide to practice in Malaysia," I ask, as if we're two strangers who just struck up a friendly chat in a bar.

"Look, I'm asking the questions here. You can't throw me off that easily. Besides, this is Boston, not Malaysia."

To demonstrate this and bring a little reality principle to bear, he goes over to the window and pulls back drapes. "See?" he says — a lit-tle too self-satisfied, I'm thinking. OK asshole, you asked for this.

"Yeah?" I reply, having gotten up and joined him at the window. "Doesn't look much like Boston to me," I say, pointing.

Across the street, a large sign on the building directly facing says First Bank of Kuala Lumpur. There are a few rickshaws in the street eight stories below. Maybe nine stories, it's getting hard to keep track. I look over and notice his face has gone ashen. Uh-oh, looks like I could be losing him.

"So hey Doc," I say cheerily, "is this your, like, diploma framed on the wall here?" I need to distract him, get him thinking about happier times.

"What's that? Oh yes, I got my degree in psychiatry from Harvard . . ." But he's still looking out the window, dangerously confused.

"Harvard?" I say. "That's not what it says here."

He suddenly snaps out of it, looks over at me. "What are you talking about?" He strides over and reads the plaque aloud, his tone increasingly querulous as he gets further into it: "Greater Des Moines Institute of Industrial Training. For Completion Of The Two-Year Associates Program In Welding, This Certificate Is Presented To David Weinberger . . ." His voice trails off.

"Zat your real name, Doc? Weinberger? Funny I never thought to ask."

He gives me a completely blank stare, then reaches into the breast pocket of his pinstripe suit and pulls out a classy looking leather billfold. He flips the little plastic card holders until he comes to a driver's license.

"Yep," I say, reading over his shoulder. "David Weinberger, that's you I guess."

He goes back to the desk and sits down heavily. Perhaps this has gone too far. But hell, I'm not sure how to get out of it now. Might as well press on and see where it goes.

"Know anything about intertextuality, Doc?" I ask, keeping the tone light, trying to coax him back from the edge. It takes a minute but he finally looks up and says "Hunh?" Not much, but it's something. Maybe I can keep him from dissociating altogether.

"Intertextuality," I repeat. "Complex references among and between written narratives. Sort of like a relational database but somebody lost all the table pointers."

The blank stare again.

"OK," I say, "I'll write this down for you. Maybe it'll come in handy later. Think of it as a Ricky-Don't-Lose-That-Number kinda deal."

"Who's Ricky?" he asks pathetically.

"Never mind about Ricky," I say. "Ricky isn't important. But this is." I go over to the desk and pick up his harpoon of a pen, an obscenely expensive Mount Blanc. In big letters on his blotter I print out:

WWW.HYPERORG.COM

He looks at the desktop, then back at me. His eyes are crazy. I almost feel sorry for him.

"Look, I know this doesn't make much sense to you now," I tell him consolingly, tapping the URL on the blotter, "but this is a big clue to who you really are. Maybe you can find someone to help you figure out what it means."

But he's gone. Tripping. Vacated. I shake him roughly. Slowly, he comes out of it, shudders like the devil just crossed his grave, takes out a silk handkerchief and wipes away the cold sweat that's broken out across his deeply furrowed brow.

"Listen carefully," I tell him, forming the words as clearly as I can. "You used to work at Interleaf, then at Open Text. You got into this profession because your mother was devoured by tarantulas in the Uruguayan jungle when you were only four years old and you witnessed the whole thing. Your father was an Andalusian monk . . . "

"But how do you know these things about me?" he interrupts.

"Don't interrupt!" I bellow, straight into his face. Then, relenting, "Well, hey, some of it's on your home page," I tell him. "You ought to read it yourself once in a while. The rest I made up five minutes ago. I've been fucking around with the paragraph to get the details right. Hmmmm, maybe it wasn't tarantulas," I muse aloud. "Maybe it was actually boa constrictors."

"Boa constrictors . . ." he echoes, putting his left hand to his forehead, radically unsure of everything at this point. Suddenly he snaps his fingers: "My god, that's right!"

"*Albino* boa constrictors," I say. "Their eyes were horrible. You remember . . . "

He begins to perspire profusely and his hands tremble uncontrollably, the panic setting in again. He tugs at his tie as if it's choking him, goes to the window and throws it open, gasping for air. Below, he sees only the familiar Boston traffic. Across the street there is no bank. In its place is a Legal Seafood restaurant.

"Not seafood!" he cries out, falling back from the window and tripping over a potted palm. He is rocking side to side on the floor, moaning softly when the attendants arrive to return me to my cell.

"Well, Doc, looks like that's all we got time for today," I say, not sure whether he can hear me. I reach down and give his shoulder a little nudge. "Say there, Doc . . . Doc?"

Oh well, no use I guess. Good session, though, I tell myself, setting the file back on his desk. I think we're finally making some progress here.

"And what about you fellas?" I ask the attendants as they lead me away, "Where do y'all hail from?"

"*Laugh-a while you can monkey boy!*"

Dr. Emilio Lizardo

The Cover Letter

Everyone needs a resume. It is a passport to crucial livelihood options, such as the ability to dine in fine restaurants rather than from the dumpster behind the local 7-11; to live in a home of one's own rather than a refrigerator shipping crate; and perhaps most importantly, to put one's personal stamp on the truck and commerce of the world at large: to make one's mark, as it were. Like you, Valued Readers, we also maintain such a resume, and like most of you — having studied our Negroponte — we have put it online in digital form.

But there is a fatal flaw in such documents. They give dates and datapoints, but rarely add up to a whole — or even barely adequate — picture of the individual they are intended to represent *in absentia*. We here at EGR World HQ have been struggling with this problem for some time. Readers who have followed the development of this excremental little zine will immediately recognize the foremost source of our discomfiture in this regard, i.e., we are plural. In contrast, the canonical resume seeks to present a profile of its subject as a predictably one-dimensional persona. As we all know, such entities do not occur in nature.

True, we *could* add a section to our curriculum vitae along the following lines:

Hobbies

- Fomenting Cognitive Chaos
- Propagating Semiotic Field Disruption
- Disseminating Disinfotainment

However, as long-time readers will instantly recognize, these various characterizations hardly do justice to the much larger agenda we have come to term, for lack of a more embracing label, "Entropy Gradient Reversals."

Finally, though, we have hit upon a solution to this thorny problem, and it comes from a most unexpected quarter: the garden variety cover letter. The purpose of such an instrument is to place the job applicant's work experience and skill base into the context of overall career goals. We realized we could leverage an enormous asset to overcome this perennial impasse: our trusty AI, BOMBAST II. Since the system had already been programmed (at great expense we might add) to reflect our assumptions, inclinations, passions, and general feelings about life, the universe and everything, what, we reasoned, could more perfectly convey a holistic impression of our True — even if multipartite — Self?

Dear Prospective Employer:

As you can see from the attached resume, we are highly qualified for the position of [insert anal retentive job title here]. However, we are bored beyond tears by your published job description. We'd like to take this opportunity to propose something a little different.

Even a fleeting glimpse of our CV will alert you to the fact that we have attempted to practice some form of marketing in organizations, which — as we're sure you'll recognize from your own long experience — could not position their way out of the proverbial wet paper bag. Of course, some of these work engagements date back to the Jurassic era, when such bungling botchery might more readily be forgiven by markets that knew the perpetrators only as four-color spreads in *Business Week*. However, now that the Internet has become home to all bipedal hominids living outside of zoos, such ineptitude has become a threat to the very survival of many corporations not unlike your own. On the off chance that your firm is not among the aforementioned class of doddering dunderheads, the following outlines several salient truths we believe we have grasped with respect to the changing nature of consumer expectations in today's increasingly online economy.

Most of these insights come from publishing what is referred to in Internet parlance as a "webzine" — a new phenomenon that differs from the traditional magazine to the same degree that anti-lock brakes differ from a poke in the eye with a sharp stick shift. We have been publishing Entropy Gradient Reversals since May 1 1996, and in that time have gathered a modest subscriber base of some 1200 souls — or 2400 "eyeballs," to again use the prevailing Internet lingo. While these numbers may appear trivial when compared to, say, the 80 million visitors per day to Microsoft's web server, we believe they represent a significant "focus group" by which certain critical inferences can be drawn about consumer attitudes in general. As we move into a far more networked business milieu, foreknowledge of this shifting mindset could well be defining of success or failure in your company's future online initiatives.

We group our findings about Internet audiences into three distinct categories:

- Overall characteristics
- Things they could give a shit about
- Things they appear to value

1. OVERALL CHARACTERISTICS

Not half as stupid as they look

The typical Internet denizen may *appear* to be as dumb as the consumer targeted by traditional media. Do not be deceived. However, many of your marketing "professionals" are deeply committed to believing this bit of wishful catechetical lore in the face of massive evidence to the contrary. Perhaps your company is a product of those very Old Media principles you cannot seem to relinquish, and thus, far less intelligent than your intended customers. If so, take a wild guess at the inevitable result.

Low tolerance for horseshit

Put simply, the New Audience isn't having any. Your corporate credibility plus a buck-twenty-five *might* buy you a cup of coffee. You are World Class. You are Uniquely Positioned. You are Sincere. "Yup, uh-huh," your market is thinking to itself: *"Losers!"*

Highly influential in their own sphere

If you had to pick just one of the new market realities to wise up to, this would be the best to heed: these folks *talk to each other*. They couldn't do that half as easily with the TV blaring or just by reading the newspaper. But online, talk they do. And if the poster/emailer/web author appears to know what he or she is talking about — or is just plain whacked enough to provide some respite from your constant barrage of commercial shovelware — then others tend to listen. Just what are they talking about, you ask? Why, they're talking about *you!* (btw, do you know what "LOL" means?)

"Trust No One"

This X-Files tagline has become the rallying cry of a whole new generation of consumers upon whose willing suspension of disbelief your company is nonetheless, as always, utterly dependent. They sometimes buy your shit, of course. But only after wading through and sorting out your outright lies and microscopically fractional truths. Internet audiences expect this of you, as you've provided them no alternative. God help your ass if some other outfit ever does.

On speaking terms with alternate realities

While hardly exhausting our possible list of New Audience character traits, this one seems to us to be disproportionately significant. These people literally do not live in the same universe you inhabit. They would sooner listen to a lengthy lecture by the White Rabbit than read another of your pathetically well reasoned homepage disquisitions. They would rather have their fortunes told by Madame Blavatsky than drop by your trade show booth. Now what does this tell us?

2. THINGS THEY COULD GIVE A SHIT ABOUT

Your products

Bo-ring! While the latest addition to your product lineup may seem *to you* to warrant all that bloody noise, most of the people hitting your web pages are throwing up their hands in disgust. In more advanced cases, they're simply throwing up. Christ, what is *wrong* with you people? Don't they ever let you cruise around out here? If you surfed a little more you might realize that your "missionary work" is tantamount to preaching virginity at an Ozzie Osborne concert.

Your press releases

Oh *yeah,* that was real interesting! These are especially fascinating when they contain executive comments of the form: "ButtWipe International is [pleased/thrilled/creaming in its jeans] to [reassert/demonstrate] its commitment to meeting [customer/client/prospect] [needs/requirements/whims] by [providing/offering] tools that [enable/promote] [efficient/effective/spasmodic] market [penetration/buggery] . . . " You mean to say that your new relationship with Pac-Rim SuperCompany X underscores your global market dominance? Well gosh. But the cat just puked up a hairball, which is a far more compelling thing to contemplate.

Your CEO's latest speech at COMDEX

It has become a cliche among political pundits that no one outside Washington gives a flying fig for the big-deal doings inside the Beltway. Why is it so hard to apply this simple lesson to the computer industry? Here's the short-form analysis your market is according you far from the hot-air hosery of the Power Circuit: "Hey man, your thing just crashed. It's dogfood. Next!"

Your competitive strategy

Yada yada, blah blah blah. However, on the other hand and notwithstanding, blah blah, yada-yada, blah. Class? Are we picking up on this? **CLASS?!?!?!**

Aristotelian logic and Cartesian dualism
Remember that what makes perfect sense to you may not compute at all in the mind of the market you hope to attract. New Media audiences are more like cargo cults than anything you've ever had to deal with before now. In fact, according to an informal survey, no reader of Entropy Gradient Reversals had the slightest notion what the above terms even referred to, and most were deeply uncertain about the publication's name.

3. THINGS THEY APPEAR TO VALUE

Disdain for authority
While ad hominem attacks are not tolerated or condoned by responsible Netizens, corporations have set themselves up in such a way that they have no legal culpability as persons. Unable to have their cake and eat it too, they are therefore flame bait for every cyber-neurotic with a deep seated grudge against Big Brother business organizations. Unfortunately for you, this group represents roughly 99.9999% of your target market. Online audiences never cease to be amused by random vicious attacks on lame-brained companies too mired in corporate protocol to rise to their own defense. You plan to call in your lawyers in such cases? What an excellent idea.

> From: RageBoy <clocke@rageboy.com>
> To: all.usenet.crazies
> Subject: net-wide flame fest set for thursday! pass it on. . .

Communicational competence
Congratulations on that new corporate homepage! You sound like a sexless droid with a badly damaged Personality Module. Anyone who can manage to come across as a human being with likes and and dislikes, hopes and fears, and doesn't appear to have been programmed in spaghetti-code COBOL has far more chance of being heard. Your

brand, you say? Save it for when you end up punching cows — shouldn't take long at the rate you're slaloming down the charts.

Big words — and lots of em

Sending readers to the dictionary would seem a fatal move with respect to an audience having the collective attention span of a swarm of gnats. We were surprised by this one ourselves. The lesson to be gleaned here is that the mass media have spoken down to people for so long that they seem to find it positively refreshing when someone talks over their heads. The only other person we know of to have figured this out is William F. Buckley — and he's an asshole!

    <!— note to Legal: can we say that here? -ed. —>

Undeserved abuse

Another eye-opener is the appallingly masochistic bent so many demonstrate in this new medium. This is probably related to the former point. Corporate communications have for so long curried favor by stroking readers' egos that the tactic is simply no longer effective. On the other hand, telling people to fuck off seems to win hearts and minds online. Who would have guessed?

Entropy Gradient Reversals

Granted, our sample for this study was self-selecting, so your mileage may vary as to the statistical significance of our little focus group. The one thing it seems to value unequivocally — with the exception of the misbegotten swine who will surely unsubscribe as a result of this issue — is EGR itself. For all the reasons suggested above, we believe our publication has been an enormously effective vehicle for magnetizing an audience *typical of the market whose trust you* **must** *win in order to remain viable into the 21st Century.*

Right about now, you're probably wondering, "But how could this work for *my* organization?" Well, good, because that's just what we've been leading up to. The simple fact is: you could virtually *own*

Entropy Gradient Reversals, locke, stock and barrel. That's right, we're putting the whole zine up for sale to the highest bidder — or perhaps we should say "up for rent." Who will "acquire" us? Netscape? Microsoft? Novell? Oracle? IBM? We're incredibly excited about the whole idea. We're peeing our pants with anticipation. And which of these organizations wouldn't share our excitement? Imagine being able to say:

Entropy Gradient Reversals is brought to you by [Your Company Name Here].

Aside from the fact that it'll cost you a boatload of cash, there's only one non-negotiable condition: we will continue to write exactly as we have to date. Think of the recognition, stature and unparalleled prestige your company will gain with online communities when we trash you right along with the rest of the Clue Impaired. And the beauty part? You get a banner on every page at *no extra charge!*

Now, perhaps, you can better understand why we are not interested in applying for your advertised position as [insert anal retentive job title here]. This is so much better! We have long believed that, as corporations come increasingly to resemble the great City States of the High Renaissance, they should also adopt one of the noblest institutions of that golden era: patronage. If you like our basic idea but would argue that your investment ought to buy you greater editorial control, think about Michelangelo for a minute. Imagine Lorenzo insisting on having "Bank With Medici!" inserted into various panels on the ceiling of the Sistine Chapel. See what we mean? It'd just wreck the whole thing.

Eagerly awaiting a response at your earliest convenience, we remain . . .

Sincerely Yours,
RageBoy®

Uniquely Qualified

"Much of our American progress has been the product of the individual who had an idea; pursued it; fashioned it; tenaciously clung to it against all odds; and then produced it, sold it, and profited from it."

HUBERT H. HUMPHREY

"There is always the danger that we may just do the work for the sake of the work. This is where the respect and the love and the devotion come in — that we do it to God, to Christ, and that's why we try to do it as beautifully as possible."

MOTHER TERESA

InfoBeat Inc.
Attn: HR Director
707 17th Street, Suite 2850
Denver, CO 80202
Fax: 303–675–2399
E-mail: jobs@infobeat.com

Dear Sir or Madam:

I am writing in reply to your job posting at http://www.infobeat.com/static/cgi/static_merc.cgi?page=/jobs.html&refurl=www.infobeat.com/
    Kee-*reist*, that's a long URL, don't you think? But anyway, in case you have forgotten, here is the material you put on your web site about the position I am applying for:

VP Business Development:

Responsible for creating and managing partnerships, joint ventures and relationships with other Internet companies as part of InfoBeat subscriber acquisition and alliance programs.

Requirements:

- Strong analytical and financial modeling skills
- Experience in subscriber valuation, risk assessment, revenue sharing, etc.
- 2–5+ years Business or Corporate Development; high-tech or Internet background
- Significant negotiating and deal-making experience
- Management experience
- MBA

First off, why the MBA? I think I would make a great VP Business Development even though I am not a member. What does basketball have to do with it?

Second off, let's talk about that risk assessment item. My assessment is this: risk is bad. Otherwise they wouldn't call it that, am I right? The implication is that something not so nice could happen to you if you take a risk, so simple: *just don't do it!* This is but one example of the analytical skills I would bring to the "party."

Now financial modeling could be another story. If this has anything to do with money, I have to level with you: it could be a weak area. Generally speaking, numbers are not my strong suit. For example, I am having a little trouble understanding how long "2–5+ years" is. More than two? More than five? Two takeaway five? Also, do you supply the modeling clay, or would I be expected to bring my own?

Actually, it was the bit about "subscriber valuation" that caught my eye as I was surfing around your — I must say way-cool — web pages. I value my own subscribers very highly, going so far as to always address them as Valued Subscribers so they'll be sure to know how I feel. Ask anyone. Of course, I also call them certain other things that

I should probably not put into this letter if I want to "land" the job, but that is just kidding around. You know? Mostly.

As to deal-making experience, well hey, you're talking about a guy who could sell ice boxes to Eskimos — just like the business you're in, in fact. I used to deal quite a bit back in the 1960s, though this was a different type of product line. Nonetheless, you can probably tell from my nickname — "Good Weight" — that my customers all thought I was pretty righteous. I would send you letters of recommendation except that most of them aren't out yet. Plus, they aren't allowed to have sharp instruments like pencils and stuff.

Another thing? I am really hot on this whole Internet deal! God, isn't it terrific? I'm on this one "list" they've got where you get different pictures every day. Some guys even put their old ladies on the thing, it's really amazing! But perhaps we should discuss my qualifications some more.

I have worked at CMP, Mecklermedia, MCI and IBM, and at all those places I was considered a "guru" with this "net" stuff. Nobody else seemed to know dick about it, which sort of surprised me. But who am I to complain, if you catch my drift. I've been working this for years, so I guess I'll do alright with you people unless you have like a test or something.

Most of my significant negotiating experience was in Tashkent, Uzbekistan (country code 3712). I trust this will not constitute a stumbling block. I see it as a plus to have had to put up with foreigners for so long and hardly ever lose my temper. If you want, I can tell you some amazing "war stories" about these people. You wouldn't believe the shit they eat over there for instance. So that pretty much covers International.

Can I ask you something? What do you *do* there anyway? I saw on your web site something about email you could sign up for, but I think there is already too much email. Therefore, I think you are headed for a problem area. I am good at problem areas like this, having been in so many in my personal career-to-date. Of course, you can't expect me to tell you the answer unless you hire me, so that will just have to wait.

What else? Oh yes, I want this job because I see from your address that you are apparently in Denver (I'm in Boulder, just a stone's throw) and therefore the driving would be a lot less than, say, Los Angeles.

I think location is very important to a business, don't you? You know what they say: location, location, location.

I believe that every cover letter should have some action points for followup. Otherwise the other person could forget what they're doing and then you're just dogfood. So here are mine:

- Let's get together and have lunch or something. Do you like Italian?
- I would like to shake hands with your CEO. Doesn't have to be anything fancy. Just want to make sure the guy has a good firm grip, if you know what I mean. It is a guy, right?
- You say nothing about dress in your want ad. Will I need clothes for this? I have been working out of my den for some time now, so I often forget. But if you're not "casual" down there, I will understand.
- How's your psychiatric benefits package? Some companies neglect this or go on about "pre-existing" conditions. Let's get one thing straight: I require a lot of care in this area.
- Will I get my own "cube"? Sharing is OK, but not if it's someone who has bad hygiene. I am a very clean person.

I'm sure you will have other questions about me, but it's pretty hard to imagine that you won't be excited to get my resume. One thing I can guarantee is that you won't ever find another candidate better suited to whatever it is you expect me to do for you.

Do you have a "web browser" there? If not, maybe someone can help you to down load this file:

www.panix.com/~clocke/resume.html

You can call me anytime except Thursday as they're coming to shampoo the rugs.

Cordially,
RageBoy®

PS: I have attached a photo that you can keep for yourself if you want.

Welcome to the Weather Channel

> "When it is evening, ye say, It will be fair
> weather: for the sky is red. And in the morning,
> It will be foul weather today: for the sky is red
> and lowring. O ye hypocrites, ye can discern the
> face of the sky; but can ye not discern the
> signs of the times?"
>
> **MATTHEW, 16:2–3**

> "You don't need a weatherman
> to know which way the wind blows."
>
> **BOB DYLAN**

Well, we've finally completed the relocation of EGR World Headquarters to beautiful Boulder, Colorado, land of mountain zephyrs and sunny dispositions! Everything went incredibly smoothly with the move (if you overlook a couple of major fuckups on the part of the Mayflower moving agent). The Holiday Inns were well appointed, the truckstop food was yummy. We rode the ferries on the Niagara, Ohio and Mississippi Rivers. We felt the booming Heartbeat of America®. Even the new job is pretty good: engaging, challenging, fraught with daily peril. Perhaps this surfeit of sheer and utter wonderfulness explains why we haven't written a bloody thing all month.

But today we awakened in a foul mood, discovered too late that the time had changed (again!), drank too much coffee, began to suspect cancer of the colon (or perhaps it's the prostate — who can tell about these things?) and are feeling especially annoyed and irritated by all this goddam sunlight. Doesn't it ever *rain* around here for christ's sake? In other words, we feel positively inspired to begin writing the issue we know you've all been waiting for!

Speaking of weather and taking the Lord's name in vain, we have lately noted a pair of linked phenomena — at least we are strongly inclined to believe they're linked, though this could be a hard one to prove. The first is the enormous and growing popularity of The Weather Channel in these United States. The second is the enormous and terrifying proliferation of TV evangelists.

The Weather Channel. Everybody's watching it. You're probably watching it right now. Or you just were, or soon will be. For clues to something, we suspect, though we're not quite sure to what.

What *is it* about The Weather Channel? Our first theory is too obvious to get very excited about, really. Everyone knows that watching Bob Dole "debate" Bill Clinton is about as scintillating as driving a rusty nail through your foot. Plus of course, they wouldn't let poor Rosser join their little Reindeer games. Too bad, too. At least the guy's a fucking screech. That twang!

> "You take your basic Weather Channel now . . . there's a refreshing departure from all this political claptrap. That radar scan makes you feel you're right on top of things. In control of the situation. Know what I mean?"

What is it about The Weather Channel that has so captured the hearts and minds of America? We'll tell you what it is. It's that you can look at the computer-generated simulation of some tropical storm down there in the distant and mysterious Caribbean that just got upgraded to a Force-4 hurricane that's gonna blow *somebody's* ass off and *know* that, for once,

IT'S NOT YOUR FUCKING FAULT!

You take your basic Bible Thumper now . . . These people would not agree with that. Know what I mean? In addition to cornering the market on TV godfomercials — and it's a big one — the Born Again are all over the web, in case you hadn't noticed, offering to relieve you of those pitiful wages of sin you've been working for lo these many years. For instance, on a page titled WHAT ALL CHRISTIANS MUST KNOW, we learn that the "Second Law of Thermodynamics is opposite to Evolution." At first we were beside ourselves with excitement at discovering this penetrating gloss on the true nature of entropy gradient reversals (though we would have put it the other way around). However, the associated statement — "Brontosaurus cave paintings in Zimbabwe . . . mean that man and dinosaurs co-existed" — made us wonder whether our enthusiasm were not a trifle misplaced. Or at least a little premature. Oh well.

What is really concerning, though, is that a whole new kind of God Squad is coming onto television via public cable channels and paid advertisements got up to look like talk shows. Typically, these guys, and so far they're mostly guys, except of course for the inevitable and fetching little Occasion of Sin whose blouse buttons you keep watching, wondering whether they're really going to pop as she enthuses away about The Rapture — oh come on, baby, breathe a little *deeper!* . . .

Anyway, as we were saying, these guys are all attempting to outdo Rush Limbaugh with their smarmy insider irony about the True Fate of the Damned and such. We were particularly fascinated by a fellow named Bob Enyart — obviously a stage appellation — who seems to be based somewhere in Indiana, but is doing a booming business in Colorado via cable. One of his favorite themes is Godless homos. For ourselves, we are much more concerned about God-fearing homos, but we'll leave that for another issue. Maybe. However, if "HOMOS MAKE YOU SICK," you'll be sure to want to visit The Official Bob Enyart Live Web Site.

One adoring fan says of Enyart: "A major part of Bob Enyart Live is the callers of the show. Callers who disagree with Bob often go to the top of the list. Watch Bob leave the liberal callers in a daze as he shoots down their arguments and reveals the Biblically-based truth with beautiful logic."

And you know, he's right. In the first installment we saw of Bob Enyart Live, he said, apropos of nothing we could discern, "Worshipping a tree is a perverse and vile thing" — and for context with respect to this sudden non sequitur, explained that there are, in point of fact, certain African tribes (perhaps those fond of repeating booga-booga all the ding-dang day) that actually *worship trees*. "That's right folks," he then added, somewhat mysteriously, "first it's god, then it's lunch . . ." It *did* leave us in a daze.

But wait. It's not that simple to write this dude off. Sure he's a homophobic psycho racist, a bloodthirsty guilt-vampire of the first water. Sure he'd have us all put to death by various interestingly excru- ciating methods. But he's certainly not stupid ("How can this be?" we asked ourselves, without getting any answers.) And most important, in a ghastly, mesmerizing sort of way, he's enormously *entertaining*. Kind of like watching a public hanging — or the Mai Lai testimony. We hung on his every word for hours over several nights upon arriving in Colorado. They just don't have the *real* stuff like this on Connecticut cable, just the same old ho-hum tits and ass.

When we first channel-surfed across Mr. Enyart, he was going on about how Clinton and his ilk are attempting to dumb down America, an opinion with which we heartily agree, though we doubt the Democrats are exactly alone in this mission. As proof of the proposi- tion, Enyart offers Clinton's evidently stated desire to have children be able to read by eight years old and to log onto the Internet by the time they're 12. Well, first off, says Enyart, everybody thought Einstein was a dullard because he was unable to read at age *seven*! "See what I mean?," he ingenuously queries his TV flock.

"Plus . . . *plus!* . . . why does he want kids to be able to log onto the Net by the time they're *12?*" Alright, here it comes, we're thinking, the whole Devil's Workshop routine complete with stark-staring perverts and buttfuckery worthy of Sodom and Gomorrah. But no. What he actually says (Scout's honor) is "Even a *carrot* could log onto the Internet!" At which point we are rolling on the floor, gasping, sputtering, clawing at the air for breath, ready to make our peace with Jesus right there and then. Or take up tree worship. *Something.*

The point is: America is dying of boredom.

And these good sincere people really do represent salvation of a sort. All they ask for great entertainment value like this — a *carrot* for godsake! — is for you to accept Jesus Christ into your life as your personal Lord and Savior. What could be simpler, eh?

Look, we understand that people are genuinely hurting out there, that the world is full of pain and misery, that injustice and evil and all sorts of Bad Things are going down in that little piece of real estate just outside the Internet they call The Real World. Well, here's a free tip from all of us here at the EGR Editorial Board: *for the most part,* and just like the weather,

IT'S NOT YOUR FUCKING FAULT!

After all, is it fair that the deepest, most intractable problems of the planet be shifted onto your already drooping shoulders, deposited like a sack of karmic dogshit on your cognitive doorstep? What, just because you got drunk as a boiled owl last night, fell down and cracked your forehead open and ended up bleeding all over that poor good-hearted hooker? Let's just say you were a bit confused.

Before we are accused of moral relativism — Heaven forfend! — we will admit that most people are doing all they can to maximize their suffering, in every way they can think up. According to our research department, here are just a few: wondering what other people think of you, especially your boss and co-workers (easy: they want you dead); asking whether you have any *real* friends (of course not); speculating as to the quintessential quality of Divine Mercy (friend, have another drink).

Now maybe you think we're taking this admittedly arcane connection between The Weather Channel and the Circuit Preachers just a bit too far. Maybe you think it's all projection — or wishful thinking. Maybe you think we've been watching too many episodes of the X-Files. But however you think about it, *think about it!* Won't you?

On Getting It

A letter, of sorts, to JOHO

OK, this one requires a little set-up. If you subscribe to EGR (and actually read it), you probably already know that I asked a bunch of people to say good things about me and, incredibly, many did. Never one to hide my light under a bushel — not even having a decent bushel handy if I wanted to — I naturally put these on the web:

www.rageboy.com/ewc/people.html

While being astounded by this embarrassment of riches (and many will feel I damn well *should* be embarrassed), I noticed that many of these quotes said "Chris Locke gets it" — or some pretty close permutation. Only the final entry sounds a slightly different note:

"He not only 'Gets It,' he has the sense to question what 'Getting It' really means."

This was from David Weinberger, longtime friend and sparring partner, and editor of EGR's virtuous twin, The Journal of the Hyperlinked Organization, or just plain JOHO.

David and I got to kicking around what it did mean to "get it" — and initially we were both of the mind that this expression reflected a potentially divisive Us-vs-Them mentality. However, I started to answer his most recent mail in this spirit and something went terribly wrong, I guess, because I ended up saying the opposite. I can't believe it! The one time I try to agree with the guy, and I mess it up. The results of this botched attempt follow.

By the way, this ramble includes several veiled and half-joking references — to things like tacit knowledge and the death of the document

— which will make little sense unless you've been following JOHO. If you haven't, there's little hope for you, but here's a last chance: www.hyperorg.com.

This is David speaking . . .

> As VP of [company name withheld] I did a video
> endorsement (a talking head shot) for [other company
> name withheld]. I was interviewed for 15 minutes
> and said, I thought, a number of pithily positive
> things that might make it into the final reel
> (which was to be shown at some product launch). But
> as I found myself saying, "[this company] gets it
> about the Web," I was washed with both a sense of
> debasement and a certainty that that's the line
> they would use. Yup.
>
> I passed this along to a friend. Within two months
> he was doing a similar interview for another
> company, and sure enough, that's the phrase that
> made it in again. As a highly paid and world famous
> marketing guru (with a tendency to exaggerate,
> perhaps), I can tell you that "X Gets It about the
> Web" is a Can't Miss marketing phrase. Apparently
> there is literally nothing that people would rather
> hear about themselves than that they Get It.

The rest is my reply. As you will shortly see, I got a bit carried away.

I have to say I do like it that so many people say I "get it" on that quotes page. Yeah, it bothers me for all the reasons we've talked about, but I think it's also current shorthand for:

"This person understands something fundamental about how online differs from previous media and knows a good deal about the dynamics constituting that difference. Moreover, he appreciates and empathizes with the frustrations of a savvier but largely disenfranchised grass-roots audience as it helplessy watches traditional corporations attempting to force the Internet and World Wide Web into the mold of mass-communication predecessors such as high-circulation magazines, direct-mail advertising and television infomercials."

. . . which, you have to admit, doesn't make half as good a sound bite for the 6 o'clock news.

Plus, I think many of us would prefer that those who *don't* "get it," according to the expanded definition above, would either a) do so quickly, or b) get the hell out of the way.

Also, there is — you should forgive the expression — a tacit dimension to this phrase. More accurately, it acknowledges that such a dimension might exist. Much reference is made to "vision" among those who "get it" — and vision used in this sense is a similarly loaded term, invoking overtones of the arcane and even mystical. Such vision spooks as much as it impresses.

It spooks the suits (another neologism in need of decompression) because it suggests an almost shamanistic ability to see into another world, a world whose logic is inaccessible to anyone who hasn't been inducted into a broad constellation of new media realities. Comparisons with the transition from Newtonian physics to quantum physics are not entirely inappropriate. There *has* been a genuine paradigm shift.

Not only does T. S. Kuhn come to mind, but also a whole raft of anthropologists. Rites of passage are highly relevant here. How does an individual achieve some measure of cultural synchrony with a larger society and the coherent set of beliefs and practices that define it?

[I would even posit that the surprisingly fast transition from old media to new has been, and continues to be, driven — to a degree that has not yet been adequately explored, and certainly not explained — by widespread disaffection with a society whose beliefs and practices have become largely *incoherent*.]

Anthropologists have also focused on the intersection of radically differing cultures, and this is germane as well — as is the phenomenon of cargo cults. How does uncritically adopting the techno-fetishism of *Wired* magazine and the atoms-to-bits catechism of Nicholas Negroponte differ in kind from worshipping an airplane made of straw? If that represents "getting it," then count me out.

But looking at the web from this perspective, the crypto-religious overtones become obvious, even glaring. To me, these at least point to the *desire* for a dimension that could be characterized as spiritual, in the sense of transcending the purely reductive and materialistic axioms of commercial culture.

And such analogies are legitimate to some degree. "Getting it" implies not just intellectual understanding but coming into deep psychological congruence with principles of operation that are largely hidden to casual view. Those who do not live in the new world, and who have therefore not been steeped in its customs, mores, rituals and expectations, are sure to be perplexed — just as the missionaries sent to "save" them were perplexed by the cultures they encountered beyond the parochial borders of 16th Century Christendom.

To someone comfortable with the world view defined and bounded by the organizational hierarchy, the telephone, the interoffice memo and the fax machine, what you and I have been doing with email and the web is nearly indistinguishable from magic. If it could be written off as mere superstition it would not be so upsetting. However, to see it actually *work* can be truly scary. I would argue that JOHO works. EGR works. And in ways damn few could have predicted.

Side Trip

Imagine attending a voodoo ceremony in which you personally witnessed the dead coming back to life. Your options at that point would be binary: choosing to ignore evidence reported by your own senses, or radically revising your fundamental notions of reality.

Does the web represent a kind of Dawn of the Living Dead? Many would agree it does — but for strongly conflicting reasons. Passive consumerism and the mass media that served it did create what amounted to a living death for anyone who might have wanted to communicate another view, create another kind of world. And in this respect, the dead have truly risen — with a little help from the web. We're not talking about zombification here, but its exact opposite: breaking a spell that has held us in thrall to commercial forces in which we have been participants less often than victims.

Note that this distancing of those who "get it" from those who don't is not necessarily grounded in the learning curve demanded by the newer tools, per se. Anyone can learn to work an email client pretty quickly. Anyone can create a web page with Netscape Composer.

Yes, there's another level of ability required. You need to get that WYSIWYG HTML page onto a server, so you need to know how to work FTP or some fiendishly friendly equivalent. Maybe you need to know something about sub-directories and file systems. And then there's the "cultural" dimension (construed shallowly and thus the quotes) involving such things as netiquette: how neither flamer nor flamee to be.

But it's not all technology and digital decorum. One can master these nuts-and-bolts principles and mechanisms — spammers do; they just ignore the injunction to be nice — without "getting it" in any meaningful sense. Knowledge of these matters does not make the knower *effective*.

Here's an interesting question for you. Is it an accident that you and I both have substantial background in what we might call, for lack of better terminology, "text management"? Or that Tim Bray and Tim Berners-Lee and (I imagine) a whole slew of JOHO readers share a similar background? By the way, I prefer "text" to "document" in this context; while the latter may die, the letter liveth.

I'm edging toward a theory here. It's still unformed, but that's always when things are most interesting — a pregnant time, as such cusps are sometimes called. So let me take a shot, even though this may amount to nothing more than premature articulation.

What if the tacitly spooky dimension of "getting it" were circumstantial evidence of a kind a folk paradigm in the making? What if it represented a popular but half-formed perception that something genuinely new had come into the world? Existing language often has a tough time capturing such events. My guess is that the empty neologism points to something that isn't empty at all. And I would guess further that what's inside is an expanded form of literacy. Expanded not in the mechanical direction of spelling and syntax, but in the rhetorical dimension.

Imagine this expanded literacy as an ability to use technology to tell a different class of stories than the story we've all been handed. Stories that draw people together around a new cultural campfire and hold their rapt attention there amid the gale-force storm of noise that's blowing down the world outside.

The spookiness derives from the open-endedness of popular narrative. This is atavistic stuff, uncontrolled and uncontrollable, connected to a collective unconscious predating any scrap of recorded history — notes from the ultimate underground. And this ancient elemental force has just broken loose in the pipes and wires of the late 20th century. Not only is it loose, it's breeding and seething at the very heart of a civilization *based on* discontent.

To a commercial "culture" whose short-term memory conjures nothing but command and control, this is nightmare incarnate, the poison-spitting Alien of movie horror, not inconsequentially black, not inconsequentially female. Bottom line: unmistakably other.

To a "postmodern" culture with practically no memory at all, it is often something altogether different — and far less frightening. The immediacy of electronic language is perceived not as threat but as invitation: to imagine, to create, to weave a very different kind of pattern into the social fabric.

text, noun
from Latin *textus*, tissue, style of literary work, the Gospel, written character (from *texere*, to weave).

I would venture that grasping this fundamental distinction regarding what really changed with the advent of an open global Internet constitutes what it means to "get it." Anyone who claims to will be branded by the still-reigning media paradigm as a "visionary" — cute perhaps, dangerous most likely, and definitely communing with Another World whose reality is fundamentally suspect.

But I live in that world. I do get it. That this world is digital or electronic is not the primary fact. What matters most is that it exists in *narrative* space. The story has come unbound. The world of commerce became dangerously permeable while it wasn't looking and sprang a leak from a quarter least expected.

Let's say it all together: Born again! Thank you DARPA!

And what is emerging is *our* story in the most fundamental sense, the human imagination weaving a vision of whatever it wants to become. The dangers of democracy pale before the danger of uncontained life. Life with the wraps off. Life run wild.

Terrifying? Why? How does the above description differ from that we might apply to, say, a virgin forest? When he said, "in wildness is the preservation of the world," I bet Thoreau wasn't just thinking about old-growth trees. He also wrote a little ditty called On Civil Disobedience. There is a connection.

Cartesian dualism and theistic religion have held the "civilized" world in their black-magic grip for centuries. We are somehow outside creation. The "laws" of "nature" do not apply to us. But what if there was no immutable law, what if there was no nature as defined to be that "other" thing that we are not? Then something extremely interesting might begin to happen.

It's happening already.

So, great! I set out to defuse the sense of mystery surrounding "getting it" and instead have succeeded in deepening the rift, justifying the fear and separation the phrase implies and identifying it with voodoo, mystical religion and magic. But I suspect my reading is more right than wrong. A reduction to more familiar terms simply will not work here. It's like trying to tell a stranger about rock and roll.

"Are you experienced?" Jimi Hendrix asked. If you had to inquire what he really meant by that, the answer was clearly no.

Maybe it's time to drop the pretense that this isn't a revolution. Maybe it's time to drop.

The Wrathful Deities of Tibetan iconography are not there to amuse and titillate, like the monsters conceived by Hollywood. They are there to protect. And what they protect is some sacred space you cannot enter with your shoes on. Can't even enter with your *mind* on.

In any genuine transition, thresholds are critical. Which side of the doorway you find yourself standing on can be defining.

To come full circle, I suspect the ideas hidden behind "getting it" telegraph a semiconscious folk wisdom relating to changes so profound we only glimpse their edges. Like clouds drifting in across the mountains. Like the moon coming out of full eclipse. Like childhood's end.

DiChirico Fends Off
the Spectral Bats of Andalusia

First off, for all of you who wondered if I was soliciting, no. Gangbangers, dear hearts, are people who belong to gangs. The state of cultural literacy is really plummeting out there. Nonetheless, you wouldn't believe how many offers I got. For all the good it would do me. Remind me to tell you sometime about the unfortunate incident at the State Fair tractor pull.

Second off, for all of you who have been kindly (and otherwise) inquiring about *Gonzo Marketing: Winning Through Worst Practices*, yes, it's done. Sined, seeled and delivered. David Goehring called me this morning from Perseus Publishing to say he liked it. Said it was a fucking work of art. Good thing too. David Goehring runs Perseus Publishing and could have easily asked for the money back. Seeing as he didn't, it'll be out in October. I'm putting together a chunk of it to stick online. Naturally, you'll be the first to know.

Third off, a French "Wired-style" publication (their description) asked me to send them something relating to the revolutionary potential of the net. I mailed them a letter bomb. The replacement editor then called and said, no, we meant an article. So I wrote this thing here. No, they said, that's too long. And could you make it a bit more concrete. So I cut it in half and took out all the funny bits (yes, there are funny bits, dammit!). They loved it, even though that version now doesn't make any sense. Frogs, what can I say? Not that this one does either, but hey, did that ever stop me from sending you anything?

btw, the first reader to correctly guess why the two lead quotes are grouped together wins a live wildebeest and a year's supply of chain-mail pantyhose. Ready? OK.

Toward a Poststructural Poetics of Cyberspace: or, Deriding Derrida and the Horse He Rode In On

"Allons enfants de la Patrie Le jour de gloire est arrivé!"

LA MARSEILLAISE

"There's nothing you can do that can't be done . . . "

"ALL YOU NEED IS LOVE"
LENNON & McCARTNEY

In May 1968 I was planting beets and corn and dropping mescaline. Later, sitting on my back porch blowing a soap bubble, I tried to imagine a world in which such a thing was possible. Suddenly and with some considerable amazement, I realized I was already in it. Needless to say, I was pretty high. At the same time, barricades were going up all over Paris, an insurrection that lives on in our collective memory like first love. In Spring, a young man's fancy turns to tear gas. A few years later, Mick Jagger, having missed all the action, lamented that "in sleepy London Town, there's just no place for a street fighting man," but demanded sanctuary nonetheless: "Ooh, a storm is threatening . . . my very life today . . ." Human culture is an endless palimpsest of commentary on the commentary written over whatever comments came before. Later, Foucault would echo the power of the pendulum, Julia Kristeva would explain intertextuality, and in time Tim Berners-Lee would implement the platform. Now — gimme shelter! — it's all connected. And we've been tripping on the connections ever since.

One of the connections to Paris '68, now hyperlinked at nothingness.org — how existential, though one suspects Camus would be scratching his head — is *The Society of the Spectacle* by kingpin situationist Guy Debord. This tract brought a heavy hit of dada and surrealism into The Movement, and argued, I think, that it didn't quite know where it was moving to — in fact (stop me if you've heard this one) that there was No Way Out. Huis Clos, baby. I have to say "I think" because I never read the book. Ergo sum a bit confused perhaps. But I did see the book jacket once on a TV program that showed it on a web page as reproduced in *Le Monde*. Debord says "The time of production, commodity-time, is an infinite accumulation of equivalent intervals." Ah yes, how true. But kind of weird because a couple years earlier Jean-Luc Godard shot a movie in Paris tricked up to look like another planet (which, I understand, didn't take much doing) — *Alphaville, une étrange aventure de Lemmy Caution* — in which a character named Alpha 60 says "Time is the substance of which I am made. Time is a river which carries me along. But I am time. It's a tiger, tearing me apart . . ." Coincidence? Yeah, probably. I never saw that movie anyway. I got the quote from The Internet Movie Database.

At any rate, situationism ultimately led to a film about the Sex Pistols in which Gary Oldman, tricked up to look like Sid Vicious (which did take some doing) sings Frank Sinatra's trademarked theme song, "I Did It My Way," just before OD'ing on heroin. *So* postmodern. All this is explained in Greil Marcus's tour de force work of pop music criticism, *Lipstick Traces*, which I do mean to read one day soon. For all his influence on the Yippies at the '68 Democratic convention (I'm guessing Jerry Rubin had spies on the Continent), Debord seems to have been a humorlessly doctrinaire sort of guy, sullenly complaining about the seamless and inescapable spectacle of late capitalism simply because he couldn't get it to do anything interesting. But art requires patience. And history is not predestined. It is, however, littered with petty control freaks peddling fascism tricked up to look like freedom — a disturbingly simple disguise.

Look: sure, we all love a good riot. However, the real problem — if I may wave my American flag proudly for a moment — was way too much Marx and not half enough synthetic psychedelics.

Not to be chauvinistic about it, but we did have the best labs over here, you know, while all you people had was that cheap opiated Afghani hashish cured in camel piss. Duck Soup will only get you so far.

Yesterday, after starting to write this (and wondering, as much as you are now, where all these random thoughts were headed), I bought a book by Peter Watson called *The Modern Mind*. It's an encyclopedic overview of 20th century memes and the rich intellectual milieu they have interacted with one another to produce. A tangled web, you might say. I bought a cappuccino and lit a cigarette — the strongest drugs I allow myself these days — and immediately turned to the concluding chapter. Dr. Watson, I presume, believes in science and rigorous analytic philosophy. He likes universities a lot but does not like the muddy sort of thinking he associates — though he doesn't say it in so many words — with the imagination. "Scientific/analytic reason has been a great success" he writes, while "political, partisan and rhetorical reason . . . has been a catastrophe." Oh dear.

Everyone is trying to control something it seems. Steer it left, force it right. The serious work of the mind is to prove that those other poor bastards are dangerous idiots, who, really, if there were a Just God, would be forever silenced — in the interests of an Open Society, of course. Ah, Popper, the amyl nitrate of rational logic! And there's a long tradition of this sort of thing, evidently. Somebody once told me Plato wanted to get rid of the poets. Did he mean kill them, I wonder? If anyone out there has actually read *The Republic*, please send me email.

Power demands to be taken seriously. But the Internet is rolling on the floor laughing, deep wracking intertextual guffaws. The web is awash in oh-please-stop-I-can't-breathe hypertext hilarity. Of course, we are not qualified to join in the more serious forms of cultural discourse and debate. We are not specialists. We are not experts. Unskilled, unschooled, our anthems come not from the hallowed halls of higher learning, but from

the vox populi arena-rock of Pink Floyd: "We don't need no education. We don't need no thought control." Oh double-dear.
Mere anarchy is loosed upon the world. Mere Napster. Mere
Gnutella. Mere-to-mere networking. Meanwhile Sony Records
wrings its metonymic corporate hands, bemoaning the fact that
we cannot hear the falconer — of copyright, ownership, control.
As e.e. cummings once wrote: "Humanity I love you because you
are perpetually putting the secret of life in your pants and forgetting it's there and sitting down on it." Meanwhile, we're going
like: "Falconer? What falconer??? Dude, what are you even *talking* about?"

Thanks to the Internet, global culture is out of control. As are
deep jungle rain forests. As are the stars, the night, the music of
the spheres. Go look at a soap bubble, as I finally did (straight)
many years later. Look closely and for a long time. Just before it
bursts, you will see millions of swirling, impossible colors.
Imagine a world in which this world is possible. Imagine the
Stones still blasting away from the past but with greater urgency
than ever, "Love, sister, it's just a kiss away, kiss away, kiss
away . . ." The barricades are gone, but the truth remains: we
won. And all that time, I thought I was just hallucinating.

We won? We who? Shit, I guess I *was* hallucinating. And oh yeah
that reminds me, I've lately been reading this terrific and enormously
fat volume, *Madness and Modernism: Insanity in the Light of Modern
Art, Literature, and Thought.*

It's part of the research I'm doing for an article that will run in
Harvard Business Review just before *Gonzo* comes out. I'm thinking to
call it "Screaming at the Demons in the Elevator Shaft: Spiritual
Proctology, Marketing Prophylaxis and Public Relations." Maybe that's
too long though. I dunno. Send ideas.

China Rising

RageBoy recently received an invitation from China. The circumstances surrounding how this came about are rich and complex (he tells us) and he is currently engaged in a great work (he says) compiling and detailing all the particulars. However, he has stipulated in his will that these documents not be given to the world until after his death, and even then, there is a strange clause — we have seen his will — about how they can only be "released by immolation" atop Mt. Pulog in the Cordillera Central of Luzon. He appears to be hugely enthused by this project and there is a new glow about him, but he refuses to say anything on the subject except that the Ministry of Culture has invited him to speak about the Internet at the Temple of Heaven in Beijing.

How he accomplished this we will never know. The lad has resources that continue to amaze us. However, while he's being very cagey about the invitation itself, he has agreed to allow EGR to publish the surprisingly brief talk he plans to give, and we therefore reproduce the current draft in its entirety below. Certain parts of it make us think RB wrote this with no prior knowledge of China, its history, its present government or its people. It certainly would not be the first time he has refused to allow deep ignorance to prevent him from making sweeping proclamations and predictions. So, for what it's worth, we present the text of his talk:

People of China . . .

Your country holds a great and priceless treasure, a jewel of immense worth and unspeakable beauty. But in the manner of your ancient sages, that is not what I have come here to talk to you about today.

At the very beginning, I want to say that there are many similarities between our governments:

- we are both led by deranged and sexless criminals mad with the power that comes from having large arsenals of nuclear weapons.
- our leaders on both sides equally value freedom of expression.
- both think only of the good of the people.

For this we should all be grateful.

Now I understand you poor sods have been laboring under the delusions of Communist ideology for quite some time. I also understand that it is part of this secular philosophy — about which we also get an earful in the West, I can assure you — to insist that human beings should be able to eat here on earth before we worry about how they will be attired in the way of harps and halos in the afterlife, or whether, as we say in English, they are headed "the other way." However, as we know from the more advanced religions — developed, of course, since your own — God loves all the people all the time without exception. And therefore, according to our more advanced political economies, God can sort em out.

But let us not dwell on politics and religion, which subjects never fail to get everybody's nighties in a knot — and I see many of you are wearing nighties here today . . .

Instead, let us speak about the Internet, that immense reticulation of new technologies that is uniting the people of Earth in ways never before possible. The Internet is relatively new to China, so for those of you who do not know what it is, let me explain. The Internet is a vast global network developed by our friends in the US Military and based on the TCP/IP packet-switching protocol that enables little surprise packages of information — also called "spamettes" — to be shot all over the place via telephone wires and optic fibers and these weird things called routers (which nobody knows what they really do), then randomly reassembled so that they appear to have been written by lower primates. These incredible capabilities wrought mostly by guys who cannot get dates are taking our civilization to a whole new level.

This puts me in mind of your great poet, Li Po, who in his latter years would get falling-down drunk and feed all his writings to the fish. Some, of course, thought him mad.

Riding atop this basic networking infrastructure are other, more complex standards, such as HTTP (Hard To Type Properly), which enables the World Wide Web. The web differs from the Internet *per se* in that it adds banner advertising and animated gifs — little wiggly pictures put there to remind us we are no longer in control of the situation.

If I may draw an analogy from your own culture, the Taoist mage Chuang-tzu once said he was unsure whether he was a man dreaming he was a butterfly or a butterfly dreaming he was a man. In the West, we have a great many young people who would have no difficulty relating to this (an idiom). However, in their case, the confusion is nearly always the result of ingesting large quantities of powerful animal tranquilizers or sniffing airplane glue.

The Internet and the World Wide Web have made it possible for the first time in the history of the world to bring network news shows, amazing multilevel marketing programs, and important information about getting out those *difficult* stains not just to Americans — which would be selfish and inconsiderate — but to all the people of our rapidly shrinking planet.

However, just as certain Third World countries have been able, in this century, to learn from Western mistakes made during the period of our great Industrial Revolution, so it may be possible for China to avoid following in the footsteps of the morons who now control the Internet. (These are easily identifiable as those individuals and institutions most vocal in proclaiming that no one owns the Internet.) Instead of using the net exclusively for profiteering and pornography as we have done, China — especially since there are so fucking many of you people — could use this unparalleled communication resource to do what we in the West have for the most part entirely forgotten how to do: tell stories.

I don't want to keep you long, as it sure is colder than a witch's tit in a brass bra here in Beijing today, so I will leave you with a very partial list of subjects and qualities your stories might include. Feel free to think up more of your own.

heaven, earth, man, woman, mountains, rivers, oceans, fire, the creative, rice, sheep, the receptive, sky, monkeys, summer, difficulty at the beginning, poetry, roosters, youthful folly, children, dogs, waiting, sun, boars, birds, conflict, rats, holding together, insects, oxen, the taming power of the small, colors, tigers, tears, sadness, treading, death, rabbits, peace, dragons, moon, trees, wind, standstill, snakes, fellowship with men, horses, possession in great measure, modesty, pride, enthusiasm, earthworms, following, sparrows, decay, trains, approach, water, contemplation, mirrors, biting through, combs, grace, hats, shoes, splitting apart, smoke, return, the usual, the unexpected, the bakery, the taming power of the great, the cat's still out, the corners of the mouth, the smell of feet, the preponderance of the great, autumn, forgetfulness, the abysmal, the barking, the clinging, wooing, pitchforks, duration, lightbulbs, retreat, breakfast, the power of the great, lunch, progress, stars, the darkening of the light, gardenias, the family, chairs, opposition, picture frames, obstruction, pearls, deliverance, winter, silver, decrease, tenderness, increase, bicycles, breakthrough, travelers, coming to meet, handkerchiefs, gathering together, toothbrushes, pushing upward, laughter, oppression, empty beds, the well, yellow roses, revolution, rock and roll, the caldron, wash basins, thunder, toilets, mountains, development, marrying maidens, holy fools, wanderers, magicians, wind, lakes, lovers, dispersion, birthdays, limitation, letters, inner truth, kites, the preponderance of the small, the morning after, wood, stone, sunset, night, loss, time, joy, oranges, music, perfume, song, dirt, spring, sex, food, breath . . .

. . . and all those useless things, which, innumerable IBM Internet advertising campaigns notwithstanding, are what make life worth living. Thank you.

[thunderous applause]

> *"I'll give you television*
> *I'll give you eyes of blue*
> *I'll give you men who want to rule the world . . . "*
>
> **"China Girl" – David Bowie**

Our Snack with André

Little known in North America today, André DeMerde was once a towering figure in French Letters. In protest over the brutal repression of Algerian dissidents, he moved from Paris to Tangiers in the mid-'50s and conducted his literary incursions against what he calls Empirical Culture from this remote expatriate base.

At first, his dispatches were prominently published in the European left-wing literary press and were responsible for vastly increased awareness of the rapidly deteriorating political situation in North Africa. Gradually though, DeMerde's voice was drowned out by a rising tide of drug-addled students, crypto-Marxist philologists and a cadre of Continental philosophes who had, in his view, taken permanent leave of their senses. By the time of the pivotal events of 1968 — now in their own turn long forgotten — it was nearly impossible to find an intellectual in Paris, much less the United States, who could recall the crucial role DeMerde had played only a few years earlier.

Always interested in contrary public voices and their fate, EGR was recently fortunate to encounter this venerable patriarch of culture criticism quite by accident. As it turned out, we found him panhandling outside the Port Authority bus terminal in New York City. He agreed to speak with us in return for a bag of fried pork rinds and a pint of Mad Dog 20–20.

WHO OWNS THE LANGUAGE?
AN EXCHANGE WITH ANDRÉ DEMERDE

EGR: You edited the seminal journal Tel Quel in 1965, played no small role in the development of semiotic hermeneutics, and strongly influenced thinkers as diverse as Jacques Derrida, Little Richard, Jorge Luis Borges, Liberace, Julia Kristeva, Ed Sullivan, Jacques Lacan, Pinky Lee, Roland Barthes and Ed McMahon. In a career that has spanned nearly a half century of literary and media studies, what events seem to you especially noteworthy in retrospect?

ANDRÉ: Before we get into all that, I must say I'm amazed. I never thought it possible that very many people — under thrall to Late 20th Century Spectacle as most are — would continue to be interested in such weighty matters. Entropy Gradient Reversals must have a very unusual readership.

EGR: Well, yes and no. Our readers are certainly unusual. But they really haven't the least interest in this conversation. Most of them have no idea what we're talking about.

ANDRÉ: Fascinating! I suspected something like this might happen. But tell me, why do they continue reading your publication then?

EGR: Actually, many will unsubscribe after receiving this issue. It happens all the time. Most, however, seem to enjoy abstruse and obfuscatory exegeses on themes that utterly elude them. They take it as a form of stand-up comedy that apparently alleviates their anxiety about not knowing anything that wasn't covered by Geraldo.

ANDRÉ: Ah! Geraldo Rivera, one of my favorite muralists.

EGR: . . . uh, you may be thinking of Diego there André . . .

ANDRÉ: San Diego you say? I been there too. Got beat up by the cops though. Really screwed up my hearing.

EGR: Yes, well let's move on to your thoughts about media evolution. How do you view recent changes in publishing and distribution, especially as these may relate to the phenomenon of online bricolage? Do you see the emergence of non-paradigmatic tropes and metaphors or iconic genre ironies?

ANDRÉ: Mmmmm, you want a hit of this Mad Dog, bro? This is some real good shit.

EGR: No, that's OK, but what about the question?

ANDRÉ: Well, while I was initially intrigued by the deconstruction of totalizing dialectics with respect to popular speech and how this implicated intellectuals in the re-visioning of more rigorous aesthetic strategies . . .
   . . . uh, what did you want to know again?

EGR: Never mind. What do you think about the Internet?

ANDRÉ: Oh that! Well the net sure fucked a lot of people up, that's for sure.

EGR: How do you mean?

ANDRÉ: Well, see, there we all were, making up these really complicated constellations of interlocking — or in most cases totally conflicting — ideas about intertextuality and recursive semeiosis and stuff like that, and then along comes electronic hypertext and p-f-f-f-f-t! That was that. You know what I mean?

EGR: Not exactly. Are you saying that the World Wide Web disproved the hypotheses being posited by literary theory?

ANDRÉ: Nah. It *corroborated* them. We thought we were saying these really radical things about hegemonic legitimation and referential indeterminacy and that whole bag of shit . . . But then Internet access started becoming available outside the University and it became patently clear that all this high-sounding speculation was just simple, pedestrian fact. It made it real hard to get grant money for research on how nobody knew what anybody else was talking about. I mean, it was just way too obvious after AOL came onstream . . .

EGR: Ah ha . . .

ANDRÉ: Now anybody can put together these kinds of theories. Peer review at least helped to keep it in the family, if you catch my drift. These days, any x-random dipshit can come off sounding profound. It's a shame really.

EGR: So looking back, would you say that Deleuze and Guattari were right in projecting the centrality of the nomadic?

ANDRÉ: Gimme a break! They lifted that whole line of thinking from Lacan — and he got it from Genet. Genet got it from a male prostitute, who also ripped off his watch and wallet and gave him a wicked dose of the clap.

EGR: So you think this was simply a reformulation of what we would nominally refer to as being "shit out of luck"?

ANDRÉ: Exactly. It all sounded pretty romantic to these faux-seditionist academics with their wire-rim glasses and tweed sports jackets with the suede patches on the elbows — you know the type. Identifying with The People and all that sorry load of tommyrot. But having been busted flat for the last 10 years, I can tell you poverty ain't really all that much fun.

So there was all that . . . And then of course, Heidegger and De Man turned out to be flaming Nazis, which naturally fucked things up even worse.

EGR: Why do you call him Da Man? Was he like some really heavy dude or something?

ANDRÉ: That was his *name*, you ignorant twit. Paul De Man. Since you don't seem to know much about modern philosophy, you may find it interesting that, despite the title of Heidegger's magnum opus, *Being On Time*, Sartre told me he was forever missing anniversaries and appointments. I gotta say I never personally met the guy . . . But anyway, I got out of the whole freaking game in '83. With the arrival of the IBM PC, it was pretty clear the shit was gonna hit the fan sooner or later.

EGR: Really? You saw the ramifications that early? That's pretty impressive.

ANDRÉ: Well look — all this mysterious crap about codes and semaphores? How long were we gonna be able to handwave that stuff? You had kids writing Dungeons and Dragons games and getting rich at it.

Literature was going to hell in hurry. We'd been saying things like "author-ity" was bogus, while slapping our personal copyright on all the journal articles we could possibly crank out. But now with this Internet thing . . . well, it was just getting too real too fast and — just like the corporations we so despised — we couldn't seem to see what came next. It was cool when Foucault laid out the power relations thing, but the whole point was to stay on the winning edge. Jameson has done pretty well — I understand he bought a Jag with the royalties from that thing he did on *The Cultural Logic of Late Capitalism*. But most of these lit-crit guys are total losers today. Christ, look at me!

EGR: You do seem a little off your game . . .

ANDRÉ: No shit Sherlock! I've got one pair of pants I musta pissed in about forty times this month, I sleep on loading docks, I drink this godawful swill . . . Other than that, it's a terrific life.

EGR: At least you don't seem embittered by your experiences.

ANDRÉ: What are you, stupid? You think this is some kind of pose? You think I'm like that wino Bukowski waiting to get discovered or something?

EGR: Was he?

ANDRÉ: I think he had it all planned, yeah. We used to get wasted together, Chuck and me. I can tell you that guy was one mean drunk. Even *after* he got an agent. Funny though, I'll give him that. One time he went into this bank and puked all over a senior vice president. He told us he was gonna do it, so a bunch of us were watching from outside. He got busted of course, but it was pretty hysterical. A regular laugh riot.

EGR: So uh . . . what advice do you have for our young people?

ANDRÉ: *Young people?* Are you kidding? Stay young. Get ahold of all the money you can and don't think about stuff real hard. Watch a lot of TV.

EGR: Nothing about the precession of simulacra?

ANDRÉ: Aw c'mon! Baudrillard drives around the States in a nice new car and gets Big Insights. Simulacra my ass! He got that from eating in too many Midwest truckstops. The guy's a hoser. You know what he *really* likes? He likes to have *Bleak House* read to him while he's getting his ashes hauled. A seriously messed up dude, no lie.

EGR: Well, thank you for taking the time to speak with our readers, André. We're sure they'll get a lot out of this exchange.

ANDRÉ: But you said they wouldn't understand a word of it. Didn't you tell me that? So, how does this work — you say they're gonna think this is funny? Do *you* think this is funny? Christ, you need help worse than I do. Why don't you go interview one of those pigeons over there?

EGR: We did an interview with a horse once. He was fairly cogent on the issues.

ANDRÉ: Yeah? Well like I said, I think you're outta your fuckin mind.

EGR: It's been suggested.

ANDRÉ: Nothing personal you understand. Listen kid, can you spare a fiver? I haven't had anything to eat in three days . . .

EGR: No, but we can offer you up to twenty megabytes of free webspace if that'd help.

ANDRÉ: That wouldn't help at all. Listen, give your freaky readers one last bit of advice from me, OK?

EGR: Sure, what's that?

ANDRÉ: Tell em to study something *practical*, like maybe hotel management or herpetology.

Death

Twenty months ago we started writing EGR, and nearly twice that many issues later, we've decided to try to find a publisher for all this crap. There are over 70,000 wordsworth here already, enough to constitute a physical tome of creditable atomic heft. A little cover art, a few testimonials from people we've paid off, and voila!: we'd get our shot at a much larger audience offline — since this one's been such a miserable bust.

So we started spamming agents. Not intelligent agents, mind you; we're talking publishing agents here. One of these recently replied: "My thought is that you'd be better off coming up with an idea for a new book rather than repackaging your web content."

While we thanked this gentleman for his speedy response and seemingly innocuous advice, we've done a slow burn in the couple days since. It reminded us why half the team that coredumps this twisted stream of consciousness goes by the name of RageBoy®. He'd almost forgotten he was angry. He'd almost begun to believe he'd found his calling as a net-centric stand-up comic, another contributor to the Niagara flood of irony, satire, parody and overall amusement that's needed today to keep us from thinking about the more important things. Like death for instance.

The other thing that triggered this sudden memento-mori flash-fest was that RB actually died last week. He was on his way down to the local hardware store to pick up some molly bolts (who knows why), and the Boulder traffic was particularly bad, as it has been all through this latest holiday season. He'd been slamming the horn non-stop and yelling out the window at the brainless sheep who pass for motorists in this part of the world, veins standing out in his neck, eyes wild and constantly darting to the side mirror for a possible opening in the passing lane, berserk, run amok behind far too much caffeine, ready for vehicular homicide. A normal day, in other words, like any other.

On getting out of the truck however — he'd picked it up for a song at a Monster Wheels rally — he felt this weird pain, first in his arm then radiating to his chest. Oh no, hadn't he read about this somewhere on the Internet? Those fucking Boulder drivers! They'd be the death of him yet, he thought, just before keeling over into one of those cute little median strip parking lot dividers they like to plant with all sorts of flowers and shit to make you think you're not *really* in a parking lot in some godforsaken strip mall in some random ratsass bedroom community for the idle rich.

Now the weather here has been particularly fine of late, like spring almost, which is why, when RageBoy went down clutching his heart, his head landed only inches from some sort of shrubbery that had been fooled by this latest evidence of global warming into prematurely flowering. "Well, will you look at that," RB thought to himself, dying there on the pavement and noticing how the colors of the petals blended delicately into one another at the margins. The sun was golden, the air was clear, the sky was bluer than usual with only wispy clouds up very, very high. A plane was going over at the moment, his last he figured, heading west. On second thought, it could be east. Who knew? Voices drifted across the lot in fragments, something about a year-end white sale.

Then a fugue from early childhood unfurled itself across his inner vision. He was standing on an overpass, idly dropping dirt clods onto the windshields of passing cars, and wondering where they were all headed off to in such an awful hurry. When I grow up, he thought, I'll have somewhere to go too. He tried to guess what he'd be and where he might be going then. Maybe a fireman, or a cowboy, or an advertising executive. Maybe to Bangladesh or Arizona. Then the scene shifted to somewhere in a deep wood, with birds calling to each other as the light faded and night came on. Where is everybody, he wondered, and why is it getting dark so soon? He tried to remember whether Daylight Savings was still in effect.

That was pretty much all the onboard recorder picked up. The rest was just static with the occasional odd image of various roadside billboards he must have seen at one time or another, plus at one point, the face of some girl looking at him oddly from a car speeding past in the opposite direction . . .

Later, at the hospital, they said he'd been legally dead for 13 minutes when all of a sudden he sat bolt upright and asked if he'd gotten any new email. A moment later, noticing the medical environment for the first time, he stopped mid-sentence and looked around, confused. "OK, where are my molly bolts, you fuckers!" he demanded.

When I got there I learned he'd been accusing everyone on the hospital staff of ripping him off ever since his nothing-less-than-miraculous revival. Finally, after soaking up two liters of a heavily morphinated IV drip, he calmed down a little, but still seemed out of it, distracted. Well, shit, no wonder.

"I had this weird dream," he said at length. "It was like I was in this huge white room and everyone I knew was there, but one guy was clearly in charge and everybody was looking at him with this kind of awe-struck wonderment. It was really creepy."

"Who was the guy?" I asked.

"That was the creepy part," he said, looking down at his hands and then back up at me. "It was Lou Gerstner."

RageBoy was lucky. This time. And the experience has clearly changed him. He's more reflective now — introspective and withdrawn. We've all noticed he's spending a lot more time in the office these days, catching up on the work he used to denigrate so vocally. Also, he's much calmer in rush-hour traffic.

A few days ago he stopped me in the hallway and said, "Listen, I think we'd better come up with an idea for a new book rather than just repackage the web content."

"Well, sure, OK I guess" I stammered. "But what makes you say that now?"

He got this faraway look for several minutes. I thought I'd lost him again into one of those comatose reveries he's been given to slipping into ever since the incident in the parking lot. But just as I was about to walk away he said, "I think we need to focus on the larger issues."

"Yeah, like . . . ?"

"Oh, I dunno, religion, art, education, politics. Something like that."

"World Geography for 200?" I asked. It was just a suggestion, but from the way he looked at me, I could tell right away that wasn't what he had in mind.

"No," he said pointedly, getting right up nose-to-nose and looking straight into my eyes. "No, that's not the ticket at all." I suddenly felt dirty. Guilty. As if I'd just been *called* somehow on a life that hadn't measured up to its God-given potential.

"Hey, back up a bit there pal. Jesus H. Christ on a Crutch! Just because you had some near-death thing doesn't give you the right to go around laying trips on people!" I was livid. How dare he? The ungrateful little turd.

It was as if he looked right through me, though — clearly he hadn't heard a single word I said. And then he was off down the hall again, stopping staffers here and there to ask if they'd ever read any Barbara Tuchman.

Deeply disturbing. But it's gotten me thinking. We originally started EGR to test a sort of working hypothesis. The Internet was relatively new and it looked to us back then as if it was a fundamentally different kind of medium from, say, television and the major metropolitan newspapers. One thing we liked about it in those days was that the only people who seemed to know how it worked were mainly using it to fuck off. However, we read something much deeper into that simple observation. We thought it was *important* to fuck off.

Maybe we'd been wrong though. I had to admit it was possible. With the prospect of the Internet attracting a mass audience, the marketing boys had been rubbing their hands in anticipation of the rank-and-file sheep that would soon be here, fat first for the shearing, then the slaughter. But hold the phone, we said, not everyone's as stupid as you'd like to think, and the options inherent in the medium will bear us out on this. Given the choice of alternative voices, The People will not choose your bread-and-circus lies, your blatherous blandishments, your empty entertainments. But what they'd do instead, we weren't quite sure. We'd wait and see. Whatever it was, it surely would not be More Of The Same. The magic was way too strong *this* time around to ever be co-opted.

That was before the banner ads, of course. And Pointcast and the Major News Sites. And Shockwave and Flashdance and the endless clever plug-ins and the browser wars. And the websites of the great technical magazines from Ziff-Davis and CMP and Mecklermedia. Not to mention *Forbes* and *Fortune*, *Business Week*, *The New York Times*, Warner Brothers, Sony, Fed-Ex, UPS, Smith Barney, Hostess Twinkies, Dell, Gateway, Orville Redenbacher, NASDAQ, NutraSweet, Harvard, Century 21, HarperCollins, TCI, Heinz 57 Varieties and Carter's Little Fucking Pills. Hey, kids, welcome to the revolution!

Resistance is still strong in the mountain regions, though, in the cultural backwaters, wastelands, along the fringes of empire. You can tell by the intelligence demonstrated in message board postings and chat room repartee, by the penetrating insight that's passed back and forth via online mailing lists, and the high humor of innumerable not-for-profit websites. Yeah sure.

Never has mechanism managed to pass so successfully for subject matter. If word processing made us into unwilling typesetters, the World Wide Web and all its multifarious attachments have transformed us into some high-tech analog of the traveling vacuum cleaner salesperson. We are all selling to each other, constantly. Encouraging our mutually pointless traffic back and forth across a digital landscape more frightening than those that cradle Dali's melting watches, cluttered with flotsam-and-jetsam pitches, late breaking scoops on matters we could give a shit about, superfluous weather reports for people who no longer go outside, and ads for articles of increasingly unnecessary clothing.

But so what? We still love the web. Where else could we rail away like this without rhyme or reason, point or apparent destination, and ever hope to get a halfway decent hearing? As to *why* we might want to . . . well, there's that nagging question about publishing once again, and that nastily insistent issue of a theme worthy of putting down in a disciplined and thematic manner upon Real Paper.

Look at it this way. When people write actual *books*, it's because they feel they have discovered something of value to share with the world at large, or at least a world larger than their local Mary Kay Cosmetics circle. This could take the form of practical advice, like Ellen Banks Elwell's *The Christian Mom's Idea Book: Hundreds of Ideas, Tips, and Activities to Help You Be a Great Mom*. Or history, like Michael Pollard's *The Lightbulb and How It Changed the World*. Or it could be a work of utterly contrafactual imagination, like a sweeping family drama that examines eight generations of okra farmers scraping a living out of the Australian Outback — their passions, their occasional despair, their proclivity for inbreeding, their substantial poker winnings.

These are but a small handful of the serious literary genres that warrant bona fide publication on acid-free pages worthy of the shelf space in such select emporia as Waldenbooks, Borders, Barnes & Noble. Not for these established outlets nor the publishing houses that serve their mass-market requirements are the tawdry ramblings of congenital retards who relegate their hastily scribbled musings to the back pages of the World Wide Web where they let just anybody write whatever they fucking feel like writing and where, moreover, any bloody rabble can already read it *free!* Publish EGR as a book? My God, what were we ever thinking?

And so, as the sun sets slowly on the West, we find our hero, back from the edge of Death Itself, pondering a theme important enough to merit the kind of Sustained Treatment that would lead to immortalization in the form of a Genuine Volume with height, width, depth, weight and its very own ISBN.

"What do you think about 'Internet for Sewage Plants: The Big Money Finally Gets Connected'?" RageBoy asks me, donning that serious mien he's lately taken on. You can tell he's really thinking about this.

"Or maybe an anthology," I suggest. "Those are big. I notice nobody's done anything yet with food-related poetry by anorexic transgendered differently-abled animal rights activists of color . . . "

RageBoy gives me the look that says "You are being frivolous again and I do not approve."

I give him the look back that says "You are a flaming asshole!"

And so, Valued Readers, we once again find ourselves at something of an impasse here at EGR World HQ. Should we continue to post these vapid meanderings to the World Wide Web, filled to bursting as it is with morons and degenerates like yourselves, or should we perhaps aim higher and attempt to produce a novel, say one that interweaves a contemplative thread on the economic ramifications of rainforest biodiversity with the sexually explosive adventures of a privileged young career woman from Darien, Connecticut, who trades off the easy money of Wall Street to devote her life to the thankless task of introducing a hopelessly backward leper colony in the darkest reaches of the Amazon basin to the wonders of modern information technology and discovers God in the process?

. . . uh, well, anyway, we figured if you had any thoughts about all this you could maybe help us out over here. Incidentally, we realize that, despite the title, this issue hasn't really been about death — not about *real* death anyway — and that this is likely to piss a couple of you off. But look, if you tilt your head and squint your eyes j-u-u-u-s-t right, you can make out the star of Bethlehem.

How'zat?

Being totally insane is hard work.
People don't realize that.

Two Guys in a Bar

So there I sat at 2:30 on a Wednesday afternoon in Phil Sharpe's Happytime Lounge on South Colfax waiting for my client to show. He was already an hour late. Sharpe with an "e" — classy touch I thought.

I hadn't picked the place. It had one of those electric signs out front in the shape of a martini glass, and at night you just knew it'd have pink and green neon bubbles rising from it, popping gaily, beckoning to the after-work crowd the way a cheap spinner lures a stupid fish. Probably lent a certain air of carnival to the fetid stench of the surrounding neighborhood. The place was already half full, and had been since 10 o'clock that morning. Nobody was drinking martinis.

This client I was waiting for had hired me a month ago to check up on his business partner. Was the guy ripping him off he wanted to know. It was an easy gig and the money was good, a grand a day plus expenses. Christ knows I needed it. Entropy Gradient Reversals Internet Detective Agency, of which I was both sole proprietor and sole employee, hadn't had what you'd call a terrific quarter. The company motto had seemed a real grabber at the time I started the thing up, but now it mocked me every time I handed out my card. "Get A Clue" it read.

"So Frankie," I'd said into the phone that morning after I got past the officious bitch who ran interference on his calls, "I think it's about time we wrap this baby up." C. Francis Booge — "the e is silent" he would tell you, but Jesus, which was worse? — Chief Executive Officer of Out of Order Legal Software, Ltd., liked it when I called him Frankie. I could tell it always gave him a little rush, as did the whole business of dealing with someone who did what I do. What a fucking dork.

"So you finally got something for me, huh? What's up?" he wants to know.

"We can talk about that when you buy me lunch today," I tell him. "And don't forget to bring the 10 large you owe me." He says he knows this great little place where nobody's likely to recognize him. After an hour sucking down the swill that passes for coffee in this hole, I can at least believe the last part. Unless, that is, C. Francis Booge with the silent "e" and Phil Sharpe, the pronunciation of whose "e" is a still a matter for deep speculation, happen to be golf buddies. Well, I think, turning the idea over idly, not giving much of a rat's ass either way, anything's possible.

As Frankie is about to find out. Not only is his partner — one Lawrence Fasterfudge, Esq. — embezzling heavily, he's also laid off a shitload of intellectual property on some pirate software tong operating out of Milpitas and is fucking Frankie's wife in the bargain. I'll collect before I let him in on this news, of course, as some of my clients are so gripped by grief under such circumstances that they forget to pay up, and kneecapping is getting way too expensive.

I look at my watch wondering if my pigeon's ever going to land and just then the guy next to me lurches up from the bar and slops half his beer down my arm. I'm suddenly busy trying to wipe the stinking bilge off my last halfway decent jacket, but I can't help noticing that the guy is hopping up and down screaming about his balls being on fire.

"Oh shit, I dropped my butt," he's yelling, clawing at his pants and dancing around like a freshly minted psychopath. Back of my mind I'm thinking he does look like a guy who's dropped his butt and now can't seem to find it anywhere. Then I realize he means his cigarette.

"Here, let me help," I offer, grabbing him by his belt and pouring what's left of the beer into his pants. Once I grasp a situation in its entirety, I'm usually quick to act. I hold him at arm's length just in case he gets any funny ideas. But this beatific smile comes across his face as he slumps down against the bar.

"Thanks buddy, you just saved my Johnson from a premature trip to hell," he says, looking genuinely relieved and massaging his still smoldering crotch. "Sorry about your jacket there . . ."

"Don't mention it," I say. "The women like a man who reeks of stale beer."

"Yeah?" he says hopefully, as if I'd just told him one of the facts of life he'd missed out on as a kid and it was just the information he needed now. "Zat right?"

"Didn't your mamma teach you anything," I say, helping him up. I want to get away from this guy as fast as I can, but human feeling and all that. I mean, he's clearly a total loser but he did just nearly cauterize his own dick. You don't see that every day.

"Lemme buy you a drink," he says.

"That's OK. I'm not drinking."

"What is that shit, *coffee?*"

"In a manner of speaking."

"Sucks, huh? Hang on . . ." and he hobbles off and exits through a side door, presumably leading to a backroom grill.

Enough excitement for one day, I think, and gather up some change off the bar. There's a pay phone on the wall behind me. Someone has scratched into the casing "Die You Motherfucking Faggot." Nice job, good penmanship. I get Frankie's office. "I'm sorry but Mr. Booge is taking a meeting," the bitch tells me. She doesn't sound sorry.

"Where's he taking it?" I ask, knowing even before the words are out that she's going to tell me.

"In his office, of course."

"Right. Well tell Frankie if he doesn't haul his ass down here in the next 30 minutes I'm selling this information to his old lady at twice the price." I hang up before she has time to ask. And here comes Guy Fawkes back from the kitchen with — I'm floored! — a gigantic cup of steaming cappuccino!

"There you go. On me. Least I can do. They got an espresso machine back there but nobody drinks here knows about it. Wouldn't care if they did. Phil's, you know, a Greek or something. Maybe eye-talian, I dunno. Pretty good friend of mine." The last delivered with some of the old pride staging a valiant comeback.

"Is it Sharp or Sharpee?" I ask, sipping the cappuccino and scalding my lips in the process. It's not bad.

"Hunh?" he says.

"The guy who owns the place," I say. "Your pal."

"Oh, that," he says. "Sharpay."

"Figures."

"Name's Clarence," he says then, as if suddenly remembering and thrusting his hand out to be shaken. This has always seemed to me an intrusive kind of behavior, even if you haven't just been trying to quench your burning manhood, but I know what's expected. I shake his hand. "Pleased to meet you, Clarence. Thanks for the coffee. Tell me, what do you do?"

If you know you have to wait around anyway — I do a lot of it in my kind of work — and you can't get away from a guy like this, what you do is you ask him what he does.

"What do I *do?*" he asks me back, "I'm a sanitation engineer over to St. Mary's School for the Blind. It don't pay much but I gotta lotta responsibility."

"Zat right?" I say, feeling more like Clarence every minute.

"Damn straight," he says, looking me right in the eye to see if it's working. "I gotta make decisions all the time."

"Don't we all," I commiserate.

"Yeah, but this is life and death stuff. Like if I leave my mops and shit in the stairwell, those kids could get killed. They can't none of em see nothin you know . . . "

"That's the scourge of being blind." What else am I going to say? I look at my watch again. Only ten minutes have elapsed since Clarence performed the Dance of Death right here in the Happytime Lounge.

"So whadda *you* do?" I realize he's asking as I tear myself away from the too-frequent reverie, the nagging questions about how I ended up falling this low.

"I'm a private detective," I say. I've learned the easiest route is to just get it out there. No use trying to make it sound like something else. Clarence is not a sanitation engineer, he's a fucking janitor. I'm not an investigative knowledge networker or some highsounding horseshit, I'm a two-bit private eye. Once I thought it had a certain romance.

"Really?" he says, warming right up to it, "you're a *private eye*? Damn, that's . . . well . . . that's pretty romantic."

"Romantic, yeah."

"Well, isn't it?" he asks. "Chasing bad guys, catching crooks. I wish I did something like that."

"What you do is just as important," I tell him. "Keeping those blind kids from breaking their necks. Remember?"

"Yeah, well, but it's not like you. You're like, well . . . you know, it's like a movie or something."

"Sometimes it is," I say, meaning it, but not the way he thinks.

"Do you find missing broads and shit?" he wants to know.

"That's not my regular line," I tell him, hoping this won't get complicated but guessing it will.

"So, what then? You track down blackmailers?"

"Something like that. Corporate counter-espionage mostly. I find out if people are stealing from their companies. The work's really not so tough, because nine out of ten times, they are."

"What kind of outfits hire you?"

"You ever hear of the Internet?" It was going to get complicated after all.

"You mean all that pussy the kids have to look at in grade school and everything? Yeah, I saw a thing about that on CNN."

He's getting visibly excited over such a vile prospect, but fortunately this line of conversation is suddenly interrupted. Unfortunately for Phil Shar-pay, it is interrupted by gunfire coming from the kitchen. On hearing the shots, I swing off the barstool and slam through the kitchen door. A guy in plaid slacks and a short-sleeved white shirt is lying on the floor with several large holes on either side of a really bad tie. I know immediately it's Phil because a waitress is repeatedly screaming, "Oh no, it's Phil! Phil's been shot!" He's still conscious and groaning — a good sign if it wasn't for the size of the pool of blood he's lying in. I wheel around and rush back out to the bar — where I nearly trip over Cousin Frankie, done up in the worst disguise I've ever seen. Wig, false mustache, the whole bit. He must have really worked at it. No wonder I've been waiting here so fucking long.

"I found out the son of a bitch was doing Gloria." Gloria being Frankie's wife.

"Who told you?" I ask, figuring I better get a little basic information quick.

"My partner. You know, Larry. Said it's been going on over a year. That dirty cunt!" The veins are standing out in his neck. "I'll kill her!"

"One at a time. Calm down Frankie," I cajole. Seems like pretty good general-purpose advice seeing how everything's totally out of control and fundamentally unsalvageable. "Take it easy."

"Take it easy my ass!" he screams into my face. "I'm gonna swing for this!" which is probably true now that he's just implicated himself in front of fifty curious drunks at the scene of serious armed mayhem.

"Look," he says, taking an envelope out of his breast pocket — despite the disguise, he's still wearing the same pinstripe I've always seen him in — "here's your money. You earned it. There's another 20k in it if you can keep this quiet." And with that he bolts out the side door.

I pocket the cash. How he thinks I earned it will remain a mystery. If I can keep it quiet. Right. Clarence, who's been watching this whole exchange from a safe distance, but who by now is so wasted on shots and beers that he probably hasn't understood a word of it, comes sidling over with his mouth literally hanging open.

"Man! So this is what you do, huh?" He's clearly impressed.

"Not usually, no." I tell him. "It doesn't normally . . ." I search for the right words to use with Clarence . . . *"play out* this way."

"Who was that guy?"

"One of my operatives," I tell him. "Unfortunately, he got here too late to save your associate." Clarence likes this, I can tell. Associate. Yes, he nods to himself, half comatose, he is a part of these events.

"So, like, your guy knew the hit was gonna *go down*, right?" Everybody's seen way too much Miami Vice.

"He knew."

"Wow."

"Yeah, wow."

Just then the cops arrived. I was cooperative of course. I told them nothing. Still, it was after nine by the time I got out of Phil Sharpe's Happytime Lounge. Phil himself took an early quit that night. I watched as they loaded what was left of him into the ambulance. As it pulled away down South Colfax, lights flashing but no siren — what would be the point? — I looked up and sure enough, there were the little multicolored bubbles rising and bursting over the neon martini glass as if nothing had happened. As if nothing else had ever mattered.

Sex Rears Its Ugly Head

It may come as a complete surprise to some, but around the same time EGR turns three, RageBoy will be celebrating 15 years of drug-free stone-cold sobriety. He hates it when we let on about this, as he has gone to great lengths in the pages of EGR to make everyone believe he begins each day with a hit of windowpane and a few peyote buttons washed down with copious drafts of Wild Turkey. Damn that sounds good! But no, he doesn't do that shit anymore, and hasn't for nigh on a decade and a half now.

We hasten to say this isn't any sort of moralistic thing, so all you boozers and dope fiends out there can relax. It's more that he just couldn't function too well at a certain point being wasted all the time and crashing into things and getting caught redhanded with women he ought to have known all along were married for christsake.

One night back around '81, John Steinbeck got him good and ripped and checked him into the local detox. Not the John Steinbeck you're thinking of. The son of the John Steinbeck you're thinking of. But that's another story. Plus, that didn't work too pretty good anyway and it was three years and change before he finally got straight, in Tokyo as it turned out. He doesn't remember the exact day, as this was after about 700 failed attempts and he'd stopped keeping track. All he knows is that it was sometime in the first week of the fifth month of 1984, as prophesied by Dylan in Subterranean Homesick Blues:

must bust in early May
orders from the D.A.

RB tends to think of "the D.A." in this case in the largest possible terms. Which is to say, he figures his Number came up in some fairly cosmic way and he just stopped. No more drinkin and drugin, no more whorin around.

He says Nancy Reagan was his inspiration. Just Say No — you remember her gift to the Great Drug Debate. But then he says he always wanted to put a bag over her head and do her with Ronnie looking on, so we're not sure how seriously to take this.

Listen, even if you haven't been there yourself, you know how this works. You go to a bunch of AA meetings in which you listen endlessly to a motley collection of seriously messed up people, chain smoke like a motherfucker and drink the worst burned-swill coffee ever conceived by the mind of man — all of which makes you want to get juiced about 100 times worse, if only to bring your ass down off that screaming jagged nicotine/caffeine edge.

At least that's how it worked in RB's time. Nowadays they probably drink Sleepy Time herbal tea or some shit and it's all Smoke Free. What a bunch of pussies.

Now it seems that certain types of people have a lot of trouble with a core AA concept: serenity. RB sure did. Like Sid Vicious, if you've seen the movie, he decided to do it his way. Or was that Frank Sinatra?

At any rate, serenity had nothing to do with it. RB got sober by getting angry. Not just a little angry, mind you. Not by stamping his foot and shouting bad words, then going like, whew, by golly, that sure felt good!

No, we mean ANGRY. His notion of a Higher Power was Shiva the Destroyer armed with Plutonium-Cobalt nukes, burn-down-the-world enraged. He got a gut-shot glimpse of how it works. The squeaky clean conspiracy of silence. The machine that eats your life and shits your soul out. He suddenly saw that what he'd been doing for 20 years was how you were *supposed* to kill yourself. All for the best, really. For the common good. For the Better Homes and Gardens vision of human being.

He turned his back on all of it, on everything. He wasn't having any and he didn't care who knew it. His anger burned and purified him.

Burned so hot it dissolved his hatred, dissolved his fear, his sad safe territorial little world. He became a black ronin boddhisattva, a serial killer without a country.

He had a sponsor back then — which is like a more experienced ex-drunk you look to for guidance — who told him this was an unhealthy attitude, that if he kept thinking that way he'd surely drink again. "Oh yeah?," RB said, looking all slanty. "Works for me." And fired the guy on the spot.

To say the least, this is not the recommended AA path.

And make no mistake, AA is useful as hell when you're white-knuckling it and can't stop thinking how good a half dozen shots of cheap Tequila would feel burning down your throat. That easy buzz, that extrasensory roller coaster first-round rush. So instead of hanging out at home with thoughts like that, you go out to some midnight meeting, where, who knows, you might at least get laid.

RB was about 18 months sober when he came back from Tokyo to work at Carnegie Group in Pittsburgh. This was like 1985 and he still had these sick fantasies about artificial intelligence. Shows you how deranged the dude really was. Anyway, one night he's invited to be the featured speaker at this monster AA meeting, mostly because he's new in town and these 300 people have all heard each other's stories already, for years. If you've heard one, you've pretty much heard em all. "Hi, I'm Chris and I'm an alcoholic. I used to drink two quarts of Bushmill's, neat, then get blasted on coke and try to screw imaginary rats." Just think how boring this sort of thing could get.

So there's RB up at the podium and not an idea in his head about what he's going to say to all these uplifted faces: gutter drunks, junkies, high society types — the ones who'd wrap their empties in newspaper so the suburban trashmen wouldn't catch on; yeah right — and he's getting that stage fright thing where your mind is looking for the exit but your body's totally paralyzed.

You know?

"I was raised Roman Catholic," he hears himself saying, "in a very religious family . . ."

People are nodding. Uh-huh. Many seem able to relate personally to this news. Their eyes are saying: "Yes, we're with you on that one, brother! We drank because those goddam crucifixes scared the crap out of us when we were kids! And how about the eyes in those freaky Jesus pictures that'd follow you around the fucking room!"

Encouraged by this largely inferred response, he continues. "So of course sex was always a big deal. I remember from when I was maybe about four years old my mother saying, 'Just wait till sex rears its ugly head!' She really said stuff like that, all the time . . . "

RB stops, thinks a second, then adds: "Hell, I didn't even know what sex *was* back then. All I knew was that it had an ugly head."

The room explodes! People are howling, pounding the tables, laughing so hard they're crying. It sweeps the hall in waves. Ah, stop! Please! Clutching their hearts. Oh no! It hurts! Some have literally fallen to the floor on all fours, gasping for breath.

This goes on for a full minute. Then two minutes. Finally, slowly, the room circles, tries for a landing. A few outliers still rocking back and forth in their seats, hooting and snorting by turns, but decorum gradually returning. Let's let the speaker continue shall we? Ahem, alright. Lots of throat clearing, eye wiping. But then some lone soul in the back turns the concept over in his mind, makes the mistake of thinking about it one more time — and cracks up at ear-splitting volume. Ahhhh-hah-hah! And they're off again. Totally. For like five full minutes. It was insane. Everyone out of control with no hope of ever getting it back together. And after a while not caring if they ever did.

Talk about an ice-breaker.

RB said afterwards he didn't think it was *that* good, and he hadn't planned it. It just slipped out. But what a trip — 300 of Pittsburgh's hardest cases losing it like that. Funny how rage and laughter go together. Like speed and whisky.

God, I love those people.

Omar Reads the Net

Your Moon is in Uranus.
Your Backfield is in Motion.
Your Personal Newsgroup is alt.binaries.pictures.lingerie.bigbutts

Psychic Hotlines are taking over the world. If you don't believe us, just check the late-nite cable lineup. And if that doesn't make a believer of you, check out the Business and Economy/Companies/Paranormal Phenomena/Psychic and Astrology section of Yahoo.

There are only about a zillion listings: Tarot Readers, Astrologers, Lucky Lotto 900 Numbers, I-Ching for the Lovelorn — every imaginable genre of Psychic Content you could ever wish for.

To bring our readers up to speed on this fast-track Internet business trend, EGR was able to arrange a rare interview with the widely famed author of "Omar Reads the Stars," an astrological column that has run in hundreds of newspapers over many decades. Whether your focus is interactivity or straight merchandising, we're confident you'll glean some savvy ideas for your own online business from this unique and penetrating exchange.

HUMBLE BEGINNINGS

EGR: Well, it's certainly a pleasure to meet you in person after reading your horoscope columns in various newspapers over the years. By the way, everything you said has come true.

OMAR: Yeah? Pretty freaking amazing, ain't it?

EGR: I'm sure our readers are anxious to hear your advice on psychic business opportunities on the Web, but first tell us a little about how you got into this whole astrology thing in the first place?

OMAR: Well, the net wasn't around then, of course. Hell, television wasn't around then either. Newspapers were the big thing. A lot more people could read, for one thing.

EGR: Yes, literacy is certainly a social hot button these days, especially in an election year. So you eventually broke into syndication with your personal predictions. But what was it that decided you on that particular course?

OMAR: Well, my father was a Sephardic Jew and my mother was a dispossessed White Russian heiress. Dad wanted to be a banker and he tried real hard, but he was seriously dyslexic and couldn't add numbers with more than three digits, so it was pretty sad overall. Mom, on the other hand used to hang with the Czarina, and her family was loaded. I remember my dad saying — this was almost every night at dinner — "If only we'd seen the Revolution coming!"

EGR: So you're saying prediction was an early concern?

OMAR: Damn straight it was an early concern! After 1917 they never had any money and I grew up with all this poor-mouth whining all the time. Christ! Nearly drove me nuts. They got off way better than the Czarina and *her* people, I can tell you. I wasn't around that early, of course, but I understand it got pretty ugly . . .

EGR: I'm trying to place your accent. What country were you born in?

OMAR: Brooklyn. Maybe you've heard of it. Look kid, "Al Weisenkopf Reads the Stars" didn't look to be a big hit in the '30s so we went with Omar to get that Mysterious Orient flavor. Got the picture?

EGR: Perfectly. OK, but aside from dinner conversation, there must have been other reasons you opted for astrology over, say, veterinary medicine.

OMAR: Sure there were! Look, you could do market research and spend a lot of unnecessary bucks to come up with a fact everybody already knows, which is that 99.99% of the people out there would give their left gonad to know the answer to one burning question: "What's going to happen to me next?" It was true then. It's true now. It's what we call a sure thing.

EGR: Interesting. But how do you convince them that you know any more about it than they do?

OMAR: It's all in the tone and the delivery. It's gaining people's confidence. Showing them you really care about them and how they're doing, how they're managing to get by. Course, you don't have a freaking clue, but you go for general kinds of things that you figure will apply wholesale, so it sounds like you're reading their minds. Also, they gotta be pretty dumb for this to work, but that's never been any problem.

EGR: Give us an example.

OMAR: Well, you can pretty much count on everybody's boss being a royal prick, so you say like: "Job circumstances improve as you learn to accommodate new perspectives." Words like accommodate are good, because nobody's quite sure what it means. Basically, in something like this, what you're really "predicting" is what they're already doing, which in this case is brown-nosing their managers. And they get a little charge out of that reinforcement.

EGR: That seems quite cynical and manipulative if I may say so.

OMAR: So what? It works. Business is about what works.

THE PEER-TO-PEER PARADIGM

EGR: But will it work online? What differences from broadcast media do peer-to-peer communications bring to the picture?

OMAR: Everybody seems to want to talk about this peer-to-peer thing. Always reminds me of a couple yokels taking a whiz out in the back forty. I will tell you what the difference is. Are you listening carefully? Nothing! Nada! Zippo! We're talking human nature here, my boy. People *need* to believe their lives matter to somebody other than themselves. Naturally, in the vast majority of cases they really don't. So what I do is provide a little harmless comfort in a world where nobody gives a shit whether you live or die. What's so bad about that?

EGR: Well, yes, it does cast things in a somewhat different light. And this is why astrology, psychic readers and so on have successfully transitioned from print media to television, and now to the Internet?

OMAR: You got it. Like I said, a sure thing.

EGR: And have you made this transition yourself?

OMAR: We're leveraging the old brand equity like everybody else, sure, but we're also exploring some new arrangements where "Omar" isn't a visible piece of the deal. I been having a lot of talks with Tony Robbins — you know, the guy with the teeth — and Cher, and of course Fran Tarkenton. These are the people who made the infomercial thing really go.

EGR: I read a piece in *The New York Times* that said Tarkenton has recently set himself up as an Internet consultant. Is this how you got working with him?

OMAR: Fran? [laughs] Oh no, I've known the guy forever. Although yeah, my people are having his people do the whole website shtick — the Shockwave, the Java applets, the promotional stuff. Like that.

EGR: Do you think Tarkenton learned a lot from the infomercial business that's applicable to the net?

OMAR: Of course he did. I mean, you can't do it justice online quite yet, but he's really got that thing down where he looks right in your eyes and says "But come *on*, this is all too good to be *true*, isn't it?" Watching him and Robbins do that routine always gives me a hard-on. Speaking of which, and much as I love the guy, I wonder whether Fran isn't a little . . . [flips wrist] You know?

EGR: Sorry?

OMAR: You know, the whole football thing he comes out of. All those beefy dudes taking showers together all the time and flicking towels at each other's butts and everything . . .

EGR: EGR has no interest in the sexual orientation of individuals, if that's what you're suggesting. Let's move on to your future plans for online. What's in the cards in that respect?

OMAR: Well, we landed the Pointcast deal and we learned a lot from that. We supply all the astrological content for them as well as Pathfinder and AOL. Also — and this is a departure for us to be sure — we're working with Time-Life on a new thing they're putting together called "The Amazing World of Animals That Eat Their Own Young." It's a kids series, for the most part, but it's got adult tie-ins too. The residuals from the ancillary merchandising alone made it a real sweet proposition. As you can imagine, we're pretty excited about the project.

EGR: And will there be a paranormal dimension to this? Is that how you got involved?

OMAR: Yeah, there's an interactive game where the kids can have like an "Avatar" I guess they call it, and ask a kind of oracle about their chances of being gobbled. We're totally focused on making it be a real fun experience for them. We got R. L. Stine working with us on the copy. Kind of a psychic Goosebumps motif. Man, now there's a guy raking in the bucks!

EGR: And how will this be released?

OMAR: Initially, it'll be a set of books like you see at the supermarket checkout counters. But there's also a Sega deal in the works and a CD-ROM. Plus of course the website — we landed a lot of the CGI work for that in addition to consulting on the psychic stuff. MCI is handling the dialup campaign: 1-800-BITEME. I'm not in the talks, personally, but evidently Microsoft and @HOME are bidding the rights straight into the stratosphere.

EGR: It sounds as if congratulations are in order!

It's been terrific of you to talk with our readers about a career that has spanned at least three major media paradigms. I wonder if you'd be willing to share your views on EGR itself. Do you have any advice for an online webzine just getting started?

OMAR: I'm glad you asked that. The only reason I agreed to this interview — as you know, I do very few — was that I was real impressed with that SmegmaWeb thing you did a few years back. In fact, an article about you in *Ad Age* was what got me to thinking that the Internet was going to be the next big thing.

EGR: Oh, you must mean MecklerWeb. Yes, an early effort to be sure.

OMAR: Yeah, that was it. Well, you had something going there for a minute but it looks like you fucked it up. Now this EGR thing, I don't know. The big thing I'd say right off is to 86 the irony. Nobody wants irony. They want straight talk they can understand with a fourth-grade vocabulary.

EGR: Well, we thought about that, but . . .

OMAR: Don't interrupt! You want my advice or what? OK, the irony thing? What do you need with that? You're just reporting real events here anyway, right? I mean, nothing I've read — and I did go over the back issues you sent me — sounds anything but factual. Then why bring a horse into it? Mr. Ed, jesus! You pull stuff like that, nobody's going to take you seriously. And who the hell is Thomas Pynchon? Look, I've read *Gravity's Rainbow* too — even got a few laughs . . . remember that song the guy sings in there about "the penis he thought was his own"? God, I about died. But so what? The hosers don't know what you're talking about. Lose the highbrow shit.

You gotta get down where your audience *lives*. You gotta know what makes em tick and stay aware of that every waking minute. I can tell you from long experience, they're a bunch of ignorant fools. Poor bastards don't know where their identities leave off and the medium begins. Well hey, that's an opportunity, son. Work it for all it's worth!

You get that formula down — and it *is* a formula, make no mistake — you'll be beating the advertisers off with a stick!

EGR: Great advice, Omar. We'll be sure to make the changes you suggest. Perhaps we can work them into our new EGR service: Your Personal Psychic Hotline on the World Wide Web!

OMAR: There you go! Best of luck with it, kid. Everybody's gotta start someplace.

Faster Horses!

Why the hell did I wake up at 2 A.M. this morning? And what am I asking *you* for? What I need is a kind of cosmic magic 8-ball site that can actually answer questions like these with — if not genuinely penetrating insight — at least a little wit and panache.

Perhaps this is somehow related to the inspiration that woke me up two nights ago. I fell asleep thinking about doing an issue of EGR called "What Consumers Really Want" and I suddenly sat bolt upright in bed with that sort of Eureka flash that comes far too seldom these days. What had yanked me out of blissful sleep was the arresting meme: foxier women, faster horses.

Now even I recognize that at least the first part of this represents a sexist notion at base — though if we are to believe Freud, we have to acknowledge that people do, on however rare occasion, actually think about sex, and that the dreams one might have in the privacy of one's own personal bed are a good place for this sort of thing and nobody else's bloody business. But you write it down and send it to thousands of people and that line of defense is suddenly missing in action.

So I played around with it a little. What about faster women, foxier horses? Possibilities there, true, but I felt it lost something in the translation. This went on for a while until the inevitable question occurred: WHAT AM I FUCKING THINKING?!?!?

For isn't it the sad fact that most of us, most of the time, simply do not know? These thoughts come into our minds. Where do they come from? Where do they go? Some have theorized that it could be something we ate. Sardines, say. But do any of us really believe this? For example, what if I were to dream about e-commerce? What would I have to eat to cause that?

A reader recently wrote to complain about EGR, not an infrequent occurrence by the way. She basically said my writing was too abstract, though she didn't use that word. She said it more by way of description. What she liked hearing about was what somebody had done — maybe gone to the zoo and seen an interesting new kind of animal (my example, not hers) — what he or she said to friends, and what they said back. You know, like real life.

I wrote back saying yes, I understood (and I really do), but my life is not like that. What I do all day and night is stare into the one good eye of this cyclopean monster we call the Internet. I earn my living this way. And it's not just the staring I get paid for, either. You think it's easy maintaining the fiction that you're a guru, a pundit, someone who knows more about The Medium than your average stumblebum on the street? No way. I have to constantly think up new analogies, metaphors, emergent trends, shit like that. And make no mistake, this is hard fucking work.

Especially when you're just pulling it out of your hat. But perhaps that reader was right. Perhaps a more interactive human exchange would better convey my point. So OK, I have this big meeting with a large and very well heeled corporation. I am thinking they can feed me for a long time. They, in turn, are thinking I plan to cheat them out of a large sum of money. In other words, your usual prospect meeting.

As it turns out, the CEO is a woman. She is trying to pretend that this is, you know, *normal*, and I am trying to pretend I'm not scared shitless of her. Just two consenting business pukes doing our jobs. Meanwhile, there are about a dozen underlings scattered around a conference table you could play football on, all of them doing a fair job of convincing me they're really quite important in their own unique way. Probably true. I'm not here to judge.

Anyway, the CEO wastes no time getting down to brass tacks. "So what do consumers really want?" she asks.

Shit, I dunno. I got nothin here. I panic. Am I really supposed to know the answer to this? How come nobody told me? Oh wait, I know!

But seeing as how she's a woman and all, I figure I better just give her the second half.

"Faster horses," I say with Total Confidence.

Across the room, someone drops a pin. Everybody hears it. They are all staring at me, dumbfounded.

"You can't be serious," she finally says. I'm thinking: how did she know?

"No, really. Faster horses." I'm sticking to my guns on this one.

"Do you have any notion of our market?" she asks, I figure rhetorically. She isn't really looking what you'd call "swayed" by my argument. "Most of our customers have never even seen a horse! For this you want us to pay you ten thousand dollars?"

Right about then I'm thinking you can keep your money, where's the fucking exit? But then I remember that I am, after all, a Professional.

"It's a metaphor," I say. That always gets em. And indeed, everyone sorta sits up a little and a few tentatively pick up pens, as if to give the impression that, if they were to hear anything potentially profound at this juncture, they might just be inclined to make a note or two.

I'm racking my brain. Jesus, how did I manage to get myself into this? Horses, horses, let's see . . . But nothing's coming to me.

"Are you implying," ventures one particularly unctuous minion, "that the speed of online transactions gates our ability to deliver total customer satisfaction?"

Say what? Bad as the horses were, this is worse. I have no fucking idea what he's talking about.

". . . well sure, that, but also the whole Portal thing . . ." I say, as if, yes, yes, it's coming to me now . . . Pens are poised.

"You see, what consumers really want is a place in the universe. A home. A feeling that they belong somewhere. They long to come in out of the cold — from the harsh realities of nomadic late–20th-century anti-intellectualism to the warm embrace of prefabricated purport."

Oooh. This could be working. I see puzzlement, but it's tinged with willing suspension of disbelief. A little anyway. OK, here's where all those wasted years of writing EGR could come in handy.

"Consumers are like newborn infants," I say, warming to it. "They wake up in mediaspace one day and don't know how they got there, where they came from." People are writing now. Hot damn!

"What do you mean exactly by 'mediaspace'?" one fetching young thing wants to know. She is so fresh and enthusiastic and her blouse is so demure. I nearly get sidetracked into unfathomable lust. But no, I must keep my mind on The Client here . . .

"Mediaspace is that concatenation of Weltanschauung, Zeitgeist and communication bandwidth that provides new opportunities for wealth creation at any given historical juncture," I orate. "It is the constellation of unbridled desire conjunct with the potential for ultimate fulfillment."

Heads nod knowingly around the table. Finally I am in my element: total bullshit.

"But what does this have to do with horses?" some asshole demands. There's one in every meeting. But I'm ready for him this time.

"Note that I said 'unbridled desire' — do you know *anything* about horses?" I ask, snottily.

"I think I see what you're saying," some other besuited weasel chimes in, saving my bacon. "It's like we need to liberate people from their repressed desires so they don't feel guilty about making what are essentially unnecessary purchases."

"Precisely!" I thunder, striking the table with surprising force and causing several people to jump half out of their seats and spill coffee down their fronts. "Get more stuff!" Nevermind that I lifted the line from R. Crumb. No one here is likely to call me on that score.

"Look," I say, demonstrating great patience, as if dealing with witless children, "it's really quite simple." But I know where I'm going with this now, and it'll be anything but.

"Before people become consumers, what are they? Just plain vanilla human beings, right? Confused, bewildered, horny for something, but they don't know what. They wander aimlessly through life filling their basic needs, sure, but suspecting that there must be something else.

Some larger plan and object to it all. And that's where you come in. The invention of purpose is a gift to humanity, an invaluable offering in the great potlatch of commercial intercourse. Semantic complexity enriches the social fabric, empowers the body politic, ennobles the spirit, enlivens the soul . . . "

"Are you seriously suggesting . . . "

"I'm not *suggesting* anything!" I interrupt back, having no idea what the guy was going to say, but not liking the sound of that "seriously" bit. "I'm *telling* you! People will kill for meaning in their lives. Not finding any after so many years, they'll naturally be grateful for any scrap of direction you can provide. Take all these people you see walking around in expensive t-shirts covered with advertising slogans. And they pay for the privilege. You can make these people do anything you want!"

I've got them now, I can tell. Time for a little personalized relevancy, I'm thinking. "Not that it matters much, but what is it that you folks sell again?"

"We produce a suite of collaborative software tools that enable productive group interaction and deliver cost-effective bottom-line results." Mother of God, where do they get these talking mannequins?

"Well then, there you go!" Before the obvious pleasure of the assembled at this entirely pointless interjection can evaporate, I quickly continue. "So that means you're competing against Lotus Notes, right?"

"That's correct."

"You should be hugely successful then. That stuff is dog shit." A new warmth circulates about the table and I am gently folded into it. I am being accepted as One of Their Own.

There is more discussion after that, but I can't remember anything that was said, so vast is my relief at having lived through the pitch. Which, by the way, was accepted in toto. What would I actually *do* for the ten grand? Oh, this and that. Advise. Shepherd their dull ideas toward some vague notion of success. "That's great, Frank. No, I really like it. Seriously."

"Faster horses!" Frank practically shouts into my face, high-fiving me with incredible we-get-the-joke-now joviality. A few months later

it's become a kind of war cry for the poor bastards. They think it's the
key to some secret knowledge I imparted. "Right on!" I say, and
"Killer!" I say, and "Hit one outta the park!"

Consulting. Man, what a racket. Why didn't I figure this out years
ago? But I almost feel unclean for doing it. I almost feel guilty. Not for
taking their money. That's just manifest destiny. No, sometimes I feel
terrible because I think maybe I really *am* helping these clueless fuckers to rape the rest of us. Giving them some empty-headed motiva-
tional excuse to weld all that avarice into an effective weapon that will
make us all salivate for spiffier software or snappier net connections or
the latest breakfast cereal breakthrough.

But what have I done, really? Tell them that people are confused
and lonely, stranded in their lives, burned out and breaking under the
strain of an insane commercial culture run utterly amok? This is news?

It's what I *don't* tell them that let's me sleep at night. Which is that
even terminal confusion is a thousand times better than spiritual
enslavement, and that I am beginning to see people — some people
anyway — waking up from the long bad Night of the Undead
Advertisers. No matter how slick the shtick, they wouldn't buy any of
this crap if their lives depended on it, which of course they do not.

"Hey Beavis, I been thinkin . . . "

"Yeah, Butthead?"

"Let's get us some collaborative groupware."

"Yeah! Heh-heh."

"Yeah! Heh-heh."

"Yeah-yeah! Heh-heh. Heh-heh. Heh-heh-heh-heh-heh-heh."

Moe Ron Hubbard on Diuretics

We feel as if we should atone somehow after our little game of hide the cyber-sausage with that eZines database site. As we suspected they might, the EGR Irregulars came through and blew the doors right offa that sucker. If you don't know what we're talking about, just count yourself lucky that you missed it. Predictably, all the people were not pleased all of the time. One subscriber called the whole charade pathetic, and while he was too kind to say it, suggested we should be ashamed of ourselves. Which we are. To try to make it up to you, we turn in this issue to a religious theme.

We were recently privileged to meet with Moe Ron Hubbard, father of Diuretics and Sayonaralogy, which, if nothing else, is fucking-a hard to pronounce. Hubbard needs no introduction, being widely famed as the only 20th Century spiritual leader to have penned a best-selling multi-volume space opera. The following exchange was taped at EGR World Headquarters in the darkest heart of the Yucatan Peninsula. We hope you will benefit as much as we did from the depth of the ideas presented by this profoundly sensitive and intelligent human being.

RAGE BOY®: Tell about the time your Momma tried to feed you to the Gila Monsters, Moe Ron.

MOE RON: Now see here, I thought you said we wouldn't be getting into all that!

RB: OK, OK, keep your shirt on. We were just thinking it might have been, you know, a formative influence or something.

MRH: No, I am Clear of those traumas now. There are no further obstructions. Of course, it did come in handy as material for my books.

RB: Well now, let's explore that a little. Is there any connection between your science fiction and your more, shall we say, serious work on Diuretics?

MRH: Yes, actually. Everything I know about people I learned over 40 years ago from a Writer's Digest book called *How to Create Really Really Believable Characters That Sell.* Reading it brought on my first numinous intimation of transcendent perspicuity.

RB: That being?

MRH: Well, that human beings are basically smooth sheep. And by that I mean simply non-woolly. But their *thinking* is woolly. Or, as we would say today, fuzzy.

RB: So are we talking fuzzy logic here? This isn't going to be like Jeff Goldblum doing Chaos Theory in *Jurassic Park* is it? Cripes, what do you suppose Crichton was smoking when he wrote *that* shit, huh? And speaking of dope, do you, like, shoot up or anything? Are you gay? Bisexual? Ooh, ooh, here's one: are you really a lesbian in drag?

MRH: You provide a perfect example of my thesis. It's obvious that you cannot focus your mind on any single thing, but instead are pulled this way and that by these . . . neurotic seizures.

RB: Why? What makes you say that?

MRH: You clearly have not read *Diuretics.* If you had, you would know that the human mind is 90% water admixed with trace amounts of Polysorbate 80. Thus that "floaty feeling" you were describing earlier.

RB: No, you're wrong. We did read some of it, and even tried some of the exercises, but it made us feel like we'd chowed on a box of cotton balls. Plus, we were running to the bathroom every two minutes, pissing something wicked. What good is that?

MRH: That's just the First Level. You get over that stage quite rapidly in our seminars where we show you how to urinate in your clothing with neither guilt nor shame. You see, most people are held back by their unexamined adherence to societal strictures that may have once been useful but become increasingly unnecessary to the evolving Alpha Betan.

RB: So these seminars must get a little messy, what with all that free-flowing evolution taking place. And people actually pay for this, don't they?

MRH: Quite handsomely. Wouldn't you pay something to reach a Higher Level of Being?

RB: We already have, to tell the truth. We are now operating on the Highestmost Possible Level of Past-All-Caring.

MRH: Or so you think in your deluded state. Sayonaralogy would help you to see that you are simply kidding yourself. In fact, you are little more than a brutish swine wallowing in your own offal.

RB: Oh really! And what makes you so sure about that, you fetid bung-wipe?

MRH: You see? You are the victim of your own unconscious programming, hurling childish epithets in defense of whatever it is you think is capable of being threatened by mere words.

RB: Oh.

MRH: *That* made you think, I'll bet.

RB: And how. So you're saying if we paid you we could, like, get over it? Hmmm . . . How much?

MRH: That depends on how Clear you're prepared to become. Not everyone is ready for the Total Sayonara of Complete Totality.

RB: But what if we worked at it really hard, renounced the psychotic zine writing and everything?

MRH: Then maybe there might be some hope for you. For ten grand you could get Clue One.

RB: And what is this Clue One, exactly, just for purposes of our little discussion here? You can tell us and we won't blab it around. Really.

MRH: Do you think I'm stupid? This is valuable intellectual property we're talking about. Receiving that transmission requires binding legal agreements that prevent it being passed on without the prerequisite training and accompanying fees.

RB: So, what . . . you like sue people if they tell, is that it?

MRH: No, we beat the living crap out of them.

RB: And you're sure the Gila Monsters don't figure in any of this? Seems to us you might want to look a little deeper into that, Moe Ron . . .

MRH: I have faced all my fears. All, that is, but one.

RB: Let us guess. You're afraid of fertile squid eggs that've been run over by a milk truck during the full moon in Sagittarius.

MRH: How did you know that? Who've you been talking to in my organization?

RB: Relax, no one told us. It's just too obvious. Ever read any Freud, Moe?

MRH: No, but I've read the complete collected works of Asimov, a far more penetrating intelligence in my estimation.

RB: Yeah, that figures. OK, well, since we're back to sci-fi, do you see anyone writing today who could take up your mantle, so to speak? Any emerging Moe Rons out there?

MRH: Oh plenty!

RB: Yeah, that's what we think too, though possibly for different reasons. Tell us this then, why did you go for the whole spiritual shtick if you were pulling down such big bucks with the off-planet stuff? Or was that it? Did you start believing your own material? Got a tad confused there for a second maybe . . .

MRH: There were two fundamental reasons for the shift of focus. The first was that we began to realize that the "fiction" was actually a Higher Modality of Perception. It was an allegorical kind of thing, but we didn't recognize it as that for quite some time.

RB: And the second?

MRH: The IRS.

RB: Ah hah. So, enter the whole money thing again, right? Why is it, do you suppose, that so many people have been willing to pay you all that dough for something that's, well . . . so dry? At least, we were pretty damn dry after that course of Diuretics.

MRH: Three things: they're scared of their own shadows, they have the approximate IQ of pygmy shrews, and they *want* to believe.

RB: And this was before X-Files, wasn't it? Amazing. But what are they looking for, precisely? Is there any pattern to it, in your experience?

MRH: Not really. Some want to get laid more often. Many are afraid of appearing silly in business meetings. Others want nothing more than a five-hour work week. It varies. In some ways, aspiring Alpha Betans share many characteristics typical of your own readers.

RB: Yeah? Well it sure doesn't have anything to do with forking over. We haven't figured a way to get ours to give us any money yet, though we are working on a political thriller cum science fiction epic called *Day of the Rotifer*, which we hope will be a big seller. The basic premise entails what might have happened if Janet Reno had joined the Branch Davidians and married David Koresh who then somehow managed to land Steve Balmer's job at Microsoft. Meanwhile Bill and Hillary and Al and Tipper are living in a commune with the entire U.S. Senate, House of Representatives and a large number of Shriners somewhere outside Albuquerque after a nuclear war. The plot's a little complicated, but it'd make a great film. We're thinking Brad Pitt for McNealy — the Brad Pitt of Twelve Monkeys, you know, with the hand thing — and either Quentin Tarantino or Christopher Walken for Reno.

MRH: Well, it's a start. But why wait? Surely you can get something out of these subscribers of yours.

RB: No. You don't understand. Not possible. They're way too cheap. Plus, then we'd have to actually think before typing.

MRH: I never did.

RB: Really? Well, we'd love to shovel all this crap into a book, but how do you find a publisher willing to take a chance on something as crass and tasteless as EGR?

MRH: Been in any bookstores lately? It's *all* crap. Plus, publishers are dumber than shit to begin with. Venal, paranoid, vengeful, yes, but generally none too bright. Of course that can work against you, too, as they kind of like to play the winning streaks, if you know what I mean. Have you thought about doing a loveswept romance type thing, but maybe give it your own special gonzo spin? Now that could fly.

RB: You mean like: "His hot breath reeked of rancid eels and cardamom as he ripped at her ample, heaving bodice like a McCormick reaper that had thrown a cylinder . . . "? That sort of thing?

MRH: It lacks a certain polish, but yes, you've got the general idea. If only you were a little Clearer, you could probably make it really sing.

RB: Ten grand you say? We'll think about it. You don't suppose we could pull off a religion of our own, do you? EGR does deal with The Larger Issues, after all . . .

MRH: Look, it was hotter than a two-dollar pistol when I got Sayonaralogy off the ground, but it's just a margins game today. You got too goddammed many players in it is what it is, and Murdoch's buying em up fast as he can. There's a nasty shakeout coming in religion. I'd say steer clear of it.

RB: Then how about the Internet? All these analysts are saying there's going to be serious money in this World Wide Web thing one day soon. They don't say how, but . . .

MRH: The Internet!!! [Starts laughing, then sputtering, then choking. Falls down foaming at the mouth in full-bore apoplectic fit. Thrashes violently, tapering off to spasmodic twitches. Finally stops moving.]

RB: Moe Ron? Moe Ron! Wake up!

MANSERVANT: No use, boss. Looks like he's croaked off.

RB: I expect you're right, Rupert. Very well then, clear away the body and bring out the tea things. There's a good fellow . . .

> *"Whatever materializes worship*
> *hinders man's spiritual growth*
> *and keeps him from demonstrating*
> *his power over error."*

Mary Baker Eddy

> *"every girl crazy 'bout a sharp dressed man"*

ZZ Top

Bopp till You Drop

"Awop-bop-a-loo-mop alop-bam-boom!"

LITTLE RICHARD

Hale-Bopp, that pre-millennial smudge on the early evening sky, has precipitated no lack of credulous rumor mongering amongst our increasingly hysteria-prone populace. And we scoff at the so-called Dark Ages! Has anyone put two and two together and come up with the inevitability of these sorts of phenomena when people are trained to react to advertising like Pavlov's salivating pooches? Blue Light Special on Salvation in Aisle Four! And next thing you know you're looking down at your dead ass on the floor — hey, my Nikes! — and your Subtle Body is doing the Apocalypse Calypso off to another planet. Or . . . something.

Apropos the Already Realized, if you check out the Urantia Book page, especially its *Slide Show on Revelation*, you will learn there that the Planetary Prince's Staff (and we'll wager you didn't even know He had one) consists of Ang, Bon, Dan, Fad, Nod, Hap, Lut, Mek, Tut and Van. As predicted in Hallucinations 12:34, this nomenclature uncannily echoes the logins of EGR's own staff — Angst, Bong, Dank, Fart, Noodles, Hopalong, Lunchmeat, Mentalcase, Tutu and Vac.

Before you get too excited though, and despite the title, this isn't going to be yet another rehashing of the now nauseatingly familiar God-as-UFO-Internet-suicide theme. How many of these have you read in the past week? Just as TV had its OJ orgy, webheads will have their 39 Demented Demiurges to talk about until the cosmic cows come home. But not us. Nope. However, we would like to suggest a similar manner of departure for a couple companies who've been waving their banners on the web of late. RageBoy® is in the back room mixing up a killer batch of seconal-vodka spritzers even as we write this.

ABSOLUT DOWNER #1

It's really something to see this Novell ad banner do its little Burma Shave impression. For those of our Valued Subscribers too damn lazy to fire up their browsers, it says in turn:

> Novell = Network
> Internet = Network
> Novell = Internet
> Is it starting to make sense?

Well . . . not quite. In fact, the question this raises for us is: HAVE YOU TAKEN LEAVE OF YOUR FUCKING SENSES? (Of course, Utah could do that to anybody.) Weren't you the clueless holdouts who ignored the net until it was too late and now your collective ass is sliding down that slippery slope to the corporate boneyard? So what's all this "Rock the Net" shit, fellas? And who's the flaming asshole in that graphic? We have to wonder whether there actually *are* unfortunates whose dementia has progessed so far that they would literally take a flying leap over something as prosaic as Novell Netware. What would you do if you saw this sort of lunatic display in the hall outside your office? Would you strangle the deviant bastard on the spot, or simply mark it up to Hale-Bopp's Evil Influenza?

Once again, for the browser impaired, the gif says "The Net's been rocking your world. It's time to rock back. Want to see how?"

Not really. But what do you suppose they mean by "rock *back*"? If you click on this bit of graphical flatulence, you'll encounter these memorable words: "The net's just a network. *A big, juicy network.*" It seems there's no small amount of projection and wish-fulfillment fantasy reflected in this curiously self-revealing Novell ad. So, no, we watched the movie and we can't take any more, guys — but come on down and get your phenobarb coolers. You earned em!

ABSOLUT DOWNER #2

Turning now to that other paragon of Netly-ness, Lotus Development, we bring you the following slice of muddled mindshare. We first encountered a print version of this Lotus Domino advertisement in *The Wall Street Journal*. Why don't we just quote a little of it:

> "IT IS A SCIENTIFIC FACT that people are nosy and the thing they want to see the most is probably the thing you least want them to see. This explains why the Web is chock-full of stuff that is so unimportant, it doesn't matter if everybody can see it. Stuff like UFO chat lines, recipes for zucchini bread and short stories that nobody would publish on real paper."

Aside from the belligerent tone of the whole thing (after all, only small minds resort to nastiness), that last bit about "real paper" reflects the ventriloquist Weltanschauung of the Consummate Moron. "Quick! Somebody tell me what to think!" If it's published on paper — like say, a Lotus User Manual — then presumably you're safe. Curiously, there's also a non-paper version of this ad in the form of an animated web banner. (. . . what the hell? What happened to that gif we just downloaded? . . . oh, christ, RageBoy's *chewing* on it! You paste that in there right now, RB, or there will be Serious Consequences!)

The choices here are offered in Simpleminded Binary. In the Yes category there's a pie chart, a nark, and what looks to be, inexplicably, a manhole cover. In the No category we see a guy with a beard, a flying saucer and an aerial photo of some really nifty crop circles. Under the picture of the dorky looking, V-sign-flashing hippy fool, the copy reads, "NO: Lotus Domino is not for those who think the Internet should be totally uncontrolled. You're running a business, not a wine and cheese party."

Ah, the old wine and cheese party gambit. Imagine for a moment the type of fascist bonehead this is meant to appeal to. "Damn straight, those commie hacker perverts with their infected shareware and slacker attitudes!" Maybe you work for someone who holds such views. Perhaps he's even asked you where "the really good stuff" is. To snuggle a little deeper into this guy's jockey shorts — and you *know* we're talking guys here, right? — Lotus offers a bookend image of clean-cut FBI agent Joe Friday from the old Dragnet show (so we're talking really *old* guys too). And that caption says: "YES. Lotus Domino is for security on the Web. Who gets the facts. Who gets the cold shoulder. And who has the authority to make changes to what."

. . . uh, Lotus? RageBoy would like a word with you . . .

KISS MY FAT

DISESTABLISHMENTARIAN

ARSE!!!

What smarmy pathetic losers. Ah fuck it; words fail us. Come get your Martian Martinis! Time to pass beyond that Final Firewall. Drink up!

We could go on . . . but why? You already see this sort of thing every day: companies patting themselves on the back for taming the digital wilderness, shooting the heathen Indians and replacing the unruly chaos of the Internet with the same lobotomized whitebread mindset that gave us strip-malled suburbs, high-tech sweatshops and mass illiteracy. We should be grateful we're in such good hands.

So to wrap this up, let's recap what we know about religious cults. Basically, they entail people killing themselves to comply with a supreme authority, which in return for unconditional surrender and unquestioning subservience, promises a stratospheric rise to unimagined power and participation in ill-defined mysteries that defy all logic. What *we* can't figure out is why Fortune 1000 cultists thought the Heaven's Gate crowd was so weird.

An Interview with Mr. Ed

Who among us could forget the eponymous star of Mr. Ed, an early television series about a talking horse that kept America on an uninterrupted laugh-track through Cold War saber rattling, nuclear tests, and the country's accelerating slide into mass illiteracy? Except, of course, the millions of Gen-X teeny boppers who have since come to the Internet, virgins to any historical context predating The Power Rangers.

It greatly surprised EGR to learn that Mr. Ed, long thought to have been put to pasture — or sent to the knacker's yard — is very much alive and kicking. In fact, Ed (he insisted we call him by his first name) is living in a sumptuous Beverly Hills mansion overlooking the sea, from which command aerie he counsels and oversees much of the global entertainment industry. His mind sharp as ever, this horse of a different color still wields enormous authority and power — albeit anonymously — over an empire that is spreading its dark wings ever more rapidly across the affairs of men — and of course, women (in this case, affairs *with* women, but as this is a Family newsletter, we have edited out those remarks).

Arranging an interview proved easier than we had anticipated. EGR turned to one of its many Industry Notable subscribers with ties to the cable industry and, after several phone calls, a date was set. We arrived several weeks later at the Ed home not knowing quite what to expect. We were pleased to find the master of the house sitting at a specially outfitted keyboard, humming to himself and surfing the World Wide Web.

Without further introduction EGR offers this historic exchange with the Dark Horse of Interactive Multimedia, as he several times referred to himself in our conversations.

ONE FOR YES, TWO FOR NO

ED: Welcome to Ed Manor, Chris. May I call you Chris?

EGR: Oh sure. Very good of you to take the time to speak to our readers. I'm sure they'll be fascinated to hear what you've got to say about the New Media — I can't help notice that you're currently in the Pathfinder site.

ED: Oh that. Yes, I've been keeping quite an eye on the Web. Who hasn't? This thing caught quite a few of us off guard — Bill Gates has been pretty forthcoming about that — but I'm proud to say I saw it coming years ago. In fact, it may surprise you that I was an early subscriber to The WELL. Do you know that system?

EGR: Really? The WELL? Why yes, of course. I believe it was Peter Lewis of *The New York Times* who called it "the toniest address in cyberspace" — or words to that effect — some years ago. Web years that is.

ED: [whinnies] Yeah, things certainly have been moving quickly haven't they?

EGR: So how did you come to be on The WELL? That was pretty early in all this.

ED: Well, Stewart Brand and I got to hanging out together at Gate 5 Road in Sausalito. This was not too long after Kesey was spreading all that acid around and Tom Wolfe was schlepping along on The Bus. What a hoot that was! Cultured, foppish little dude among all those howling drug-crazed maniacs.

Anyway, Stewart introduced me to some of the movers and shakers at that time. The people who really had their ear to the ground, you might say. Portola Institute, Global Business Network . . . Most folks don't realize how much this whole thing has been carefully planned behind the scenes. I'll bet you don't know that Tim Berners-Lee and Lou Rosetto — you know, the *Wired* guy — were doing 'shrooms in Yucatan with Tom Pynchon back in '66.

Did you ever see *The Yage Papers*? Well, no matter. It was a pretty obscure little volume. Letters between Bill Burroughs and Ginsberg. They'd discovered certain telepathic effects of iboguine, some jungle psychotropic they'd stumbled across via a couple of pretty hip shamen who'd been gigging in the city with Sun Ra. Turns out it wasn't just Bill and Allen doing that back then. There was already a kind of wireless network you might say.

It was a time of creative ferment, that's for sure. But you didn't come here to hear an old horse reminisce . . .

EGR: No, that's fascinating. And you were in on this scene while you were still shooting episodes?

ED: Oh yeah. We were totally ripped on the set most days. I mean, how else could you do something as utterly mindless as Mr. Ed? And it was wild, because America at that time was, as you know, totally straight. There we were riffing on the cosmic verities and planning a revolution in media that wouldn't happen for at least another 20 years.

HORSING AROUND

EGR: Well, since you bring that up, let's fast forward to a couple years ago. From where you sit now, what was it that turned the corner in that respect. What really kicked the whole New Media thing into overdrive.

ED: Well, we tried with CD-ROM, but you saw how slow that was to catch on. It's doing OK today, but a lot of people lost a lot of money on that in the early days. Bill used to regularly come around crying about Bookshelf and how it was relevant as hell, and educational and all. Poor Bill. He still doesn't quite get it. But at least he's not sniveling as much in public these days.

I'd have to say it was really Jim Clark. Of course, everybody knows how he scored Andreessen and that team from NCSA and set up Netscape. Stroke of fuckin genius, that was. But most people on the outside don't know that Pynchon was a *major* backer of SGI, which is of course where Clark got the bucks in the first place. Clark was the guy got Tom started on that whole post-horn paranoia that comes out in *The Crying of Lot 49*. God, that was a funny book.

EGR: . . . uh, that's real interesting, Ed. You seem to be quite well literarily connected. I'm sure that's an aspect of your career most of our readers wouldn't have guessed at.

ED: Well, you know, the entertainment biz is like any other. You gotta keep ahead of the curve. Always be watching for the Next Big Thing and all that. You look back, you find the artists are way ahead of the market research crowd. Every time. So I've always maintained certain connections to the weirder quarters of the literary scene. Now you take a William Gibson — there's a boy that really had his finger on the pulse of things to come. Too bad they cast Keanu Reeves in that *Johnny Mnemonic* flick though. What a butthead! But I guess he's big with the chicks . . .

BRANDWIDTH®

EGR: Getting back to the New Media, though . . .

ED: Oh yeah, well like I was saying, Netscape clearly tipped the scales and put the whole web thing over the top. Got it outta the goddammed universities. As to where it's going, nobody's really sure, of course. I can give you some off-the-top opinions though.

EGR: That's precisely what we're here for. How do you see Online evolving in say the next two-to-five years?

ED: I'm not sure you can frame it temporally. Things are moving a lot faster than they did in my day. For instance, I don't see a talking horse series being a real killer draw on the web, though I've got my agent looking into it.

To see the shape of things a year or more out, I think you have to look to the fiber guys. Did you see where MFS just did a tie up with UUNET? Now there's one to watch. Metropolitan has more miles laid than the telcos and is moving more IP in the background than most people realize. But still, that's commodity-level stuff.

EGR: How so?

ED: Well, it's just pipe. The transport layer is obviously something you can't do without, and Internet GUIs have given the folks a real big appetite for bandwidth, no denying that. However, the real challenge is where the value-add is going to come from. You can bet the answer isn't a bunch of wireheads cutting cable trenches or wiring prototype set-top boxes.

I think you've got to look at what Turner's doing with this @Home thing. Course, they've bitten off quite a bit there — a new fiber IP backbone infrastructure, basically. Gonna cost Ted a bundle and the risk is high, but if he can pull it off it's the Holy Grail. I like to call it Higher Brandwidth.

EGR: Interesting turn of phrase, Ed. Tell us more about that.

MAKING OUT OK

ED: Well, look, everybody knows nobody's making any money on this yet. Other than the HTML-cum-Photoshop hackers, I mean — a bunch of ad agencies have jumped into this and are time-slicing with a freaking microtome . . .

EGR: Just parenthetically, can you unpack that one a bit?

ED: Sure. The agencies saw their bread-and-butter accounts going Internet and it scared the living crap out of them. So they hired a pack of longhairs and stuck them at terminals in the back room and said, hey look at us, we're in the World Wide Web business! We can have your site online and pulling down megabucks in three weeks flat! Of course, it's all bullshit for the most part. I've been in some of these shops and seen copies of *Teach Yourself CGI in 21 Days* lying around. It's pathetic really. Most of them don't know enough perl to code "hello, world."

EGR: But about the microtome business . . .

ED: Oh that. Yeah. You see, these agency web butchers are just responding to corporate demand, which is right now completely off the charts. It's a huge opportunity for them. But they don't have the staff to really service it. So what they do is dangle the carrot bigtime, sign up more accounts than Carter's has pills, then jerk them around with fancy administrative handwaving combined with enough dog-and-pony to wow the most jaded corporate honcho. These guys are past masters at this routine, believe me.

First they storyboard some trivial shit that has real flash value in PowerPoint. It'll never play on the net, and they know it, but that's OK by the agency people because the way they time-share their services — with about 1000% more clients than they can adequately handle — it's going to take a year and a half to get the site online anyway. And by that time, they figure, the tech will have changed so drastically they'll have to start the process all over again. Gravy for the agencies, of course, as it's all being done on a billable-hours or cost-plus basis.

When any one of these clients gets too frustrated with this churning, the agency slaps up some pages a four year old could've produced with Navigator Gold. A lot of them I know hack these up in the first week as a contingency, then trot them out only when they're about to lose the account if they don't show *something*. And everybody knows that the corporate execs they're typically dealing with are so completely clueless they rarely if ever suspect they're being milked. It's a great scam, really, so who can blame them?

In the big picture, though, this is just penny-ante poker. The serious bucks are riding on high-speed delivery options.

TELEVISIONATION®

EGR: Well, let's explore that. You mentioned TCI and @Home. Why is Turner betting the ranch on a project coupled with such high risk? Has he slipped his cable? Or does this involve the Grail Quest you alluded to earlier?

ED: The latter, absolutely. It's about advertising. Always was. Always will be. Let's face it, the Internet is a shitty place to advertise. Nobody ever wanted to see your toilet paper spot — and online they don't have to. The air mouse was bad enough, but this is ridiculous.

EGR: Air mouse?

ED: You know, the remote. The thing you use to click to another channel when the sponsor's ad comes on. Wasn't like that when we were doing Mr. Ed. No sir! When you had to get up, and walk across that room, and turn a dial? No way! You were going to sit there like a good little consumer and watch the repulsive crap about the washday miracle or the toothpaste that got you laid or whatever. It was beautiful. The air mouse really put a big crimp in that though. And the Internet blows the doors off. I mean these kids aren't giving us enough time to download the graphic. They hit the next link and they're gone!

EGR: So how does net-via-cable change all that?

ED: Simple. At 40 megabits a second you can cram full-motion video down the pipe. No more of this reading bullshit. People don't want to read, they want a circus! They want to be razzled and dazzled. They seem to be happiest when the technology is essentially raping whatever cognitive apparatus they have left. And we simply can't rape them at 28.8 — I mean it's like saying "Would you like to take off your shoes, first?" That just doesn't have the immediacy of say, a film, where we can give you fifteen violent deaths and three explosions before the opening credits are done rolling.

EGR: So you're saying speed is important to grab people . . .

ED: Grab em and *hold* em, son. That's the thing. Addict the bastards. Keep em coming back.

Today's web pages are like public libraries. You know the books are there. You think it's culturally relevant and a Great Thing for the Community and all that. But do you ever go there? Of course not. You go to the video store! Or maybe the movies. Fuck the library!

[As if to punctuate his strong feelings, Ed at this point in the conversation took a — literally steaming — 20-pound dump right in the middle his living room. He didn't miss a beat as his Eurasian houseboy hurried in with a silver shovel, but kept right on talking . . .]

Same thing on the web. You see something marginally useful so you bookmark it, hotlink it, whatever. Right? But do you ever go back? Unlikely. And if you do, do you stop to read the ads? Not unless it's for some freeware download that's costing somebody a bundle but has a lower ROI than human kindness. Nobody's making a nickel at this game. It's all jockeying for position. Not that that's not important, mind you. But there had better be a payoff here, and soon, or a lot of corporate cyber jocks are gonna be peddling their resumes down at the Rent-a-Suit office.

The trick is to push the medium to its full potential, which is of course, television.

EGR: You mean that as we get faster Internet connections, higher bandwidth, we are approaching TV?

ED: You got it, kid. Remember how FM radio used to be different from AM? More interesting stuff, sure, but no market for it. Well, we fixed that. Nothing sacred about TCP/IP, either; it's just another neutral conduit straight into The American Dream.

The point is to make it real-time so they can't just click away. If they do, they miss the next close-up evisceration, the C-4 explosion taking out the grade school, the super-horny degradation of the whore with a heart of gold — whatever gets us a strangle-lock on those atavistic passions this medium is so good at stirring up. Doesn't matter that these are hopelessly worn clichés — what's important is that they're not worn *out*! They work like a charm. They mesmerize!

What @Home and similar efforts promise is to make it even less rewarding to change channels than it was when you had to heave yourself out of that comfy armchair and walk over to the set to twist the channel knob.

You accomplish that and — Bingo! — you got your advertisers back!

EGR: But what about interactivity?

ED: Oh please! Interactivity can kiss my serene Illinois ass! So we give em a back-channel, big deal — 28.8 is already better than they're getting on those over-saturated T1s companies are giving their migrant knowledge workers.

Give em freedom of speech too. Who cares? Have you seen anything really seditious on the net recently? It's not like the government is exactly about to fall from organized rebellion. Most of these people couldn't organize a trip to the water cooler. Fact is, we manufactured that whole Communications Decency Act business to give the kids something less dangerous than reality to focus their youthful energies on.

[Glancing at massive 24-karat Rolex] Look, I'm sorry about this, but I've got Al Gore and Newt Gingrich scheduled in ten minutes, so we're going to have to wrap this up.

EGR: We appreciate the time you've taken to share your unique view of where we are, where we've come from, and what we can expect to see next. I'm sure our readers will find much food for thought in what you've told us. Do you have any final words of advice you'd care to impart?

ED: Well it may sound trite, but I believe the one big thing to keep in mind is that Money Talks. It's all very well to ponder Change and Social Impact and Big Ideas, but at the end of the day, nobody's going to listen to you if you haven't made a bundle of hard cash. Look at me. I'm a goddam horse for christsake! Yet, in the final analysis, that doesn't matter one bit. I've got a shitpile of money and that's what people respect. Same with your big CEOs — most of them I've met are no smarter than a crate of rocks, yet people suck up to them all the time. Why? Simple: because they're loaded! And that gives them a lot of power and makes them dangerous.

Always go back to the simple things. It's like Ockham's Razor, you know what I mean?

EGR: Thanks, Ed. Those are certainly words to live by.

ED: No problem, son. Been a real pleasure talking to you. Good luck with EGR and those IPO plans you were telling me about on the phone. Gimme a ring when you get the underwriter lined up.

Talking Cure

It is the day after Christmas and the New Year looms ominously, the last in the present millennium. And what a millennium it has been, from the Norman Conquest to the invention of dry cleaning. However, this late-December cusp has never been a particularly good time for any but those witless scions of normalcy who would be better off dead in any case. So why is it so much worse this penultimate time around? That is the theme of today's little meditation.

We know there are certain Valued Readers who hate it when we interview ourselves in this fashion. But then, some percentage of you hates at least one of the many genres with which we have experimented over the years, so it pretty much doesn't matter which form we choose. Of course, you don't have to read this tacky suite of interrogatories, and for that you should count yourself lucky. We, in contrast, did have to write it. We had no choice in the matter. It was either write or die of ennui. We can only hope the following will provide others some solace — that they *are* other, and not identical with any of our several selves.

CHRIS LOCKE: I gotta tell you, RB, I am truly bummed.

RAGE BOY®: Yeah? Me too. Maybe it's that SAD thing — Seasonal Affective Disorder or whatever. Whaddya think? That's sorta tony these days . . .

CL: I dunno. I hate those crypto-medical explanations. Sure, maybe it's just depression, but what does that really mean? It just seems like a fancy way of saying you're bummed out. I'm bummed out.

RB: So if not S.A.D., then what? Been grappling with the Grand Narratives again, have you? The One and The Many? The Great

Chain of Being? History? Death? The Afterlife? All those head crackers they put inside the bindings of *The Great Books*? You *know* that shit'll fuck you up.

CL: No, that's not it. I stopped thinking about all that. At least I think I stopped thinking about it. Do you think that thinking you've stopped thinking about something is just another form of thinking about it?

RB: Let's not go there, OK? Every time you start talking like that you *really* bring me down. Maybe it's something simple, like The Holidays. That ever occur to you?

CL: Could be. It feels more cosmic than that, but maybe you're right. There are so many hidden hopes and impossible expectations that sneak in at a time like this. Maybe it's a kind of Currier & Ives hangover. Maybe I'm crashing off a Norman Rockwell high. Chestnuts roasting on a open fire and all the good times skating down at the pond with the neighbor kids in that idyllic little New England town we used to live in, remember?

RB: No.

CL: Oh right, I forgot. That never happened, did it? More culturally imprinted wonderfulness. No wonder we're fucked up, RB.

RB: Speak for yourself old man. You know I don't go in for all that crap. Let me guess. It's the day after Christmas and you've got that empty letdown thing after all the buildup of wondering what Santa was gonna bring you. Am I right?

CL: Well, no, I don't think so. Santa actually brought me something cool. Wanna see? It's called Duck on Bike.

RB: Oh. Does the little propeller beanie whirl around when you wind it up? Oh wow! It does! Man, how could you ever be down with something like this? Can I have it?

CL: No, RB, it's mine. This tin duck is the only thing that makes me smile anymore. Look at the happy colors it's painted, see? It's so simple, so wonderful. I think I'm going to cry.

RB: Jeez, man. Why does it make you want to cry if it's the only thing that makes you happy. You do see the logical inconsistency there, don't you?

CL: You're a fine one to talk about logical inconsistencies. But you're right of course. I guess it's because it reminds me of all the shattered dreams of childhood, of when the world looked so big and shiny and new and . . .

RB: And you hadn't read any Derrida?

CL: C'mon, I still haven't read any Derrida. Or Lacan or Foucault or Lyotard or Rorty or . . .

RB: Yeah, but you *pretend* you have. You have to admit that's significant, right? Maybe you're bummed because you never got that Ph.D. Never wrote that overarching synthesis of all human knowledge that you used to dream about, eh? I remember those whacked-out fantasies you used to get carried away with about book signings at Brentano's and all the chicks you'd get from NYU. Could that be it?

CL: Nah. I gave up on all that. At least I think I gave up on all that. Though the idea of being a serious scholar does still have its appeal. Did I miss something there? Could be. The academic politics, the infighting . . . [eyes glaze over in wistful reverie . . .]

RB: Yeah well, publish or perish the thought. I'd say stick with the duck, pal. It's a cool duck. Uncomplicated. That's what I like about it.

CL: You seem so balanced sometimes RB. And when I think that about you, that's when I really get scared. Because everyone knows you're totally insane.

RB: Well, being totally insane is hard work. People don't realize that. They think it's all fun and games and just a full-time hoot. It's not.

CL: Yeah? And this is why you're down too? Because it's hard being nuts all the time?

RB: I guess that's partly it. But it's also the choices Modern Man is constantly faced with.

CL: Modern Man? Are you yanking my chain? Are you making fun of my deep sadness?

RB: No, I'm serious. And that's interesting. You didn't say you were sad before, just bummed. Sadness implies something more . . . intimate. Could it be you're avoiding something you haven't mentioned here? Something so terrible and profound you just can't allow yourself to confront it?

CL: Probably. But it's so terrible and profound I just can't allow myself to confront it. And I sure as hell don't need you confronting it for me, OK? So just back off!

RB: Touchy, touchy! But all right. I can dig it that you need to keep being repressed and lying to yourself about it. Sure. Knock yourself out. It's a common neurosis.

CL: And you have uncommon neuroses I suppose. So what are these choices you speak of? Is that the big deal? That you can't decide?

RB: Actually yes. Life is generally a simple matter for me. I don't get into all that intellectual stuff you do. All that philosophy. No wonder you're feeling messed up. For me, it's different. It comes down to conflicting alternatives — which things I can do and, because I can't do all the things I'd like to, which other things I won't be able to pursue at all.

CL: So depression basically boils down to a time management issue for you, is that it? We're talking setting priorities here? This is a side of you I don't think I've ever seen. Give me some examples.

RB: Well, OK, but before I can decide which things to do, I have to decide how each of them fits into some larger scheme of things, right?

CL: Right, that makes sense I guess.

RB: So like I wonder about Dynamic HTML. What's up with that, you know? Is it just a plot to make shit more complicated? Or is it a leading-edge technology I should jump into with both feet?

CL: Jesus, RB! You really think about stuff like that?

RB: Sure I do. And it's not as simple as it sounds, either. I mean, take Javascript for instance. Will there ever be an implementation common to all the major browsers? Will the W3C prevail or just keep adding stuff to the standard to foil the ability of greed-head companies to deliver something we can actually use?

CL: I don't believe I'm hearing this.

RB: Are you kidding? It's a huge issue! Client-side scripting gives authors far more control of their content. Of course, I could learn Perl and CGI instead, but that's not exactly apples to apples, is it?

CL: You got me.

RB: Or Visual Basic. The new 6.0 package is supposed to have some very cool new features, plus it has an Integrated Development Environment that beats anything the Perl community ever came up with. But I ask myself: will it handle full regular expressions?

CL: What the fuck's a regular expression?

RB: Well, they're a sort of finite automata that operate over string data. That's clear enough, right? Imagine being able to specify, for instance: bring me all the redheads living in the 212 area code who like to attend dog racing events in New Jersey but who do not have serious eating disorders.

CL: Yeah, OK. I can see how that would be handy. But what would you do with that information?

RB: Good question. Because this is where things start to get complicated. As you know, we're all still waiting for web log REFERER fields to capture hair color, and that's just the beginning. Then we need a commonly accepted mechanism for correlating that data with HTML formatting preferences so that we can develop a strict mapping between pinpoint social demographics and effective page layout schemes.

CL: I'm not sure I even know what you just said. But why would you want to do that, whatever it is?

RB: Cascading Style Sheets! These are a great advance, there's no doubt about it. A whole site can be redesigned in minutes by changing a single style sheet that specifies how certain kinds of structures should be rendered by the browser. For instance, we could create an object class called block_tiny that would force all paragraphs so marked to appear as indented 2-point heliotrope Transylvanian Gothic. Or maybe one called interview_response that would make our initials show up in red to indicate who was saying what.

CL: But I just Viewed Source, and we're not doing that here.

RB: Precisely! Because the time investment in a CSS approach begs certain questions that can't be adequately answered without a substantial amount of demographic information — and that's simply lacking without better ways to collect it than are currently available.

CL: So what are you saying exactly? I'm getting lost here I think . . .

RB: Well, look, should our initials be red or blue or chartreuse? We just don't know what would be most pleasing to the audience we want to target.

CL: And what audience is that?

RB: Well, I already gave you the non-bulimic redheads example.

CL: But RB, that's not our audience! Are you completely out of touch with reality?

RB: What is reality?

CL: Nuh-uh, you're not getting me started down that path! Just forget I asked. So these are the terrible choices facing Modern Man? Is that what you meant?

RB: Precisely. We know the web is here to stay, and we know it can't just keep being fun. There has to be a *reason* for all this. Plus, of course, 5-GL tools for manipulating huge corpora of textual and fixed-field information.

CL: By "5-GL" you mean meta-languages? Tools to manipulate tools that manipulate lower-level data structures and like that? It all gets so abstract.

RB: Abstraction is power! We live in a hall of mirrors. Get used to it.

CL: But what are we talking about? What are we actually saying? I don't think we know anymore. It's all representations of representations. That's partly what's got me feeling so down.

RB: Oh bullshit! You don't know what to represent any more than I do. What is primary? What is most fundamental?

CL: You mean does zero beat one like rock beats scissors?

RB: Well, yeah, something like that. What would you ground everything else on if you had to choose an axiom base? And you do, you know . . .

CL: That sounds like philosophy.

RB: No! It's utterly practical. What comes first? Is it hunger, sex, religion, science, Thursday night's TV lineup? Or is it something more fundamental, like representability.

CL: RB, "representability" is not a word.

RB: Is too. Besides, even if it wasn't already, it is now.

CL: Says who? And what for?

RB: Says your spell checker, and because I just needed it to prove something. I used it to represent the whole notion of the effectiveness of representation.

CL: What does that prove?

RB: Well, nothing really, but it does take us in the direction of finding a way to examine and weigh what is adequate and inadequate in what we posit proof of anything to *consist in*. Think of it as rigor.

CL: I am getting a serious headache now.

RB: Oh sure, just ignore the whole problem! That is so like you!

CL: *What* problem?!

RB: I thought you said you woke up feeling bummed out, right? Didn't you say that?

CL: Yeah, I said that.

RB: So there must be a problem, am I right? Look, this is just Logic 101, nothing too mysterious about it. I'm not losing you here am I?

CL: No, I understand that part, sort of, but Jesus H. Christ, RB, how'd you get from that to Dynamic HTML and client-side web page programming?

RB: Well, follow me here, OK? Tell me when the chain breaks for you. Ready?

CL: Yeah, OK, ready. If you must.

RB: Consciousness, perception, feeling, emotion, intellect, knowledge, understanding . . . with me so far?

CL: Well, that's a mouthful, but yeah I guess . . .

RB: . . . communication, frame of reference, semantics, phoneme, morpheme, token, hieroglyph, pictogram, alphabet, letter, digit . . .

CL: Yeah, all right. I think. But I also think you skipped something in there.

RB: What?

CL: I don't know.

RB: *AHA!*

CL: What do you mean, "*AHA!*"?

RB: Yes, what do I mean?

CL: I asked you first.

RB: OK, I mean you have to have some method. Some way to represent what is most fundamental about experience.

CL: Why?

RB: Why? *Why?* Because how else are you going to be able to describe what's missing? What you really want? How else could you begin to identify the giant lacunae in your life?

CL: Is that anything like a Giant Squid?

RB: Decidedly not.

CL: Well, whatever it is, is it really so important to figure all this out?

RB: It is unless you intend to go around whining all the time about how bummed out you are and never have a clue as to what the problem is!

CL: But maybe there really isn't any problem. Maybe we just think there is.

RB: What do you mean by "we"?

CL: Well, you know, you and me, people in general . . .

RB: *AHA!*

CL: I wish you'd stop doing that. But I know you're gonna tell me why you keep doing it. Tell me you're gonna tell me . . .

RB: I am going to tell you. But that's just it. How will you know what I've said is true?

CL: RB, this is philosophy. Now you're bumming me out for real.

RB: No it's not. It's market demographics! You're a writer, right?

CL: I like to think so.

RB: Well, what's the first question a writer has to ask himself?

CL: Or herself?

RB: Sure, or herself.

CL: Is my computer turned on?

RB: No, asshole. It is: who is my audience?

CL: I do ask that. Then, after I don't get any answer, I write something. I had a dream last night that I wrote this long rambling confused screed and posted it to a bunch of mailing lists. I woke up wondering if there were any responses that would help me understand what I'd written, which I couldn't remember. In the dream, I didn't get anything back but flames. It was horrible. I totally ruined my reputation.

RB: You realize that if you publish this, your dream is going to come true. And by the way, what reputation?

CL: You're asking *me*?

RB: Never mind that. Look, here's your problem. You don't know what you're saying, you don't know why you're saying it, and you don't know to whom you're saying it.

CL: Saying what?

RB: That's just it. You have no idea!

CL: Oh.

RB: Let's go through this one more time, shall we? You say you're feeling bummed out. Do you examine this "feeling"? Do you inquire into its origins? Do you ask of what it is constituted? No. You talk about it as if it existed in a form that could be grasped by others who hear you whining about how bummed out you are.

CL: They understand. All God's children get bummed out sometimes.

RB: How do you know that?

CL: They tell me so.

RB: And you accept these reports at face value? You think these others are bummed for the same reasons you are?

CL: Well, I'm not sure. I'm not even sure why I am. So how could I know if they were "the same"?

RB: Uh-huh. Now we're getting somewhere. And how do you and those who "tell you" exchange these clueless cries of tortured malaise?

CL: Email usually.

RB: And now? What is the format you are typing into right this second?

CL: HTML?

RB: Very good!

CL: So what you're saying, in effect, is that I am using a representational schema which, while it transmits a recognizable set of characters in an accepted interchange format — in the case at hand, low ASCII — nonetheless lacks the semantic coherence necessary to construct a common basis in shared experience and is thus impotent with respect to genuine narrative conveyance. Is that it?

RB: That's it!

CL: And you think this could be established via better *technical standards*?! You really are insane, you know that?

RB: You have to start somewhere.

CL: So, by carefully building representations of representations of representations of . . . *something* you think it's possible to arrive at precise and unequivocal communications between human beings?

RB: What else have we got?

CL: That's it. You've put your finger on it. That's why I've been so depressed!

RB: Oh breakthrough! I'm so happy for you.

CL: There's no need to be snide about it. I actually feel much better now that I know what's been bugging me.

RB: And now what? You'll send this out to the Valued Readers and they'll all unsubscribe.

CL: No, I don't think so. Some will, of course, but those are the ones who just don't get it.

RB: Get *what* for christsake? What are you *talking* about???

CL: Well, I think some will say that I really put my finger on something here.

RB: But I thought you said *I* put my finger on whatever it was. Didn't you just say that?

CL: Yeah, but everybody knows we're the same person. They don't nit-pick these fine distinctions the way you do.

RB: And this, to you, will pass for communication? That a handful of readers will go: "Hey, you're as fucked up and confused as we are. Way to go!"?

CL: I see it as a kind of higher, co-emergent wisdom, you could say. A mutual recognition of the human condition, don't you think?

RB: Actually, I think it's a sad commentary on the human condition.

CL: Well, we're all entitled to our little opinions.

RB: I give up!

CL: Good. You want to play with Duck on Bike now?

RB: Yeah, sure, Duck on Bike, why not . . .

Tonight on Cary Ling Jive!

Tune in tonight as Cary Ling talks to the enigmatic and reclusive RageBoy® at his never-before-filmed Mayan pyramid command post deep in the heart of the Yucatan peninsula. In 1996, RageBoy was just beginning on the road that would eventually make him the most powerful — and most feared — "Spiritual Executive" the world has ever seen. Now, only five years later, he reveals to Cary the secret plan he used to effect his astounding rise to Universal Domination. Don't miss this historic interview! 9 P.M. — 8 Central.

CL: Mr. RageBoy, sir, it surely is good of you to agree to come on the show, and to invite us into your — I must say — *sumptuous* home here. I understand it is customary to kneel and kiss your ring . . . [kneeling, kissing ring].

RB: [proffering hand, looking bored] Actually, it is more customary to kiss our ass, but we're sure you'll be getting to that later. And by the way, you may call us RageBoy. Just don't let it go to your head. Did you enjoy our little Geisha enclave? Loosened you up a bit, did it?

CL: [blushing] Well, yes, you certainly have spared no expense on the palatial accommodations. But let's get right down to what brings us here. How did you manage all this? [sweeps hand around in arc as camera pans interior of the RB mansion] Everyone knows who you are today, of course, but you came out of total obscurity just before the turn of the century, and very few understand how you accomplished that. Was it all planned or would you say you were just lucky?

RB: Lucky, Mr. Ling? Surely you know enough about The Teachings of RageBoy to understand that we recognize no such force as "luck." It is merely a question of who does the planning, if you catch our drift . . .

CL: Hmmm, I'm afraid I really don't, but let's not get into the meta-physics just yet. When did you first know you would end up where you are now, as Supreme Military Commander and Most Humble Minister to the Global Flock? Of course, it isn't necessary to mention that you personally control 80% of the world's wealth . . .

RB: Well, the Plan first came to us shortly after we began writing Entropy Gradient Reversals in the Spring of 1996. Our paramilitary Church of Entropy knows these today simply as The Scriptures. Several entire libraries have been devoted to the exegetical writings they have generated — one in Rome, and as you know, the most recent in Bangkok. But as to your question, it had been clear to us for some time that conditions were ripe for the emergence of either a messianic spiritual leader — the real McCoy, you know, not one of those Corn Belt Bible thumpers — or a wildly popular fascist dictator. The real inspiration, if we may say so, lay in realizing how seamlessly the two could be integrated.

CL: And did you see yourself in that role?

RB: No, no, not initially. [laughs] We simply found ourselves waiting for something like that to happen.

CL: So what was it that turned the corner for you?

RB: Well, we finally realized that we weren't alone in this expectation — that there were a lot of other people similarly poised for Something Big to take place. One incident, especially, brought this home to us. Do you recall the day in 1997 that Hong Kong reverted to China? We were looking for news on this hugely important power shift, but all the TV anchors were going on and on about that boxer Mike Tyson biting this other guy's ear half off. It was clear to us then that people were starved for meaning in their lives. Remember, this was moving onto the cusp of the millennium, and people have historically become rather strange around such numerologically significant thresholds.

CL: Did you personally believe the year 2000 was significant in some spiritual sense?

RB: You mean like Harmonic Convergence or something? No. None of that stuff means jack shit. Perhaps you haven't read The Scriptures yourself . . .

CL: Uh, well, I've looked them over in a cursory sort of way, but no, I have to admit I haven't studied your teachings.

RB: Then perhaps there is still hope for you.

CL: Yes, I think I see . . . But back in '96 you say you saw an opportunity to combine politics and religion. Tell us more about that.

RB: So, right, you had your millennial fever going, but as the historians will tell you today, it was the Internet that put the whole thing into high gear. Curiously, many had argued that the Net would make people smarter, more informed — you know, the whole One World trip. But in fact it did just the opposite. You have to wonder why it took people so long to realize what was happening. All those rumors circulating, all those conspiracy theories, all those people literally breaking down the fabric of reality with their balkanized and solipsistic little opinions about everything. You remember what it was like by '99 — no two people shared even a remotely similar ontology and there was open warfare over things like shoe color. Our personal favorite was the debate — it didn't turn bloody until later — about whether toaster ovens had souls.

CL: But you were still just observing at this point?

RB: Well, yes and no. We were writing the Entropy Gradient Reversals and began to realize that the early readership was divided into two distinct camps, if you will, though "camps" is putting it too strongly at that juncture. We didn't institute the actual camps until later in 1998.

CL: And how would you characterize these two groups?

RB: Actually, it caught us quite off-guard that there *were* two. But it soon became impossible to ignore the fact that a certain percentage of the subscriber base was taking EGR a bit more seriously than the others. We began to get these very interesting confessional messages, and the way this works is that one piece of email generally represents anywhere from 10 to 20 lurkers who feel the same way but are too chickenshit to say anything.

CL: What were they saying?

RB: Oh, you know, things like "what is the meaning of life *really*?" or "why don't we all just kill ourselves?" or "why don't we just kill everybody else?"

CL: And you thought this was odd?

RB: [sighs] We understand that it's hard to remember back to a time when this might have appeared a bit unusual. But yes, we thought it was pretty fucking weird. Remember that EGR was basically just an over-intellectual comic strip for bored First Worlders.

CL: So one part of the readership was deeply confused and highly aggressive it sounds like. And the rest?

RB: The rest got what was going on from the beginning. That's how the thing took off in the first place. We started with this boast about getting two million readers in 14 months, but it actually took nearly three years.

CL: *Two Million?* But you have over a billion today!

RB: Yes, things did get a little out of hand there didn't they? [chuckles]

CL: So what about the ones who "got it"?

RB: We cut them in on The Plan, and most were game. They were all spooked about the advent of global fascism and RageBoy looked like a far better bet than some. Also, we built in some pretty sweet incentives, so that helped a lot too. You have to understand that these people were very well placed, some of them anyway. So when we were ready to move, things happened quickly.

Ah, here's some refreshment. What can we offer you, coffee, tea, orange juice, heroin, cocaine? We don't partake ourselves but we understand some people find it soothing.

CL: Just orange juice would be fine.

RB: Thank you Rupert, that will be all for now . . .

CL: Was that Rupert *Murdoch*?

RB: Yes, I'm afraid so. He hasn't fared too well in the transition has he? Oh well. We encourage him in his little hobbies. He likes to write haiku and feed them to the koi in the Japanese gardens. But the poor fellow hasn't any talent. One of our people found one recently — evidently the fish throw up after they eat them. Would you like to hear it?

CL: Why yes. Haiku are short, right?

RB: Seventeen syllables, traditionally. But with Rupert, you know, who's counting anymore? It went:

> I think that I shall never see
> a bird as cool as B Sky B.

CL: That's it? But that's not a haiku, is it? It's doggerel!

RB: To him, it is beautiful. And isn't that what counts, in the end?

CL: Yeah, well, I guess . . .

RB: So we organized the CyberJihad. All that's a matter of record at this point, of course, but it was pretty exciting when we brought it off.

CL: I'll say! 30 days from anonymity to total world domination. Did you know you would be successful? Had you failed, the consequences to yourself would have been . . . well, dire.

RB: Oh yes, but we were fairly confident it would work, right from the start. We also timed things to take advantage of the Y2K confusion.

CL: Y2K?

RB: You know it as the Millennium Bug.

CL: Oh yeah, when all the computers went down. So you saw that coming?

RB: Anybody who wasn't deaf dumb and blind saw that coming, are you kidding? Of course, from the position we had taken by that time in global information systems, we were able to help things along substantially. What no one other than ourselves predicted was the Cold Turkey effect that would kick in after the net crashed on January 1.

CL: You mean The Day of the Stare?

RB: Yeah. We stepped in and provided Strong Opinions over the private backbone we had set up beforehand. It wasn't much but it was all there was, and as you know, people couldn't get enough of it. We did this Push thing that gave you something to think about, something to argue about, something to organize some semblance of a personality around. Before that, most people didn't really understand that information is a drug. We knew, so we were ready.

CL: And this was free, right?

RB: It didn't cost any money if that's what you mean. We weren't interested in money. Never have been.

CL: You are now the richest man in the world, and you are telling me you aren't interested in money? How can that be?

RB: The first principle of entropy gradient reversalism is not giving a shit. This is a fundamental pillar of The Teachings.

CL: Not that we fully understand that, but alright — what *was* the cost then, if not measured in dollars?

RB: In order to get on our feed, people had to agree to perform certain favors in return.

CL: Such as?

RB: Oh, such as crippling the firewalls on government computers and media-industry web sites. Plus, we had a lot of fun with the monetary system.

CL: And there was hardly any resistance, was there?

RB: None to speak of. Even now, just a few years later, it's hard for people to remember how powerfully they were affected. The Day of the Stare was no joke. When 200 million Americans realized AOL just wasn't coming back up, they sort of snapped. The Army was useless. Ditto the National Guard. Only the Marines kept it together. None of them can read . . .

Oh say, Bill, I wonder if you'd have a look at that Pac-Rim server, it's been a little twitchy the last few days . . . [Bill exits bowing.]

CL: Was that Gates? My god, you've got the Old Guard on your household staff!

RB: Yes, we *are* rather proud of our people here at EGR World HQ. Bill is an interesting case. After the Change, he was found wandering around on the outskirts of Seattle mumbling something about Visual Basic. Poor guy, he was pretty shaken up by the whole thing, as you can imagine, but he's doing much better now. We've given him a slot on the Malaysian Help Desk and he's not half bad at customer service. Who would have guessed? It just goes to show what kind of results are possible when you give people a fighting chance.

CL: That's very good of you, RageBoy. So tell us, who else do you have working for you here?

RB: They're not all here physically at our Yucatan base, but we do have an impressive international organization. Boutros Boutros-Ghali is covering our natural resource exploitation initiatives. We converted the Joint Chiefs of Staff into a pretty crack marketing unit — they've been hugely effective as you can tell from our 99.7% global market penetration. We've got Janet Reno working network security. Of course, there isn't any network security anymore, but she hasn't figured that out yet. Maya Angelou is our Poet Laureate — Rupert is studying with her in fact. And we put Bill Clinton to work in PR. Actually, that last one's not working out so well, but he can't really do much harm there either, as the Church has virtually immunized the planet to that sort of rhetoric. Ted Turner manages our Human Resources Division — you know, new hires, bennies, all that. Plus I understand he's about to make Archdeacon . . .

CL: Unfortunately, we don't have a lot more time, but do tell us a little more about the Church of Entropy. I take it this was part of your vision about the widespread longing for some sort of messiah.

RB: Precisely so. You see, everybody already knew that religion was crap, science was crap, politics was crap. We just elevated those beliefs and organized them around a few easy-to-grasp tenets.

CL: Which are?

RB: We call them The Five Auto-Revealing Insights of the Anointed:

- Never Believe Anyone
- Never Take Yourself Seriously No Matter What
- Don't Harbor Gratuitous Cynicism
- Don't Be An Asshole Unnecessarily
- Be Nice

CL: Well, four and five seem kind of similar, but you're right, that's fairly simple. Isn't there a paradox or two in all this, though? You've practically deified yourself. You rule the world with an iron fist and brook no opposition to your financial predations. And, please don't take offense at this, but we understand you're sometimes anything but nice.

RB: [testily] Hey, shit happens, OK?

CL: Well, uh . . .

RB: Look. There is world peace. Hunger is nonexistent. The trains run on time. Plus, you gotta admit the content is a whole lot better.

CL: True, all true. And yet, what about things like self determination?

RB: Self? What self? That was the whole problem for christ sake! All these people bumbling around like chickens with their damn heads cut off trying to "find themselves" or some shit. All we said was look, if you can't find yourself, then you are really truly fucked up. There you are, right there! We had to hold a mirror up to the worst cases and say, real loud like, "*See?*" If that didn't work we either put them on high-tofu diets, just to get even, or we popped a cap in their sorry ass.

CL: You mean you had them shot. I see . . .

RB: You got a problem with that? Say, I been meaning to ask you, how do you like running CNN? Zat working out for you OK?

CL: Yes it is, RageBoy, and thank you so much for making it possible. I really can't adequately express my gratitude . . .

RB: See, we told you you'd get around to kissing ass sooner or later. It's OK. But lookit pal, we gotta book. It's time for our afternoon benediction in the Plaza of Mere Mortals and we really shouldn't keep the faithful waiting, now should we?

[rising] Rupert! You wanna clear this stuff up here?

CL: [shaking hands] Thank you for inviting us into your home, RageBoy. This little chat has been a real eye opener.

RB: Yeah, I'll bet.

"You Can Be What You Want To Be On Cloud Nine"

The Temptations

Writer's Bloc

"To be great is to be misunderstood," wrote Ralph Waldo Emerson. If he was right about this, I must already be headed for the Internet Hall of Fame. If you know what I'm saying here. Ah, but perhaps you don't. The beauty of Emerson's insight, though, is that ultimately it doesn't matter. Works out for me either way.

I am desperately trying to complete my book, *Gonzo Marketing: Winning Through Worst Practices*. I tell myself I'm trying, anyway. I'm certainly desperate. I should have finished the chapter I'm working on three weeks ago. No, three months ago. It's about social marketing and public journalism, concepts which may be new to you. They were to me when I decided to write about them. Which is why I've had to do a lot of, you know, research. But the time it takes, my God!

Take yesterday. But first some necessary background. I've been writing about Oliviero Toscani, the guy at Benetton who ran advertising spreads of people dying, being born, horses fucking in a field. That sort of thing. His AIDS and death-row ads are prime examples of "cause related marketing." Welding a brand to some worthy—not to mention high-traffic—social issue has achieved a certain critical cachet among marketing consultants, many of whom are furiously pitching it to their well-heeled corporate clients. AmEx gives spare change to the homeless. IBM opens Lou McGerstner House for autistic Fortune–500 executives. You've seen this stuff. But nobody wants to talk about Toscani. He has given the practice a bad name. He doesn't play by the rules. It's possible he's insane. This does not endear him to the marketing crowd, or for that matter to squeaky clean non-profits intent on presenting human suffering in a more attractive package.

But I find myself deeply drawn to his work for this very reason. I must know more!

Learning that he's produced two books, I immediately go to Amazon.com and single-click them into my virtual possession. Then I wait. Ta-dum- da-dum-da-dum-da-dum. What use it it to write before consulting my primary sources? Finally, the UPS guy brings them yesterday morning, just as I've managed to bang out three consecutive sentences . . . "We'll soon return to the vexing issue of objectivity, but for now let's agree with Rosabeth Moss Kanter of Harvard Business School. She's right: an increasing number of corporations want to proactively align themselves with the common good. However, it's none too clear to whom this 'common good' is common."

Excited to hear the doorbell ring—in fact, for any distraction from this vaporous blather—I eviscerate the Amazon package and open the first book . . . to a full-color photograph of . . . no wait, this can't be right . . . rhinoceros shit. I stare in amazement, flipping the pages, incredulous that I have paid good money for this crap. Lion crap, tiger crap, giraffe crap, camel crap, it goes on and on. In the single-paragraph trilingual introduction, Toscani writes, "Let us celebrate shit (scheisse, merde)!" And on the back inside cover flap he somewhat less than helpfully explains, "All that glitters is not gold."

This is a truly disgusting book. I have wasted not only my money, but my precious, dwindling time. My publisher's iron-clad delivery deadline looms ever nearer as I peruse page upon page of noxious animal and human excrement. I ask myself how this will help me explain to the managerial cadre of the Global 1000 the unsuspected opportunities awaiting them on the World Wide Web. To be fair, I also ask myself what I was really expecting when I ordered *Cacas: The Encyclopedia of Poo.*

The same day, I wrote a highly speculative piece on a question that has greatly intrigued me of late. To wit, what if the marauding bands of Canadian geese that are currently terrorizing my apartment complex are really alien invaders from outer space bent on destroying our way of life and all that we value as a species? Sort of like advertisers. I thought I could maybe work it into the book, but it's not looking good.

So you see? Everything is grist for the writer's mill, yet not all the avenues one thinks to explore turn out to be productive ones. I know now that I should have allowed more time to accommodate this bitter truth.

This morning I promised myself I would write non-stop all day. No excuses. No getting side-tracked. First, though, I had to check my e-mail. Oh Christ, another spam from Matt Herlihy and those maniacs over at Sweet Fancy Moses. And look, here's one of those clickable URL things. My resolution instantly forgotten, I'm game. I go to the site. I read. I laugh. This is much better than writing. But also germane to my theme, I suddenly realize. Yes, that's it! I snap my fingers. With the Toscani thing having panned out as a dead end, I'll use this as an example.

But an example of what, precisely? Hmmm. Finding the right fit could take further thought. Then again, perhaps not. Let's see . . .

In general, Vice Presidents of Marketing working in large corporations think we are morons. Takes one to know one, I guess they figure. For decades, they have been sponsoring "content" that fits their bell-curve-driven dreams of mass market penetration. Bend over, here comes another sitcom. They will tell you they only sponsor this sort of thing for the mindless, shuffling Thorazine-drooler category, which however, comprises 98.74% of all Americans. Because when they ask them "Who wants to be a millionaire?" every hand in the house goes up. Of course, they'd get the same reaction if they said, "Who wants to go to Arts and Crafts now?" or "Who needs to use the bathroom?" But the marketeers will tell you they've conducted extensive, expensive research. They'll tell you this is what the people want.

Yeah, but look who they asked! Forming a focus group is like jury selection at the O.J. trial. "Not that one. He sneered. Swear to God, I saw his lip curl! And not the one laughing into her laptop, either." They never ask the smart people. They never ask *us*. And you know why? Because they know what we'd tell them. To stick it up their Nielsen ratings. Sure they do these multiple choice questionnaires. "Do you like Friends better than Cheers?" And maybe for the octogenarians: "Did you like Cheers better than Mork and Mindy?" But they never give you any real options, like: "If given half a chance, would you strangle Robin Williams with a length of rusted barbed wire dipped in botulism toxin?"

And so the same old tired stereotypes are perpetuated. But not on the Internet. Oh no! Here, the really interesting demographic—the pig-in-the-python disposable-cash crowd—is attracted by the weird and unseemly, the offbeat, the lowbrow, the downright offensive. Which is why sites like this one have a bright commercial future. If corporations had a lick of sense, they'd realize that top-down mass marketing is over—so 20th century—and instead, that it's around whacked-out fare like this that the most powerful new markets are emerging, bottom-up. They'd realize that these markets are coalescing around a new breed of intelligent writers and artists who actually, you know, like think about shit.

That's why, in a couple more months or quarters or—who knows, these marketing types are none too swift—maybe years, you shouldn't be surprised if you're reading the usual blow-it-out-your-nose screed on Sweet Fancy Moses and suddenly you get interrupted by some voice-over XML-javascript flashbot announcing: "We'll be back right after this important word from IBM and Lou McGerstner House . . . "

**So now I'm an expert on flying.
Sure, ask me anything.**

Foreigner

I went to google.com tonight and plugged in the query: "I am dreaming of C4." You can imagine why. I was trying to imagine too. Something must have gone wrong with the process, because all I got back was shrapnel.

. . . I am not. I cannot distinguish between. Hence, reasonable grounds for doubt cannot be contained. Turing dreaming today's fortune cookie, writing a logfile script. Am I dreaming, or could it be something more expensive? I am unsure of the model. Active imagination is driving my car. Overcome with paralysis, I study the medium tessitura. A night in the park. I am dreaming there, stark naked, running, reading with a bad attitude, changed. I walk to The C4 Hotel to pick up all things that work. Am I creating a character? Codeine, hmmm. I am sorry to hear that. Every day I hope I am dreaming and will wake up. Then I begin to manipulate the story: object abduction experiences. "I feel as if I am dreaming now," she says. Almost everything you know requires waking at 4 A.M., ingesting the tape recorder, the reputation of being. Yes, I am disappointed. Lucid dreaming monsters these engines apart — blindfolded, official, phenomenal. And I am on dangerous ground.

I drove home dreaming a wall of Marshall amps lined up along both sides of Interstate 25 synchronized to detonators wired to 38 tons of C4 strategically placed along the structural girders of Denver office buildings. Partly because of their name, I picked Foreigner, and partly because that's what came on the radio just then. It could be a lounge act in Vegas. Partly because of that. At 300 decibels, anything sounds hip. I push the first plunger and the amps kick off, rocking 18-wheelers into the oncoming lanes.

I WANT TO KNOW WHAT LOVE IS . . .

. . . the second, and all the glass blows out of the U.S. West tower and 30 other buildings down there. Whoosh. Kaboom. Instant rainbows just before 100 million tons of nightmare begins its stately slow-mo dance with gravity.

I KNOW YOU CAN SHOW ME . . .

For as it is written, charity without good works is dead, though it speak with the tongues of men and angels.

Trip Report

Because I have trained you far too well to not believe me, you will not believe me, but it's true: I carry you everywhere. Thousands of people I do not know, how could you be so important to me? But you are. I think: oh, I must tell the Valued Readers about this place, this thought, this person. Then I think about how I will describe these things, and I think about it so long, there's no time left for the telling. Only things I have written to you in my head.

Then I begin to get email from certain of you, as I have been lately, saying hey, are you OK? What's up with you? When are you going to write again? Have you forgotten about us? Because I have trained you far too well in a particular form of skeptical cynicism, you will be skeptical and cynical and will not believe how much I love you. This is the result of implacable karma, from which none of us escapes unscathed. We can only wonder at our helplessness. And perhaps tell another story. Whether terminal madness or luminous sanity, it is all just stories within stories within stories. Deus ex machina, world without end, that's all she wrote. Amen.

So when we last saw our hero — which is to say, myself, as I get to make this stuff up as I go along, no other options being available — he was darkly intimating heartbreak and sorrow, but saying precious little as to what that was all about, and here will say precious little more, except that to open the heart may cause some breakage or at least routing errors. Some settling in transit. Some pain that seems to be there always and everywhere underneath events no matter what choices we make. There is no perfect path — understanding which constitutes supreme great enlightenment and the fulfillment of all desire. Meanwhile, we keep on trucking and trafficking in endless confusion. How wonderful. No, really. Ever invisible, her smile is your smile is my own.

Goo goo ga joob. May all beings be happy. God bless America. Etc. This intelligence is highly sensitive, fragile and temporary. For your eyes only. Which I here imagine laughing. I wear your ornaments. I speak your language. I begindylsen war Ordet, og Ordet war hos Gud . . .

Since last writing, a month ago now, I have traveled to Maui and Washington DC, Las Vegas and Copenhagen. I have seen more of the world than I thought there was, and am happy to report it is bigger out there than I'd imagined. And more fractal. Wheels within wheels. Stars within stars, new universes popping up everywhere. Simply amazing how it works. Though I could be wrong about what I've seen. How would I know? Oh dear, this is not coming out right at all. . .

Sending from Maui

sitting in the lobby
of the Grand Wailea
there is no inside or outside.
the sky comes right through
it's a breeze.
everywhere clouds
water flowers
one world continuous
no edges.

so much
so much has happened here
and on the way to this place
which has taken a lifetime
to arrive at.

last night I rode in the prow
of a 90-foot motor launch
hanging over the edge
feeling the waves slip under me below.
feeling the night come on
the endless deep.
and stars in ancient mythic constellations
unknown to me
marking the way to destinations
yet to be discovered.

I prayed into the water
to take my heart
accept my little life
my little joy, my little sorrow
and fill the space of this loneliness
until it bursts, flows over
returns to its source
completes the circle
floods me, drowns me
takes me home
into its enormous spiral star-strewn
ocean heart.

I walked barefoot in the surf
asking for the courage
to feel the pain again
that I forgot
when I forgot
you.

and it came
like a knife
like a poison wind of despair

*and I opened my heart to it
opened the place in my chest
that I have wrapped myself around
so long, so long.
and I felt it go all the way through
until there was nothing left
of me
of you.
only the blinded night
only breathing still in the abandoned
world.*

*but breathing
still. but breathing still.
and free.*

*no signs, no maps
no clear way to turn.
but awake in the darkness
seeing myself at last.*

*and a deeper forgiveness
how far can this go?
a deeper forgiveness
than I ever thought possible.*

*what I saw was that I love you
and I let myself love you
even more
without reason
without holding back anything
because of the world
because of the ocean
because of life*

because this heart
is endless boundless
because of love.

I cannot tell you
but I know you know.
and I don't need to tell you
anything.
but I tell you anyway:
this blessing is deeper
than any I have ever known.
it leaves me exactly where I am.
and you the same.
it is a mystery to touch
without touching.
but I see these orchids
in front of me
stained deep yellow and purple
in their fragile white hearts
and I offer them to your eyes.
and the wind, the sky
the great heart of the world.

sitting in the lobby
of the Grand Wailea
there is no inside or outside.
so much has happened here.
so much.

So that was what happened in Maui. A little intimate, perhaps.
From my "personal life," as we are wont to say in these strangely
twisted times. But I've been thinking: what other kind of life is
there?

And to the engineers I said, no corporation has ever fallen in love. But they had no idea what I was talking about. I said, what is happening on the net is people falling in love with the world again. Listen.

I refined this a little in DC, talking to the Federal webmasters and agency chieftains. I said this is a radical conspiracy that you may have heard of, called democracy. But that didn't sound right to me. Not even half dangerous enough. So in Las Vegas, because of the venue and in honor of Elvis I said, I sang (I actually did) Suspicious Minds from the podium to Sun Microsystems and their largest clients and I said no corporation has ever fallen in love and that is why corporations, which have never really incorporated in the true sense, are so suspicious of the net. Words to that effect. And I gave them shit about being "the dot in dot-com" and who really gave a rat's ass about that? They laughed. They sorta got it. And I thought to write a poem called Viva Las Vegas, in honor of Elvis again, of course, about how all the stupid things in the world add up to a world that isn't stupid at all if we could only see it from high enough up. I was in an airplane at the time. But I never wrote that one because I was crashing.

So I crashed and I wrote:

> *if you hear me in the silence*
> *then am I real.*
> *if you see me in the darkness*
> *then am I music*
> *to your music.*
> *if your heart is empty*
> *yet fills with joy*
> *then are your colors*
> *my colors.*

Something is shaking, uncovering itself. Is it just me? Or have you sensed this too? I felt into it deeper. I went to Denmark.

Nanna couldn't meet me at the airport, but was sending "an investor" she said. Oh no! I was there for a conference called Reboot

3.0. As it transpired, however, this was no ordinary investor. We became instant friends, which never happens to me with guys, so it must have been something in the air or possibly the water. His name is Morten, and as we got into town, he said he thought I should see a special part of Copenhagen called Christiania — not sure if I'm spelling this right; it's pronounced chris-jane-ya. And he mumbled something about drugs being legal there, but I wasn't really paying attention at that point. So when we got to Pusher Street (actually called that, which is sort of quaint) I was thoroughly amazed to see blocks and slabs and slices of hashish — dozens of kilos of the stuff — laid out ever so tidily for the inspection of casual strollers along this surpassing strange alleyway in the middle of a big Western city. I picked up a loaf of Afghani black and took a huge whiff. I haven't seen that much shit in one place since 1969.

Oh.

So that wasn't anything I was expecting. Then I met Morten's wife, who *is* expecting. She will have a baby in August. A girl. I saw the sonograms pinned to the kitchen corkboard in their flat. She is studying Communications.

The TV said there was rioting in the streets. Football hooligans — they always call them that over there, which speaks volumes, I think. I think it's a funny word. But not so funny in fact. Turks and Brits fighting over who would win the final game that night and calling each other terrible bad names. They'd all been drinking since early morning and singing in the streets. Morten and I had seen them as we sat drinking coffee along the river — singing in the tourist boats and marching over the bridges. I couldn't understand what they were singing, but it was probably along the lines of "we are the champions of the world . . ." Sports fans everywhere seem to sing that one — though I've always had a completely opposite take on what Queen was talking about.

Later, we all met for dinner in a funky industrial loft. Except inside there were white tablecloths and candles and wine and good talk. I don't drink wine or beer or Aquavit or alcohol of any sort, or smoke hash or take anything, really, for the pain, or the joy — unless you count coffee and cigarettes. Too bad, as Copenhagen seems a wonderful place to do all those things. In abundance. To excess. But I do talk, as you know. Endlessly.

Jerry Michalski was there with his wife Jen. And Peter Merholz and Ann Winblad plus many other speakers. And our wonderful hosts: Thomas and Morten and Nanna and Nikolaj and Christian and Joe and many more whose names I couldn't remember even then. And Ann Winblad came up to me and started telling how, when she arrived at her hotel, she realized she had a perfect view of the riots from her balcony. And her eyes lit up talking about what the rioters did — part of which was to slam chairs into the ground, which she thought somewhat missed the point — and what the police did to keep the drunken Turks from killing the drunken English, and vice versa, the final upshot of which was that the cops fired off a lot of tear gas and everyone ran away. Including Ann, who was by that time getting gassed on her balcony.

I asked Nanna where the toilets were, feeling it was too silly to ask for the bathroom. No one says bathroom. And why should they? We are so stupid. Come with me she said and showed me, down iron stairs and around the corner, where they were. But we got talking and she told me she was once in the fashion industry but is now studying economics, more inclined, she said, to the fringe, postmodern aspects of that subject. I wondered about this and asked what kind of fashion? And she said, oh, for surfers and extreme skateboarders and such. In France and around Europe. You know, this and that. So sure, postmodern economics. Why not? But by this time it was becoming a little too obvious that I was falling in love and she reminded me that I'd been looking for the toilets. Oh yes.

I went back to the hotel early that night and on the way told Morten and this other guy, a very cool guy whose name I have spaced, once a journalist he said, but now in venture capital, about a dream I had a couple weeks ago that involved being nearly gang raped by these very nasty Aryan Nation skinheads. It really freaked me out, I told them, and they thought this was pretty funny. Maybe you really like guys, they suggested. No, I assured them, I tried that a couple times, but could never get my head around kissing someone with a beard. Too scratchy. I was pretty sure I liked women a lot better. And I was thinking, though I didn't say this until now, possibly women into some exotic combination of extreme sports fashion and postmodern economics — odd juxtapositions counting for a lot in my world. And getting to count more so every day it seems.

I went to bed and slept. For about 20 minutes. Then the jet lag kicked in, I guess, or it could have been the cappuccino, and I was off to the races, revising my talk in my head, again and again all night, in a state of total fugue. Maybe Christiania had more effect than I thought. Maybe I'd taken a deeper whiff than I intended. It wasn't burning. But I was. These people are so wonderful and strange and open and straight ahead, RageBoy argued — for RB had arrived in full regalia sometime during the night — that it was clear (to him at least, in that mad way he has of being utterly certain) that he must give the talk the following morning, and not I.

I never should have agreed to this, of course, but by 4 A.M. I was too exhausted to resist. RB knew he'd won — and forced me to drink three double cappuccinos to celebrate his victory. The keynote kickoff was at 9:30, by which time I was thoroughly wasted — and terrified at what I knew by this time he was going to say. He started off with a bang. The Big Bang, in fact, with a detailed account of some naive but hyper-mystical theory of proto particle physics, equating the ultimate First Event to a cosmic orgasm, then doing the entire history of life up to that specific present moment. "When we look up into the stars and see their light," he boomed through the great hall, "when we see the light in each other's eyes and see it is the same light, then we recognize each other. People of earth . . . remember . . ."

2000 people were looking at me dumbstruck. Who is this maniac? I don't think they believed for a second we are two separate people.

It was utter madness, of course. But it got even worse from there. He said no corporation has ever fallen in love. But if I say this, he said, that they are heartless, they say but look at all the money we've given to Charity. This is only fighting metaphor with metaphor, he said. It's hopeless. We need something stronger. Try this: corporations have no sex. And of course, we do. If you don't believe this, RB said, here's a simple experiment we can all do right now. Reach over to the person next to you and determine for yourself whether he or she has a sex. There were various forms and degrees of laughter by this time, and I said, or maybe it was RB, it was getting hard to tell: you're shy, I understand, but if you'd just go along with this little demonstration, we could forget all the talk and cut straight to the party. This was greeted with cheers if nothing else.

Somehow, I managed to get through it. "What's going on has nothing to do with e-commerce or broadband or any of that. Those are just tools. Like the horses we painted in the caves at Lascaux, like the bone axes and bows we made, the religions and mythologies we invented, the literatures, arts, intellectual disciplines. Just tools. What they are for is to help us fall in love with the world again, and again, and again forever."

"People of earth!" he ended, splaying his right hand as on that capsule we once sent out into the stars thinking someone might recognize five fingers as an unmistakable sign for human being.

Then RB, satisfied, released me to wonder at the terrible spectacle I'd made of myself. I have to say I was mortified. And then came the press interviews. Who are we talking to, the journalists asked, Chris Locke or RageBoy? I tried to sound businesslike, but I'm afraid it may have been too late. Later, I fell asleep in the press room. Thank god. I went back to my hotel before the big party, which lasted all night. My new friends got home at 6 A.M. they said — but they were there at 11 for lunch and cruising around Copenhagen telling bad jokes and RB recounting his wildest drug escapades, and a lovely six-course dinner in some elegant cellar of a restaurant in which we had a private room that night. I felt I'd known these people all my life. The women were too beautiful and half of them were pregnant. I let my hair down and showed everyone how much I look like the Mona Lisa, which I do that way, and everyone was choking with laughter. Leaving, I saw Nanna in her pink corduroy jacket for the first time. I like you so much, I said, come home with me. She didn't, but it didn't matter. It was an extreme, one might even say postmodern, pink.

The next day we all met again and went to Louisiana. This will sound strange unless you understand that it's an art museum. We saw a show of Andy Warhol stuff there, including many inflated silver pillows, one of which Nanna released into the museum proper. This caused some consternation among the guards we were told. We wouldn't have known, as we immediately ducked out the back way. Then we all sat on the stairs outside overlooking the ocean and drank whatever we each liked to drink and talked and talked and Nanna told me about Heidegger and Foucault. I was more interested in how many ways her face had to express amusement, joy, concern, delight, flashing across her features so quickly, like water in water. What a wonderful country.

And then we drove to the ferries — I wanted to go to Sweden, but there wasn't time — and past Hamlet's castle, which we decided none of us really wanted to go into, but we parked and went down some cobbled alleys instead to a place that had the best ice cream in Denmark we were assured, and walked around eating it in the twilight making fun of the Swedes, which seems to be a local sport. Then into the car again and back to the city — I forgot to say this was up the coast a bit — and more coffee and beer and Jerry made us all play Concentration with this postcard he found that divided into little squares, pairs of images you had to match. I was very bad at this, not being able to remember from second to second who'd turned over what. Same as it ever was. The place was called Summer Shoe, they said, and across the street was Flying A, which Nanna told Jen was the best store in all of Copenhagen, though it was very tiny. The things women know.

And as if that weren't enough, they said now it's time for us to take you to Tivoli, the centuries-old garden in the heart of the city, but we had to kill time, as the lights are, of course, better at night — and it doesn't get dark there until about 10:30. Nanna said she was there when she was three and her mother bought her a beautiful balloon, but a man came up and popped it. On purpose. Her mother got very angry and yelled at him — which Nanna demonstrated rather convincingly. We were all sad for her. I took her around the waist and said come with me, little girl, and walked her over to the balloon stand and let her pick one out. At first, she had her eye on a silver spaceship, but when the balloon vendor said it was really just an airplane, she chose a ladybug instead, which she later (we conferred about this first) gave to a little girl, whom she said looked very much like herself when she was three.

We ate Chinese in some fake Chinese temple, with lights and lanterns starting to come on everywhere and spoke fake Danish and made more terrible jokes. Nanna insisted on getting a huge cotton candy, and the sight of her devouring this was truly other-worldly strange. Mmmm! Sugar! Then Thomas said we had to take an "experience ride, not a thrill ride" — I'd been making it painfully clear to everyone that I had no interest in going on rides whose sole purpose was visceral terror. And it looked to me as if there were quite a few of those. I was in a distinct minority in respect of this fear of fear. But anyway, thus Thomas's proposed experience, which turned out to be the Valhalla ride. After various special effects involving raging giants and angry gods, they bolted us into these rows of seats and turned the whole fucking building upside down several times. I'm going to kill that Thomas, I promised myself. But when we got outside, he said the ride hardly moved at all and it was all psychological. Could be an analog for something, I guess. Then Christian blew everybody's mind by ringing the bell 12 times in row on one of those things you have to pound on with an enormous wooden mallet and even huge hulking guys couldn't make the bell ring even once. Reboot, we cried. Reboot! We were all so proud of him. Later, he told me there is a word in Finnish for people who die of drowning during a mid-summer festival in which the men get totally stinking drunk, go out in small wooden boats in groups of four, stand up and try to piss into the ocean.

Then we went to see the famous Tivoli fireworks, on the way to which I posed by a poster of the real Mona Lisa, letting my hair down again, and perfect strangers were stopping along the path to crack up at the weird people taking pictures of each other. Boom! Hiss, splash, ooooh! The fireworks were great! And then we needed more coffee as it was after midnight. Back at the hotel, I slept a little. Then Joe and Thomas and Nanna came again at 9 to take me to the airport. We said goodbye. We hugged each other. And here I am, back in Colorado by way of London.

EGR has a new office in Copenhagen, about which you will certainly be hearing more. As well as more about Reboot America. It's definitely time to reboot America.

I'm sorry I haven't written in so long, but I was working through some some painful stuff, you know? Like why are we here? And what are we for? And what is love? I figured it out, though. It's so simple. We are the champions of the world.

Celebrate Responsibly

You know that book you won't let me talk about? It just got ranked #6 on *Business Week*'s list of top books for 2000. It's in the current (February 19, 2001) issue, which I'm sure you'll all want to run out and get ahold of. What this says to me, more than the fact that business people will buy nearly anything, is that all those reviewers can just *kiss my ass!*

Heh. But on a more sober note, I was just driving back from Blockbuster — it's a long story, which, if you're not lucky, I'll tell you later — when an ad came on the radio for Bailey's Irish Cream. Now if there was ever a pussy drink, this has to be it. Give me a case of Mad Dog 20-20 any day over that swill. Not that I drink anymore, but still. Jesus. Bailey's. Retch! That's not the point though, of course. It never is. You think it might be, it could be maybe, but then . . . well, what can I say? Time marches on. No, the *point* was the end of this otherwise brainless ad in which some fetching chick is telling you about the hunka-hunka burnin' man in her *dance class* — oh yeah, I can relate to that — who actually likes women, she says, and asks her out — and wow, I'm thinking, they're actually talking about queers. What next, Negroes? But nevermind that. The real part I wanted to comment on was at the end when she says "Celebrate, but celebrate responsibly." And I want to comment here, because while I think this company and its product are both lower than homemade shit, this is an important message for today's young people, and I'm concerned that they won't fully grasp what she was telling them. Celebrate responsibly? So listen up if you're a young person, because what it means is: DO NOT DRIVE HAMMERED.

I used to do this, and I can tell you from experience, it is dangerous. I can remember having to hold a hand over one eye so there would be only one road. Otherwise, I couldn't figure out which one to drive down. Of course, this meant I had to drive one-handed, which made it really hard to hit off the fifth of bourbon and roll a joint at the same time. God only knows how I did it. Somehow I managed.

But one thing I *never* did, even back in those days — and *especially* if I was the designated driver — was to take more than ten hits of acid in any given four-hour period. Ten was my limit. If someone offered me another tab, I'd just say, "No, man, I can't. Love to, but I gotta drive." Only it would come out sounding more like "whaaaaa???? who are YOU, maaan?!?!" I was *thinking* it though. I found if I went over ten I could get into certain existential uncertainties about the difference between myself and the fuel molecules exploding in the piston chambers. For some reason, my ego would always get tangled up in the whole internal combustion thing and I'd be flying out the tail pipe instead of paying attention to oncoming traffic. Vrroooom!!!

So kids, do like the lady says and celebrate responsibly. We know you're going to get snockered out of your skull, but for Christ's sake, hire a chauffeur or something, OK? I have long wanted to say this, so thanks for indulging me.

What else? This morning yeah. Actually, it was almost noon when I woke up because I was online all night signing up for DVD clubs. Thanks to the wonderful Google search bar I recently installed in my browser — no shit, it's great — I found these Columbia House DVD Club coupon cracks on the Evil Zero forum at

Evil Deals: Deals So Good They're Evil
http://evilzero.com/ubb/Forum8/HTML/000001.html

. . . posted there by one Jago, who seems to have earned the title of "Overlord." Suffice it to say that this individual has worked it *out* in an impressively rigorous and scientific way. Personally, I'm proud of our young people and the advanced skills they're acquiring on the Internet. Though I know you're wondering why I, author of a best-selling business book, would give two shits about the sniveling cretins over at Columbia House. And of course I don't. I guess it all started several months ago (jesus god, this could really get long) when I first stumbled onto Netflix:

http://www.netflix.com

I was intrigued with their, you know, business model. How could they make money offering fixed subscriptions with no late-fee penalties? The latter item interested me especially, as Blockbuster keeps breaking my balls for forgetting to bring their tapes back. Look, I'm a busy man. I can't keep track of every little thing I did in 1998! Lately, however, these fees have begun to amount to a tidy sum. So Netflix looked good. Problem was, all they offer is DVDs and I didn't have a DVD player. Now, I'll be goddamned if I'm going to do a bunch of fucking e-commerce research and not be able to watch the occasional Steven Seagal movie, like *Under Siege*. I know you'll say it's just a *Die Hard* ripoff, but that part where Tommy Lee Jones has got the Tomahawk missile pointed at San Francisco and goes into that Road Runner routine, man, that is pure art!

Deciding, therefore, that I simply *must* equip myself with the latest video technology, I went off to Amazon to look for a cheap DVD player. Well, cheap is relative, isn't it? I mean, what's technology without All The Latest Features? Things got worse and worse and I ended up buying this entire stereo system:

Philips FWD5 Shelf System with Integrated DVD Player
http://www.amazon.com/exec/obidos/ASIN/B00004U54N/

This way, I figure, I can bring the JVC RV-DP100 Kaboom box up here into the command aerie. Listen to some good head-slammin' tunes while I'm having to write all this business shit. If you're ever looking for total raw wattage, look no further than the RV-DP100 Kaboom — plus it's got these really cool decals so it looks like flames are shooting out of the front. Very tasteful. Here's a 360-degree view you can fuck around with:

http://www.etronics.com/product.asp?stk_code=jvcrvdp100&sv bname=162

[A rather amusing aside here. If you click on the "Detail View," as I did, you will see labels that say things like Superwoofer Volume, Mid/Treble and the like. Wondering where these buttons were, I looked all over my RV-DP100. I thought perhaps I'd bought a different model, until I realized, oh christ, I lost the remote!]

Anyway, cool, huh? Looks sorta like a low-yield nuke. And get this, it has an integrated scratch pad, a drum machine and a *guitar jack*. Because, you know, sometimes when it gets dull around here, I like to hook it up to the old Roland guitar synth. . .

talk to me baby!
http://www.rolandus.com/images/VG–88_L.jpg

. . . and blow the walls out. Truly unbelievable what that box can do. You might think the proximity of neighbors would pose difficulties, but not really. They're stone deaf after the first few hundred decibels, and after that they don't notice anything out of the ordinary. Until they look in the mirror and see they're bleeding from the ears. But is that *my* problem?

All this because what? I forget what I was going to tell you. Oh yeah, I'm almost finished with *Gonzo Marketing*, and it's a little, shall we say, strong in places. I'm afraid reviewers will call me a Communist, like last time. But I ask you. You read about all this crap I buy online. Do I *sound* like a fucking communist??? No. What I am is the perfect fucking *consumer*, though I fear this may be lost on some. I am struggling with how to clarify this for readers without saying fuck too many more times, but it's tough.

Despite these last-minute misgivings, Perseus seems excited about the manuscript. Evidently, they like the idea of publishing the first business book with a parental advisory warning on the cover. This was my idea, but their marketing people went nuts when they heard it.

I don't know. I may need to revise.

I also need to go watch the movie I just rented from Blockbuster before they decide I owe money on it. I was going to tell you how I reserved it over the web — something you can only do in the Austin and Denver areas, so tough shit for you, but of course they fucked it up anyway; more research — but maybe another time.

Meanwhile, here's a note about Monday. Seeing as most of you hosers log off on weekends anyway, this will probably still be news by the time you get this send. So for the few, the brave, the proud who actually read this far . . .

```
Big news, Moses fans. Big news.

Starting Monday, your wit will be dispensed thrice
weekly. It will be packaged in a brilliant new
design, and have several new features. You will love
it.

We'll kick things off in grand style with a new
essay from Christopher Locke, co-author of The
Cluetrain Manifesto.

Read it here: http://www.sweetfancymoses.com

Enjoy, now.

Matt Herlihy
```

Sweet Fancy Moses is really good. I don't get nothing from no one for saying this, by the way. In fact, I don't get anything for plugging anything in this issue except maybe if you buy the Philips player from Amazon, which dig it people, wouldn't exactly kill you, now would it? Or could I perhaps interest you in something for the *smaller* apartment?

EdgeAudio SW–12 320-watt Powered Subwoofer
http://www.amazon.com/exec/obidos/ASIN/B0000542A9/

But will you bite? Highly unlikely. You never buy dick! What fucking good are you? One of these days, I'm going to delete the whole lot
of ya's. In the meantime, don't make me come over there. If I decide
to whip out my 12-inch long-throw woofer, things could get ugly fast.

I didn't really tell you about Columbia House, but after I used one
of those fake codes to rip them off, I then hassled them for good measure. Why not? Everyone hates these moronic cocksuckers. So I sent
them this:

> How come your web page didn't let me select a 6th
> DVD for $14.95, like it promised?
>
> also, what's my Account# ??? you didn't assign me
> one so how am I going to log in and buy more stuff?
> I'm trying to get rid of a whole lotta money over
> here. help me out!

I thought this would whet their appetites, you know. But while it
did elicit a response — surprisingly, from the long lost love child of
Henry Mancini and Jello Biafra — I was a bit crestfallen that no one
really took the bait.

> Thank you for your e-mail message.
>
> We regret the problems you have encountered with our
> on-line service. We are working to correct them, and
> your comments have been forwarded to our systems
> analysts for review.
>
> When submitting an application on-line, please allow
> ten business days for processing. After this time,
> we will be happy to check the status of your
> application. Please resubmit your e-mail message
> along with your name and complete mailing address.
>
> If we may be of further service, please let us know.
>
> Sincerely,
>
> Henry Biafra
> Customer Service

Ten business days. What do these systems analysts do over there? Makes you wonder, doesn't it? What in Christ's name are they even talking about for that matter? Fuck if I know.

Finally, on a more serious note, the political climate in this country is turning quite chilly due to a certain dumb motherfucker who will have to go unnamed for the present as I just learned all our email is being monitored by the NSA. I just got the news in the URL below and was going to tell you about it in the first paragraph. In fact, this was *all* I was going to tell you about tonight, but, what with one thing and another, I guess I got carried away. Anyway, this report is extremely disturbing. If you haven't heard about this yet, I urge you to inform yourself. And to pass this link along to everyone you know.

http://www.rageboy.com/badnews.html

. . . uh-oh, someone's trying to get in the back door. I'm going out the window. this may be last you hear from me. don't give up, though. no matter what. remember: constant struggle!

No Justice, No Peace

Clues You Can Lose

Are you sick of hearing about *The Cluetrain Manifesto* yet? Well, I am. Nonetheless, here comes more of it in the form of an interview clocke did a week or so ago with Amy Gahran of the zine Contentious:

> "It's possible to sound human and sound stupid at the same time. The trick is to really communicate — and that means having something worthwhile to say, as well as having a real ability to write."

What a self-serving buttwipe this guy is! Who does he think he's kidding? Oh, excuse me: *whom*. Have you checked out any of his puerile EGR spew lately? I don't know what *your* definition of "worthwhile" is, but c'mon! Only the lowest form of bottom-feeder net scum would ever read that garbage.

Locke and his pals are clearly out to fucking lunch on this whole thing. We don't need to "speak with a human voice" or some other nicey-nice ever-so-Nineties New-Age nonsense. What we *need* is for some advanced off-world sentience to carpet nuke planet Earth from high orbit. Call it Equal Opportunity Ethnic Cleansing. I mean, racism is so petty. Why play favorites? I say take em *all* out! No more spam, no more useless debate, no more "Honey, could you take the trash out?"

No one has bothered to ask *me* what I think about all this. So yes kids, it's time once again to conjure up an interviewer with the jumbo cahones necessary to confront RB on the *real* issues. Ready? Dubious at best, but here you go anyway.

REALLY CONCERNED THOUGHTFUL JOURNALIST: So about this cluetrain thing, RB . . . By the way, do you mind if I call you RB?

RAGEBOY®: On my home planet I am traditionally addressed as Your Exalted High Holiness, Keeper of the Scrolls of Gonzo Immortality, but sure whatever. RB's close enough.

RCTJ: Well, uh . . . OK then RB, what do you make of this cluetrain manifesto? Is it having any real impact out there?

RB: Impact? Yeah sure, lotsa impact [yawns]. As an example of drive-by semiotics, it's first rate. Woulda made a great post to some newsgroup like alt.effluvia.extralarge.boxershorts — in fact, it's generated quite a bit of discussion there.

RCTJ: Oh? And what are they saying?

RB: Basically, the whole thing has devolved into a debate about the relative merits of PowerPoint. Some say — following cluetrain's suggestion — that we should burn all such presentations. Others argue that it's OK to use them as long as you're wearing mismatched argyle socks during a new moon.

RCTJ: And what do you say?

RB: Well, I think we need to ask ourselves what the socks are *made* of, and *where* they were made. Cotton, maybe OK. Synthetics, I'd have to demur. Akron Ohio, fine. Some slave-labor sweatshop in Kuala Lumpur . . . well, you see where I'm coming from on this I'm sure . . .

RCTJ: Certainly, yes. And would these socks be one-size-fits-all or sized for specific individuals? Are there gender issues to consider?

RB: Yes, yes, now we're getting somewhere! That's the heart of the problem really. We have all these companies sending us commercial messages online, but how many fully realize that our feet are different sizes? Or that some of us have athlete's foot?

RCTJ: Cluetrain has been criticized for not including examples of good and bad business practice.

RB: And rightly so. As I see it, the fault is mostly Locke's. He thinks in abstractions to the point that he's not . . . how shall I put this . . . let's say there's a question of whether he's um . . . living among us, if you take my meaning.

RCTJ: A little light in his intellectual loafers, could we say?

RB: Something like that. Have you ever talked to the guy?

RCTJ: I tried calling but he said he was on the other line with *The Wall Street Journal* and could I call back next year.

RB: Typical. He's a total media whore. And those pals of his, who are they? Dr. Weimeraner? Rick Leviticus? Doc Martin? Did anyone ever hear of these guys? Sounds to me like Locke bought into a Yiddish shoe store.

RCTJ: I know you have strong feelings on this RB, but let's veer away from the ad hominem, shall we? I want to ask about the notion that online markets are getting smarter faster than corporations.

RB: Well, yes, that's true. As far as it goes.

RCTJ: How far *does* it go?

RB: Well look, ants are also smarter than thumbtacks, but what does that prove? You can't use an ant to pin up a postcard of your adulterous fling in Bimini, now can you?

RCTJ: I've never tried.

RB: What, to score?

RCTJ: No, I mean, like you said about using an ant . . .

RB: Oh that. Well, just try it sometime. They bend when you try to force their heads into the corkboard. This is something the clue boys obviously never thought about.

RCTJ: So is Bionomics relevant here, would you say?

RB: Of course. Thumbtacks not only work better, they're cheaper too. Have you priced Ant Farms lately? I mean, it really doesn't take a rocket scientist to figure this shit out.

RCTJ: And how would that work in with the sock thing?

RB: Well, you've had ants in your pants before, I assume, so you know what that's like. Socks represent a closely analogous case. There are just so many questions cluetrain begs — and weasels out of, I must say — one hardly knows where to begin . . .

RCTJ: Let's turn to cluetrain's focus on discourse. What point is the manifesto actually trying to make about the "human voice"?

RB: 'the fuck would I know? I mean 95 Theses? How many people do *you* know who think that's even normal, much less human? And "discourse"? Give me a break! Nobody talks that way. Except maybe academics, and they can hardly be classed among the standard hominids . . . Which reminds me, I have a paper coming out soon on Barbie Doll dentition. Fascinating study actually.

RCTJ: Yes, that's all very interesting, I'm sure. But getting back to your main point, you're saying you don't agree with the idea that we should all number our sentences?

RB: I think you need to look at the issue on a case-by-case basis. Sometimes numbering is useful. Like say you're ticking off the various medications you're currently taking. In my case:

1. Marijuana
2. Tylenol
3. Heroin
4. Psilocybin
5. NyQuil
6. Viagra
7. LSD-25
8. Prozac
9. Jack Daniels
10. Vick's Vap-o-Rub

11. Vicodin
12. Dimethyltryptamine
13. Tums

. . . and so on.

RCTJ: That's quite a list, and I can see how you'd need the numbers to keep straight, so to speak. But in other cases not?

RB: Of course not! If you were Julia Child, would you say:
1. Carrots are vegetables.
2. Vegetables grow in the ground.
3. The ground is basically dirt.
4. People get dirty when they pull up carrots.
5. What has a carrot ever done to you?
6. Leave those carrots alone you dirty fucker!

RCTJ: Good example. But what about conversations as such, forgetting about the numbering scheme for a moment? Are online person-to-person conversations any more informative, really, than reading the tag on a mattress?

RB: You mean the ones that say you can't remove them under penalty of law?

RCTJ: Right.

RB: Is that really true? How do they actually *know* if you take them off?

RCTJ: There's a tracking device keyed to the UPC barcode they scan when you buy the mattress. They know where you live from your credit records and if you take it off, you get a little visit.

RB: I've heard about disappearances. Anything to that, you think?

RCTJ: Well, funny you should ask. I was just reading something in alt.mattress.tags.no.no.no that said the Department of Alcohol, Tobacco and Firearms has put tiny nanotech cameras in those tags and they can see right up your asshole!

RB: Wouldn't surprise me one bit.

RCTJ: But companies just don't get this, do they?

RB: About our assholes?

RCTJ: Well, that, yes, but more the whole cluetrain thing that says we're onto them and they can no longer get away with this sort of thing.

RB: I doubt many Fortune 500 companies are even selling mattresses any more. Now they're mostly using them internally.

RCTJ: How do you use a mattress internally? Seems to me it would be hard to eat the whole thing.

RB: No, no, I meant: using them inside the company. To take little naps on and such.

RCTJ: Ah, I see. Sorry I misunderstood you.

RB: Well there you go. That's part of the "human voice" too. All these morons playing Telegraph out there — no offense to you. How is this supposed to add up to greater knowledge? Locke knows all this, of course, but he also knows a good media play when he sees it. The guy has no integrity whatsoever.

RCTJ: But so many seem to agree with the cluetrain ringleaders, as they call themselves. Could they all be wrong?

RB: Are you kidding? Of course they could all be wrong! Cluetrain has had an effect, no doubt about it. But let's put this in perspective for a moment. I suspect cluetrain amounts to no more than .00002% of the cognitive impact of, say, a single Sprite ad on daytime TV.

RCTJ: So perhaps we should be having a conversation about Sprite . . .

RB: If it's all the same to you, let's not. Obey your thirst.

RCTJ: You're basically saying that the entire notion of smart networked markets is suspect, is that correct?

RB: It's utter bullshit! Look, on my home planet, a human being would not be able to carry on a coherent conversation with a doorknob.

RCTJ: The doorknobs talk?

RB: It's actually more of a psi thing. I was just back there recently for debriefing, and as I was entering a room, one delivered quite an impressive disquisition on free will and predetermination. I had to totally revise my entire Weltanschauung.

RCTJ: That must have been painful.

RB: They have surgery for it now. A sort of spiritual liposuction.

RCTJ: OK, well that's about all we have time for, but thanks so much for sharing your views on cluetrain. I'm sure they'll add much to the ongoing discussion.

RB: Christ, I hope not.

RCTJ: Why do you say that?

RB: If it's not already obvious, then I guess there's no way to explain it. Uh, say look, Locke is due back here any minute, so if he like, finds us talking, you pretend to be the Orkin Man, OK?

RCTJ: The Orkin Man?

[footsteps]

CLOCKE: [entering] RB, what are you doing at the terminal!? And who is this fellow?

RCTJ: Who me? I'm the Orkin Man.

RB: Yeah, he's like the Orkin Man, man.

CLOCKE: I wasn't aware we needed an exterminator.

RB: It turns out you had a rat . . . in your, uh, operation . . .

CLOCKE: Get out of here, both of you!

RB: OK, OK. Touchy, touchy!

RCTJ: Well, I better go now.

RB: Yes, er, goodbye and thanks for smoking out the rat.

RCTJ: By the way, what did you do with it?

RB: Hung it out to dry. You'll see.

CLOCKE: RB, that doesn't sound good. What've you really been up to?

RB: [looks innocently blank]

CLOCKE: Oh, nevermind. Go back to your dungeon immediately!

RB: Yeah, boss. Pickin it up here, boss . . .

CLOCKE: Damn, it's always so hard to know how to end these things. OK, what the hell. Cut. Print it.

> *"colonel mustard?*
> *in the library?*
> *with the lead pipe?"*
>
> **anonymous**

Red Shift Blues

I should do the dishes instead of writing this. OK, I'll do the dishes in a minute. Let me just see if I can get something started here. Today got off sideways. How does that happen? First not enough coffee, then too much. A half-hour interview with KTALK AM 760 radio in Denver about, sigh, that book. Yes, markets are talking to each other as never before. And what are we talking about out here, where we don't see ourselves as markets at all? About the burning issues, that's what. Like for instance, today, for me: Why is this all so fucking boring? Why can't I get it up?

Something was happening there for a second and then I came down. Sure, it's OK, I'm used to it. We're all used to it. Life going flat. The champagne left over from last night's party. Not that there was a party last night. Not here anyway. And the glasses are all lying around and the sunlight streaming into the whole mess, bloated cigarette butts staining perfectly good Mumm's the color of ginger ale. That was a great party though, wasn't it? I mean, wasn't it? Let's do it again. Or not. Or maybe wait a while to see if the moon comes into that particular configuration again. Looking to the skies then. Studying the charts. And Jimi singing from the land of the dead: let me stand / next to your fire.

But also: I don't live / today. / Maybe tomorrow baby . . .

And the big old snake of the world, Uroboros, coils and uncoils, I can feel him sliding around himself down there, opens one jaundiced eye and winks — what does it mean? — goes back to sleep. The sound of lawnmowers in the American suburbs on a beautiful Spring morning. A Saturday. Memorial Day weekend, on which I can remember only traces of traces. Ashes to ashes. Funk to funky.

Let me stand . . .

But nothin doin.

Ah, it would be a good idea to do the dishes then, wouldn't it? Something practical and grounded. Waiting for the sun. Waiting for life to begin again. No more arguments. No more complications, deals, arrangements. In the beginning was the arrangement, and the arrangement was complicated. And the arrangement had endless complex ramifications.

Let's nuke that universe, start over.

Three kids just rang the doorbell. Hello? Who's there?

There's a baby bird under your porch, the oldest one said, a girl. And it was in the middle of the street and can't fly and can you help us get it so it doesn't get run over?

Oh boy, I thought. Where is it?

Under here? See? And sure enough, there's a fledgling blackbird hopping around under there.

It's not hurt, I said. It just can't fly yet. The momma bird probably kicked it out of the nest so it would learn.

They are looking at me like: the momma bird? Are you nuts? The two boys are maybe five and six. I can tell from their eyes they've been watching too much MTV — though the youngest looks at a hedgehog-shaped iron shoe scraper on the porch with broom bristles sticking out of its back and wants to know if it's real.

That depends, I start to say . . . then realize this will probably not lead in a productive direction.

No, it's not real.

Oh.

Sometimes it's helpful to be definitive even when you're radically uncertain. Like now, I'm thinking.

So do you have some gloves? the girl is asking me. She's maybe 9 and very down to earth. No nonsense. I tried to catch it, she says, but I'm afraid it will peck me.

Listen, I say, I know a lot about these things, and I think the best idea would be to leave it where it is. This bird is learning to fly, but it's freaked out because we're all looking at it and it knows you're trying to catch it. If we go away, it will come out and fly away by itself.

I invoke an analogy. Remember when you were learning to ride your bike and at first you couldn't and then suddenly you could. Flying is like that.

So now I'm an expert on flying. Sure, ask me anything.

So what about the gloves, she says. And instantly I know, along with everything there is to know about flying, what it will be like to be married to her ten years from now. I go and get gloves. I'll probably never see them again. The gloves, the kids, the bird.

It's quiet out there. They must have caught it. They are going to put it in their back yard, they said, so a cat can't get it. And try to feed it worms, probably. Life. It's amazing we've made it this far.

I just need another cup of coffee, that's all. Another smoke. Another paragraph. Or maybe a nice nap. Yeah, but not here. Not in this chair in front of this terminal. Under a tree somewhere. An apple tree. In Maine, I had hundreds of them and in the Spring the blossoms were impossibly large, as in a Japanese print. A modern one where the flowers are big and splashy, not delicate and precise. Zen but not Zen. You know? You probably don't. I was maybe 14 and I was reading Alan Watts that summer, D. T. Suzuki. I was listening to Bessie Smith. I had this calendar with those kind of flowers on it. I was thinking about it yesterday. Thinking what was it about those flowers? And once back then I fell asleep in the woods and a guy I just recently reconnected with after almost 40 years told me his wife had died just a few weeks ago and that she'd said she remembered me from those woods. I didn't think anyone knew. Her name was Susan. She was very beautiful.

Broadcast is the meme that wouldn't die. I want to lay my head in your lap and fall asleep like that. I want to get lost in your rock and roll / and drift away . . .

It won't die because it has blacked us all out like bad poison magic and all we can remember is two dimensions. Flat life. Flat desire. Just enough to make us want the very thing that obscures us and makes us seem to each other so bright and lively, like the goddam Pepsi generation. Coke's the one! So vivacious. So plastic. So dead. And it sounds so dated to even say it. So socially conscious, so unhip, so yesterday. Guy Debord said it better: you can't revolt or even criticize. You can only feed the spectacle. In Sanskrit it's called samsara, the endless seamless round of birth and death, enthusiasm and frustration, hope and despair. Sisyphus raised orders of magnitude. Now we have Samsara by Guerlain. They turned it into a brand of perfume. Floral, the ads say. Oriental. Feminine and romantic.

But something very unspectacular has been leaking through your email lately. Yes, the stuff you send me — this is realtime, personal, not some abstract observation. More dimensions. Greater life. And oh man, here I am right back at a very old fantasy, because that last one, greater life, is the offer and bond of the vampire. Let's get really funky then. Why not? Where is there to go otherwise? What left to lose? Questions of a thousand dreams, none of them rhetorical.

So there are a couple rules for vampires, which sadly, they don't teach in the schools anymore, along with Latin and Greek and rhetoric, my craft. All of them my craft, if you must know. Though I don't read Latin and Greek, but more sense them, understand how old my tools are. And the first of these rules is that you must invite the vampire across the threshold separating you. Protecting you. He can't cross it unless you . . . let's just say "subscribe." After that, of course, there's no netiquette. No way to stop whatever it is that comes next from coming. Choosing my words here carefully (see rhetoric, above). We're talking sexual, but more than sexual, more shocking. Whatever it is that opens your eyes and snaps your head back and suddenly you know it ain't no movie. Baby.

Let me stand next to your fire.

And the other rule, though it's not really a rule, but more a sort of binding promise, is that the reward for such a dark and dangerous path is greater life. And what's interesting is that everyone understands this immediately. Everyone I want to be talking to, anyway. If you're saying, gee, whaddya mean "greater life"? What's wrong with a sunny Saturday afternoon (by now) in the suburbs — and after all, my God! the *Boulder* suburbs, themselves one big sprawling subdevelopment of the soul, and what could be bad about that? — then you really need to unsubscribe right away before anything more contractual takes place. Not that it really could, this being only email and all. Right?

Are you with me here?

Because you could be. All the old stories say it: it is a great sin to wake up. It is unforgivable to awaken to greater life. To open our eyes and see each other's nakedness. It is shameful. Odious. It is an abomination.

There is a trick of the light here, though. Ah, the light! That's a good one. And we always want the good one, the better, the best. To always be on the side of the angels, of heaven. This is why broadcast will never die. It slots into our genes the way morphine slots into endorphin metabolism. Give us some commandments, Oh Lord! Give us your Eternal Work Orders! And we will be flat, Dear God, and stupid all the days of our lives. And blind.

Whether of light or dark, there is always the vampire. Which makes it hard to know who your friends are. And doubly critical. The myth lives on because it is not a myth. Look now at what is fastened to your neck, feeding. It has been feeding there always. Sucking your life away. And for what? A sound-bite trickle-charge of desire. Just enough to make you wet. Just enough to lubricate the wheels of commerce. A desperate dream of happiness that comes complete with its own laugh track.

Whether or not we have forgotten, there is greater life.

Broadcast will die, the unequivocal stentorian voice that has echoed in our heads from Eden to E-Commerce. Everything dies eventually. With certain exceptions, let's just say. It's dying now. We're dying now. And the death spasms will be truly spectacular.

Please allow me to introduce myself / I'm a man . . .

Cross my threshold.

Music Appreciation

I'm so tired of seeing this kind of crap. It's wearing. I'm listening to the Moonlight Sonata to try to calm myself down. And I just fucking hate Beethoven. Ah, good thing Nirvana's next up on the playlist. Teen Spirit fits my mood better: stupid and contagious. Here's the latest Amazon.com review of that book I never mention anymore.

```
[one star] Like, duh., January 3, 2001 Reviewer:
Sydney (see more about me) from Oceanside, CA

I originally bought this book thinking that it might
contain some useful business information. Surprise!
It doesn't! Cluetrain Manifesto is nothing more than
the ramblings of a number of self-appointed dot-com
smart guys who have little or no experience in the
real world of profit and loss. As the recent and
ongoing dot-com implosion so aptly demonstrates, this
balloon — and this book — is filled with nothing
more than hot air.

Don't bother.

Was this review helpful to you? [YES] [*FUCK NO*]
```

An albino, a mosquito. (Voting suggestion asterisked above.) But Sydney seems to have lightened up a couple days later, giving TWO stars to *this* execrable piece of shit: *Care Packages for the Workplace: Dozens of Little Things You Can Do To Regenerate Spirit At Work.*

```
There are better books on the topic . . . January 6,
2001

This book is just okay. There are a lot of examples
of how to improve morale at work, but the writing
isn't that great, and the book isn't very well
organized. There are much better books on the topic
```

```
. . . try Managing to Have Fun by Matt Weinstein or
1001 Ways to Energize Employees by Bob Nelson.
```

I'll energize him alright. I'm gonna call the motherfucker up. Right now. I'm dialing, hold on. . .

"Hello, Sydney. What's your favorite scary movie?"
"Who is this? How do you know my name?"
"Because I wanted to know who I'm looking at. . . "

Well, OK, maybe not worth the time in Joliet. But really. I ask you. Shouldn't we do something about people like this? Genocide is too good for them, but I'm thinking. One thing I'm thinking is that most of these sorts of proposals are way too reactive. You know, too after-the-fact. What we need is a more *actionable, proactive* approach. It's just a start, but I did have one good idea this week. The next car I buy is going to be a black Lincoln Continental like the secret service guys drive. And I'm going to get it fitted out with flag holders on the front fenders, like you see in those presidential motorcades. Except I'm going to have special flags made that say:

FUCK OFF!

Imagine me tooling down Broadway like that! Driving with one hand, my arm straight out, other arm over the seat back. Lookin good and knowin it. Maybe some cool shades. Yeah. That'll keep some of these people away. Of course, it may attract other sorts of undesirables. Like cops. But anyway, like I say, it's a start. And I'll have the windows down and the radio cranked. Like the secret service.

"No pill's gonna cure my ills.
Doctor, Doctor, gimme the news. . . "
"No I don't have a gun.
No I don't have a gun."

Ah, Nirvana. As it turned out, though, he did have a gun. Why'd he have to go blow his head off like that? So sad. So unnecessary. I mean, I can relate to the pressures, but some people overreact really badly. Me, I try to aim for balance.

For instance, while lots of people don't realize it, art is something that's important to all of us. You have to keep your hand in. Self and I came up with a great idea the other day. Self is my daughter, who is now like 10 and five-eighths. Sometimes I call her Selene. Well, we were pulling up to my apartment and we couldn't help notice the several million geese that are wintering here and crapping all over the joint. I said, "Hey, I know. What if they're really aliens from outer space?"

Selene started laughing, so right away I knew we were onto something. Sell the kids for food. No, wait. That's the MP3, isn't it? Anyway, we started thinking up titles for the movie. Here's what we've got so far:

1. Day of the Anatidae
2. Night of the Living Anatidae
3. Earth vs. Anatidae
4. Attack of the Anatidae
5. It Came From The Pond
6. It Came From Canada
7. Killer Geese From Outer Space

So far, I like #6 best, but as you can see, we need your help on this. Self is working on the storyboards, which should be pretty simple. Just shots of the goose hordes walking around the apartment complex, intercut with panic scenes of people running for their lives, looking over their shoulders and screaming in horror, "They've landed! They've landed!!!" (We're looking for extras, by the way.) Cut back to geese tearing this guy apart — we'll put day-old baguettes into some old pants and a shirt. His head will already be eaten away. Terrible, terrible. Carnage everywhere.

Their headquarters on our vanquished planet is the Anatidae Citadel of Empire, or, as they call it, the ACE. Cut to ACE Hardware store with ominous theramin music and voice-over: "The invaders met in High Council to decide the fate of the Earth . . ." Cut to Al Gore smiling stupidly for no reason. Cut to George W. Bush looking scared as shit, doing lines and slugging back a 16 oz. Colt–45 with his special nuke key pushed into the slot, waiting for General Colon Trowel to tell him it's Their Last Hope.

Then, there'll be dialogue. Two Imperial Guard-type geese are attending the fearsome Anatidae Overlord, who has RED EYES and POISON GREEN WEBS. When he speaks, it sounds like he's got a lawnmower carburetor over his face.

"Bring the prisoners to my quarters."

"Yes, Your Overlord."

"But first make sure they've been, heh-heh, properly prepared!"

"Yes, Your Overlord."

"And one more thing . . . "

"Yes, Your Overlord?"

"We are the Sultans of Swing."

"Anything you say, Your Overlord."

Maybe we'll have to work on that a bit, but you get the idea. One cool thing is that we don't have to worry about making their lips move. Geese don't have lips. Of course, having to finish the *Gonzo* book is really slowing down production something awful. But like I always say, you gotta do what you gotta do.

Welp, that's it for me, then. Back to the old salt mines . . .